THE BATTLE OF BRITAIN
NEW PERSPECTIVES

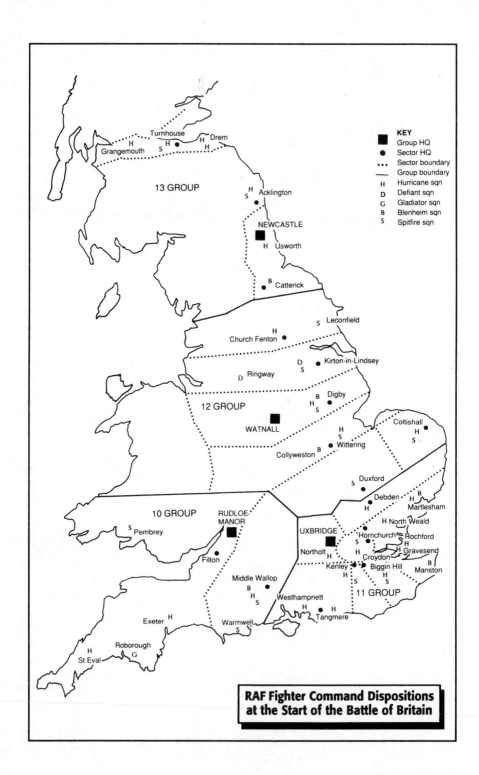

RAF Fighter Command Dispositions at the Start of the Battle of Britain

THE BATTLE OF BRITAIN

NEW PERSPECTIVES

Behind the Scenes of the Great Air War

JOHN RAY

'Dowding should go.'
Salmond to Trenchard,
25 September 1940;
see page 139.

Brockhampton Press

To Jack

Arms and Armour Press
A Cassell Imprint
Villiers House, 41–47 Strand, London WC2N 5JE

British Library Cataloguing-in-Publication Data: a catalogue
record for this book is available from the British Library

Designed and edited by DAG Publications Ltd.
Designed by David Gibbons; edited by Philip Jarrett;
printed and bound in Great Britain by
Creative Print and Design (Wales), Ebbw Vale

Jacket painting by Jim Mitchell.
Limited-edition prints of this picture are available from
Mirage Fine Art, 26 Megacre, Woodlane, Stoke-on-Trent,
England.

This edition published in 1999 by Brockhampton Press,
a member of Hodder Headline PLC Group

ISBN 1 86019 937 2

CONTENTS

ACKNOWLEDGEMENTS

Thanks are due to a number of people who have provided help and advice in the preparation of this book, which has developed from my doctoral thesis, written at the University of Kent. First among them I must place the late Squadron Leader Bruce Ogilvie, who provided friendship, encouragement and contacts at the start of the research.

Of those who served in the Battle, I am particularly indebted to Air Marshal Sir Denis Crowley-Milling, whose reflections on No 12 Group have brought balance to my assessment. Others who have helped, either with recollection or judgement, by interview or correspondence, are: Squadron Leader Denis Armitage; Air Chief Marshal Sir Harry Broadhurst; Mrs Joy Caldwell; Richard Collier; Sebastian Cox; Air Chief Marshal Sir Kenneth Cross; Group Captain George Darley; Captain Alan Ellender; Dr Martin Gilbert; the late Group Captain Tom Gleave; Wing Commander Hal Ironside; Professor R. V. Jones; the late Air Vice-Marshal George Lott; Wing Commander Laddie Lucas; the late Dr H. Montgomery-Hyde; Dr Vincent Orange; Air Marshal Sir Kenneth Porter; Denis Richards; Andrew Roberts; Alec Ross; Squadron Leader Frank Usmar; Mrs June Ventris; and Professor Donald Wiseman.

I also acknowledge a debt to the following people and institutions for their assistance with comments or submissions for text or photographs, or permission to reproduce extracts from documents in their possession: Professor Richard Crampton; Dr Julian Hurstfield; Dr Michael Dockrill; Wing Commander P. J. T. Stephenson; Chriss Goss; J. Corbin; Squadron Leader C. S. Bamberger; Wing Commander N. P. W. Hancock; Fred Beacon; Wilf Goold; John Ridgeway and Jim Mitchell; Foster Services: Wing Commander G. C. Unwin; Squadron Leader J. R. Kayall; the Air Historical Branch, Ministry of Defence; the House of Lords Record Office; the Battle of Britain Fighter Association; the Trustees of the Imperial War Museum; the RAF Museum, Hendon; the University of Kent; Churchill College, Cambridge; the Bodleian Library, Oxford; the Liddell Hart Centre for Military Archives, King's College, London; the Australian Archives, Belconnen, Canberra; the Conservative Political Centre; Lady Douglas of Kirtleside; Mrs Tania Paddison; the Staff of Arms and Armour Press and of DAG Publications Ltd.

No one deserves greater praise than my wife. She has been a constant help and scribe in gathering information about a battle under which we both lived and which is still refought when those who were involved meet.

John Ray, Tonbridge, Kent, March 1994

INTRODUCTION

At 10.30am on Sunday 30 October 1988, the Queen Mother arrived outside St Clement Danes, the Royal Air Force church in the heart of London. Beneath crisp autumn sunshine a Guard of Honour from the Queen's Colour Squadron presented arms as the RAF Central Band played the National Anthem. After a short speech of welcome from Air Chief Marshal Sir Christopher Foxley-Norris, chairman of the Battle of Britain Fighter Association, Her Majesty was escorted to a nearby statue and plinth, which were shrouded in velvet. She drew a cord and the drapes fell away, revealing the figure of Air Chief Marshal Lord Dowding, formerly Commander-in-Chief, Fighter Command. To a number of his old pilots it appeared that, as in life, 'Stuffy' was looking down with a blend of surprise, severity and faint disapproval at both spectators and proceedings.[1]

Thoughts of the variations in treatment meted out to serving commanders were uppermost in the minds of a number of those present. The British can be generous to heroes. In their day, Marlborough, Nelson, Wellington and Haig were all adorned with honour and rewarded with wealth and high rank by a grateful nation. After the Second World War, Alexander and Montgomery, Cunningham and Tovey, and Portal and Tedder were among commanders who reached the highest pinnacle in their respective Services and received the accolade of ennoblement. Even Slim, commander of 'The Forgotten Army' was finally remembered. Why then, they reasoned, was Dowding, whose victory in the Battle of Britain stood unequalled since Trafalgar, treated less generously? In 1943 Churchill offered him a barony for his services three years earlier;[2] he was never promoted to the rank of Marshal of the Royal Air Force.

Nevertheless, many with long memories felt that at last some justice was being done. A degree of fair play had finally triumphed, as royal approval was accorded to a man who appeared to have been snubbed both by colleagues and politicians ever since leading 'The Few' nearly half a century earlier. Dowding had received neither palace nor estate, no special pension or earldom, yet in the opinion of his supporters had done at least as much as any previous hero to save his native land from the grip of the enemy. For his pains he had been the victim of a vendetta that denied him full reward and honour.

They believed that, after leading Fighter Command to a narrow victory over the Luftwaffe from July to October 1940, and having thereby prevented a seaborne invasion of Britain, the Commander-in-Chief was summarily dis-missed in November. Against his will he was despatched to the USA on a mission to obtain aircraft and equipment.[3] Later he was offered no more than minor appointments within the RAF until his retirement in 1942.

For the Dowding camp, his removal from office was tainted with plot and intrigue.[4] In their view, the case against him revolved around differ-ences over daytime air fighting tactics. He, together with his protégé, Air Vice-Marshal Keith Park, Air Officer Commanding, No 11 Group, Fighter Command, refused to employ Big Wings of at least three squadrons of fight-ers to counter large formations of Luftwaffe aircraft during battles.[5] How-ever, Air Vice-Marshal Sholto Douglas, Deputy Chief of the Air Staff, together with Air Vice-Marshal Trafford Leigh-Mallory, AOC, No 12 Group, were advocates of Big Wings and disagreed with Dowding's policy.

The C-in-C's supporters believe that, during the quarrel, Leigh-Mallory used political influence to advance his cause. He did this, claim his accusers, through Squadron Leader Douglas Bader, the chief practitioner of Big Wings, who commanded No 242 Squadron, stationed in No 12 Group. The Adjutant of Bader's squadron, Flight Lieutenant Peter Macdonald, was also a Member of Parliament; he was persuaded by Leigh-Mallory, Bader, or both, to meet the Prime Minister and expose the controversy. In this version Churchill followed up the matter with customary vigour, and steps were soon taken to accelerate the removal of Dowding and Park. A conference was held at the Air Ministry on 17 October 1940 at which their tactics were criticized, while the use of Big Wings was approved. Changes of command followed shortly. On 25 November Dowding was replaced by Douglas, and on 15 December Leigh-Mallory took over from Park. The accusers had not only removed the two commanders, but had also purloined their jobs.

This conspiracy theory has been nurtured ever since and, like Falstaff's buckram men, has grown with the telling. The bitterness engendered by their removal affected both men for the rest of their lives. Park interpreted events mainly as a personal contest between himself and Leigh-Mallory, which the latter, using devious tactics, had won. 'To my dying day I shall feel bitter at the base intrigue which was used to remove Dowding and myself as soon as we had won the battle,' he wrote in 1968.[6]

Dowding also believed that dirty tricks had been used by the Air Min-istry, with whom he had suffered an acerbic relationship for several years. He carried his disappointment with dignity, yet was prepared after the war to allow two authors to set out his cause. The first, Basil Collier, wrote an authorized biography in 1957 and, although the book is a balanced account of the Commander-in-Chief's career, the writer lacked access to several doc-uments which have, more recently, placed different emphases on the battle and on Dowding's subsequent treatment.[7] The second work, produced in 1969, was a panegyric written by Robert Wright, who, for a short time, had been Dowding's Personal Assistant. The book, however, was often less than accurate, and was critical only of those Wright considered to be Dowding's enemies. Its pages certainly reflected the C-in-C's subdued anger at the treatment he had received over his final four years in the RAF. Unfortunately others still believe the charges, and have used them in their own writings, so that they are widely held to be accurate.[8]

What of the opinions and recollections of Douglas and Leigh-Mallory? Douglas's autobiography is generally non-committal on the matter, and attempts to distance the author from what he describes as a 'clash between the personalities' of Park and Leigh-Mallory. He claimed to have been drawn 'against my wish' into the controversy, and refers to Leigh-Mallory's 'rather over-forceful contention' over the employment of Big Wings. Douglas gives the impression of having been an unwilling participant in the quarrels of others. That certainly was not accurate.[9]

Moving blame in the direction of Leigh-Mallory was hardly the most difficult strategy for any later writer, because he alone of the principals involved did not outlive the war. On 15 November 1944 he was killed when his aeroplane crashed in the French Alps.[10] Suspicion arises, not unnaturally, when blame is apportioned to a man who had no opportunity of presenting his case. The reminiscences of other litigants are then open to question.

The background to the accusations has seldom been explored. Were they myth, or truth? Did Leigh-Mallory and Bader collude behind the back of their C-in-C and use variations of the 'Old Boy network' to bring him down? At the time, were the principals scheming against each other as strongly as they were fighting the Germans?

Certainly some people, not present at the unveiling ceremony, believed that an exaggerated tribute was being paid to Dowding. In their opinion he was a conscientious leader, lacking in flair, who had been rewarded sufficiently at the time. Wartime Service leaders had judged his contribution fairly and had placed him correctly in the hierarchy of honour. A number of those who had worked with Dowding found him to be intransigent and unimaginative.

Over the years a few books have refuted the charges laid by Dowding's supporters. 'Laddie' Lucas, Bader's brother-in-law, has explained in some detail his view of the controversy, and denies that either Leigh-Mallory or Bader was responsible for Macdonald's intervention.[11] Lord Balfour, who in 1940 was Under-Secretary of State for Air, also spoke for Dowding's opponents in his autobiography, although the work suffers from some inaccuracies.[12] Sir Maurice Dean, formerly a civil servant at the Air Ministry, wrote a pithy summary of Dowding's relationship with his employers.[13] In 1980, Group Captain Haslam unveiled a new aspect of the argument by suggesting that Dowding's removal owed more to his inability to counter the night Blitz than to any other cause.[14]

Which view moves more confidently along the narrow tightrope of truth?

One aim of this book is to show that, in reality, there were seven reasons why Dowding was replaced in November 1940. Three existed even before the Battle of Britain started. First was his age; at 58 he was an old man at a time when younger officers were being promoted to senior posts. Second was the fact that he had led Fighter Command for over four years; he was tired, and the need for change was felt. Thirdly, his relationship with other senior officers in the Air Ministry had often been contentious since 1937; in their opinion he was stubborn, aloof and on occasions unwilling to co-operate.

As the air battle developed between July and October 1940, four other reasons emerged. Firstly, in the eyes of the Air Staff Dowding showed poor leadership by failing to resolve the controversy over the use of Big Wings, which grew bitter between Park and Leigh-Mallory, his two subordinates. Next, with the arrival of the night Blitz from September, he appeared not to appreciate the need, widely shared by the Air Ministry, the Ministry of Aircraft Production and politicians, for an urgent response. Thirdly, by the end of the year, as the RAF was moving to an aggressive role, a more dynamic leader was sought for Fighter Command. Lastly, Churchill and Beaverbrook, his two powerful political patrons throughout the daylight battle, came to appreciate that a new man was needed. Unless these seven factors are examined and weighed it is difficult to unravel the truth of what happened among the top echelons of the RAF during the second half of 1940.

Nonetheless, such explanations cannot disguise one sad and important issue. From the end of 1940 Dowding was treated less than honourably by senior commanders of the Service to which he had given so much. At some later stage, when the importance of the Battle of Britain emerged from the fog of war, he could and should have been offered an earldom and, in spite of lack of precedent, been promoted to the rank of Marshal of the Royal Air Force. There is difficulty in believing that those senior officers of the RAF who at that time were opposed to Dowding's policies and who later reached the pinnacle of the Service – Newall, Portal, Harris, Douglas, Tedder and Slessor – achieved so much more in keeping their nation in the war.

Bearing this in mind as a background of apparent rejection and neglect, it is possible to understand the depth of emotion felt by the elderly survivors of 'The Few' as they watched the Queen Mother paying her tribute to their former chief. Almost half a century had passed before recognition was given, but the reward was all the more gratifying when it came.

1
DOWDING'S POSITION IN JULY 1940

PART 1: QUESTIONS OF LEADERSHIP

The campaign to replace Dowding was well under way even before the opening of the Battle of Britain. What happened in October and November 1940 was no more than a culmination of long-standing dissensions over the leadership, strategy and tactics of Fighter Command.

Differences over Dowding's tenure of office can be seen at the highest level on 10 July, the very day he later selected as the start of the main air battle.[1] Churchill felt compelled to send a private and confidential letter to Sir Archibald Sinclair, Secretary of State for Air and, considering the impending threat of a German assault upon the United Kingdom, the opening sentence was remarkable. 'I was very much taken aback the other night,' he wrote, 'when you told me that you had been considering removing Sir Hugh Dowding at the expiration of his present appointment,' then added that Sinclair had agreed that 'he might be allowed to stay on for another four months'.[2] The Prime Minister rose to Dowding's defence, describing him as 'one of the very best men you have got', a judgement made after knowing him for two years. He said that Dowding was both gifted and trusted, and should be kept in office indefinitely while the war lasted. Churchill then went further. Bearing in mind the forthcoming replacement of Sir Cyril Newall, the Chief of the Air Staff, whose popularity was fading, Churchill even suggested promotion for Dowding, who had been innocent of 'proved failure or inadequacy'. The letter expressed a firm and unequivocal belief in Dowding's suitability, and left no doubt over who should be leading Fighter Command.[3]

In assessing the career and subsequent dismissal of Dowding, it is instructive to estimate the reputations of Sinclair and Newall at that stage of the war. Both were held in low esteem by several politicians. For example, Stanley Bruce, the Australian High Commissioner in London, met Beaverbrook on 2 July and later wrote; 'We were in complete agreement that Newall had not the fighting weight necessary for the position of CAS'. On 10 July, the very day that Dowding's future was under review, Bruce discussed Newall's abilities, or lack of them, with Sinclair. Bruce told him that he had always had 'the gravest doubts' of Newall's competence and, referring to the French campaign, that 'the difficulty in getting decisions was an obvious indictment of Newall, who after all was responsible'. Sinclair, in defence of his CAS, called him 'a first class Staff Officer', yet claimed that if he 'was not the man to be Chief of the Air Staff' he would remove him.

Bruce, a shrewd politician, added an assessment of Sinclair. 'I have great doubts, however, whether he would take such definite action whatever was the result of such examination as he is making'. This was Bruce's second expression of reservation over Sinclair. On 10 June he had written; 'While a perfectly nice person I do not think Sinclair is much good or has any particular force and drive'. Bruce's papers underline the fact that political interest in, and effect on, the activities of the RAF at that time was very strong.[4]

Churchill's letter was only one in a long sequence of correspondence concerning Dowding and his future. It fitted into a cluster written around the start of the Battle of Britain, but can also be linked to a series of notes and letters dating back three years. Taken together, they form a catalogue of controversy and act as guides and pointers to his removal from office, his replacement by Air Vice-Marshal W. S. Douglas, and to the strategic and tactical role of Fighter Command both before and after that date. Without a study of this relationship, the fate of Dowding and, by extension, that of Park, cannot be seen in perspective.

For Dowding this was well trodden ground. On 30 March 1940, only one day before an earlier date for retirement was due to take effect, the Commander-in-Chief had received a note from Newall asking him to serve on until July, when he would have held his Command for four years. The note praised Fighter Command's efficiency and Dowding's part in achieving it, but the true reason for the request was that 'we may be on the verge of intensified air activity'. Newall added that he sometimes had the 'uncongenial task' of replacing senior officers to provide promotion for others, then offered the date of 14 July for retirement, although the RAF would 'greatly regret' the move.[5]

Ever punctilious, Dowding agreed immediately to the Air Ministry's wishes and asked the name of his successor, an enquiry that remained unanswered. Subsequently, in the early days of July, with his time almost expired and the Luftwaffe sitting at the gate, Dowding contacted Newall, seeking guidance on what was to happen. According to Wright, the exchange concluded when he sharply told the CAS; 'If you want to get rid of me, then get rid of me, but don't do it in this way'.[6] After contacting Sinclair, Newall wrote back on 5 July, asking the C-in-C to stay on because of 'present conditions' and offered to extend the appointment to the end of October.[7]

Dowding's tenacity over what he saw as a point of principle was as great as in any struggle against the Luftwaffe. He replied with a detailed account of his running battle with the Air Ministry, showing a powerful memory of real, or imagined, blows received. Newall was invited to cast his mind back to February 1937, when Sir Edward Ellington, then CAS, had informed Dowding that he would not be succeeding him, but that his rank should guarantee employment until the age of sixty, an anniversary that would be reached in 1942.[8] Dowding, who had expected to get the post, was hurt when it went to Newall, who was junior to him both in age and length of service.

Later, in August 1938, the Air Council had told him that his services would not be needed after the following June.[9] To add to his confusion, Dowding claimed, in February 1939 the *Evening Standard* had announced his impending retirement, even naming his successor, yet on the following day Newall had said that the Air Ministry would make no change that year. During an interview in the next month, Dowding continued, he told the Secretary of State for Air, Kingsley Wood, that he would not stay without the backing of the Air Council, previously denied to him. On that point he had received verbal assurance, but a week later he sent a reminder that an answer was awaited. That was followed on 20 March by the request from Newall that he should serve on until the end of March 1940.[10]

This date rested in Dowding's mind until, only one day before its arrival, Newall set the new date of 14 July. The passage of correspondence and action that followed led to Churchill's intervention with Sinclair on the very day that the main air battle started. Dowding's letter referred to the discourtesy and lack of consideration which he felt had been shown. No fewer than five retirement dates had been offered and, he reminded Newall, he would have been pleased to go before the war started. Now he was anxious to remain because he believed that no one 'will fight as I do' against proposals to reduce defence forces 'below the extreme danger point'.

Dowding never hesitated to speak his mind, a quality not universally admired. Here was an oblique reference to a two-pronged controversy which had existed between him and the Air Staff. First there was a disagreement over the number of fighters needed for the defence of Britain, the Home Base. Second was the attempt during the recent French campaign to send extra squadrons to France. In Newall's opinion he, as CAS, had resisted these moves, with Dowding's support; the C-in-C, however, was convinced that he alone had opposed them while the Air Staff hedged. Dowding's words, therefore, were a barbed reminder of contention, a point he well appreciated.

Dowding's letter concluded with the claim that he should not be asked to resign, except at his own request, before 1942, or the end of the war, 'whichever is the earlier'. This was a remarkable and unreasonable claim from a senior commander who should have appreciated that, in the exigencies of war, no commander or politician had an irrevocable right to any position. The letter was sent to Newall and a copy posted to Sinclair. Dowding was determined that his exasperation and sense of injustice should be widely known.[11]

Sinclair's reply was dated 10 July. Evidently he had discussed matters with Churchill in the meantime. His letter attempted to show an authority of office that some believed he lacked. 'I can only say,' he wrote, 'that the Chief of the Air Staff consulted me before asking you to retain your Command'.[12] The relentless Dowding, nonetheless, was in no mood to let matters rest, and maintained the chase in another letter which told Sinclair of events 'before you assumed your present office'. He pressed further, seeking an apology and confirmation that he was to retire at the end of October.[13]

Sinclair was noted as a paragon of good manners and master of tact, as might have been expected of an experienced politician. His response was in three parts. First, he avoided dealing with matters that occurred before he took office; he was concerned only with a decision for which he was answerable in Parliament, namely that Dowding should remain until October. This reinforced the final responsibility of politicians for Service appointments. The second part was a prophetic judgement, Sinclair adding that he did not look beyond October because he believed that by then the issue of the war would have been decided. He insisted that his only motive was to have the best leader at Fighter Command. His third point, on the proposed length of Dowding's service, was categorical – 'That decision must stand'. The letter promised diplomatically that, in future, Dowding's opinions would be consulted in good time before decisions were taken.[14]

Nevertheless, it is illuminating to note the mood of the Air Ministry at the time regarding Dowding's employment. Sinclair would not agree to the C-in-C's request, but remained firm on 31 October as the target date. This was confirmed by an official letter sent the same day.[15] Dowding's response was an acceptance, but instead of agreeing to the suggested date, he cannily inserted the words, 'for so long as my services may be required'.[16] The Air Ministry's reply was equally shrewd, avoiding the mention of any further date, but noting 'your willingness to continue in your present appointment'.[17]

Far more satisfying for the C-in-C was a conciliatory letter from his old rival, Newall, who mentioned as an explanation the inconvenience and lack of consideration caused by the stress of events since 1938, and then offered his 'sincere apologies'. Newall added that he had had the difficulty of providing opportunities of promotion while maintaining continuity at Fighter Command. Then he crossed swords over which of them had really opposed the dissipation of fighter aircraft during the French campaign. 'I was glad to have your support', he stated, a remark guaranteed to infuriate Dowding, who believed that he alone had saved them.

Newall went further to explain the extent of the Air Staff's responsibilities and dilemma, a factor often unacknowledged both by Dowding and his later champions. They had struggled to conserve forces for defending the Home Base, yet had a duty to implement Government decisions. It is noticeable that Newall, while applauding Sinclair's expression of confidence in the C-in-C, would also not be moved on the new date for retirement.[18]

The tennis-match of correspondence, so revealing of Dowding's slender hold on his position at the start of an air campaign for which he had prepared during the previous four years, was not finished. On 14 July Dowding wrote two further letters. In one, to Newall, he seized on and accepted the apology offered but then continued combatively by suggesting that they could not be expected to see eye to eye, and that further discussion would be unprofitable.[19]

An apparent confusion between Churchill and Sinclair over Dowding's future was displayed in the C-in-C's second letter, written to the Secretary of State.[20] It opened by claiming that, while dining with the Prime Minister the previous evening, he was told that he had secured confidence and that Churchill wanted him to remain on the Active List, with no retirement date offered. Churchill also told him that he had written to Sinclair on the matter.

Yet this does not tally with a comment written in Sinclair's hand on the letter he had received from Churchill. Sinclair claimed that the Prime Minister had agreed to matters resting 'at the point reached in my letter to C-in-C', and that a reconsideration could be given in about a month. Did Churchill change his mind? There is no written evidence to show what passed between Sinclair and Churchill at the meeting. Possibly he gave a different interpretation to each man, or, as both were desperate for the Prime Minister's approbation, they seized on any remark which appeared to support their particular case.

Churchill at that time had faith in what Dowding was achieving at Fighter Command. After the C-in-C dined at Chequers on 13 July, John Colville, one of the Prime Minister's secretaries, noted Churchill's comment that the previous four days had been glorious for the RAF because 'the enemy had come and had lost five to one'. This acceptance of a ratio that in reality was two to one may explain the Prime Minister's enthusiasm. Dowding also assessed the merits and weaknesses of Hurricanes and Defiants. Referring to Luftwaffe aircraft, he was surprised that the Germans had not yet protected the rear of their engines with armour plate; if that were done, RAF tactics would have to change. An augury of troubles to come for the C-in-C arrived when there was discussion of the German beam which could be used to lead bombers over their targets in darkness. Dowding's closeness to the Prime Minister allowed him to relate that recently 'he dreamt that there was only one man in England who could use a Bofors gun and his name was William Shakespeare'. No reaction to that remark is mentioned.[21]

In his letter to Sinclair, Dowding tried to avoid accusations of currying favour. No minister, he said, had learned from him of the approaching retirement. He concluded with grim satisfaction by mentioning Newall's apology, which he had accepted. Why did he write to Sinclair on this occasion? Probably he believed that the Prime Minister was an ally at a time of considerable strain between the Air Ministry and himself, one whose support he wanted to advertise. He did this to shore up his position in Fighter Command against those considered as enemies. Dowding obviously was very sensitive over the matter, as he emphasized that he had done nothing underhand to gain that support, a point made unnecessarily by an officer noted for honourable conduct and straight dealing.[22] The episode shows that he was more deeply affected by fears for his personal position than is generally acknowledged.

This passage of correspondence has not been assessed in earlier biographies of Dowding. Collier mentions the letters but barely explores them. Wright refers at length to the C-in-C's jousting with the Air Ministry, but does not mention Churchill's correspondence with Sinclair, which adds a further dimension to the controversy. These communications show explicitly that Dowding felt aggrieved by what he considered to be years of shabby treatment suffered at the hands of the Air Ministry. Also they display a lack of friendship between Dowding and Newall, who had been promoted over his head in 1937; in Dowding's recollection, some rivalry had existed even in their young subaltern days in India. However, they also demonstrate clearly the Air Ministry's intention at the start of the Battle of Britain that Fighter Command should have a new leader by the end of October at the latest.[23]

Dowding at this stage was fighting a double war. Firstly, he had no more than a tenuous hold on his position at the outset of a campaign for which he had prepared for four years, and was having to use considerable time and thought to defend himself. Secondly, he was attempting with limited forces, which had suffered heavily in the French campaign, to hold off probing Luftwaffe attacks against Channel convoys. Between 10 and 14 July, while he was busily sending and receiving letters concerning his own past and future, Fighter Command lost 14 pilots and 20 aircraft, while shooting down 44 enemy aeroplanes and killing 114 aircrew. Regardless of where the fault lay, the twin demands on Dowding were considerable at a time when his undivided attention should have been given to the defence of the Home Base.[24]

PART 2: DOWDING AND THE AIR STAFF BEFORE 1940

To gain a balanced view it is necessary to know not only Dowding's opinion of the Air Ministry, but also what the Air Staff thought of him. In their minds by July 1940 there were three valid reasons why he should be replaced.

The first was his age. Dowding was 58 years old and the senior RAF officer holding an active Command, while there were several staff some ten or fifteen years younger who were ready for advancement. The RAF has always offered opportunities to staff in their mid- or late-forties, a successful policy; examples include five who finally reached the rank of Marshal of the Royal Air Force – Harris (b.1892), Tedder (b.1890), Slessor (b.1897), Douglas (b.1893) and Portal (b.1893).

Second was the fact that Dowding had been at the head of Fighter Command since its foundation on 14 July 1936. The Service custom was for an officer to hold a post for two or three years before going on to gain further experience, so his period of four years was an exceptionally long one.[25]

He was 32 at the start of the First World War and had been, first, in the Royal Flying Corps, then in the RAF continuously since then. Even his closer contemporaries, Ellington (b.1877) and Ludlow-Hewitt (b.1886), had moved on from Commands, while Newall (b.1886) was near the end of his time as CAS. Salmond (b.1881), the only officer older than Dowding in age, rank and length of service, was working for the Ministry of Aircraft Production. These factors help to show how, in the view of many younger officers, the C-in-C represented the 'Old Guard' of the RAF and must surely be near the close of his service.

However, the third and main reason why the Air Council wanted Dowding to go was connected more with personality than with age. Particularly from 1937, when he failed to become CAS, Dowding developed an increasing disrespect for the Air Staff. He claimed that they failed to share his enthusiasm for the cardinal importance of fighter defence, and regarded them as vacillating in policy and incompetent in its execution. His outlook, nonetheless, was clear in a narrow field, sometimes becoming tunnel-vision, while theirs was necessarily panoramic and tended to blur when options competed or overlapped. For years they had suffered from lack of finance, the effects of the Ten Year Rule and the stagnation of the Depression; when the nation awoke to the need for rearmament they had to compete with other Services for resources. Then they had to place in perspective all of the requirements of the RAF, from building aircraft to providing supplies, from training aircrew to developing Radio Direction Finding (RDF) and from providing Intelligence services to the construction of airfields.[26]

These and many other commitments descended daily on their desks – and sometimes their heads – in an unremitting dive-bombing of urgent requests. Dowding's needs had to be placed beside those of others, seldom to his satisfaction – or to theirs. Therefore he increasingly viewed the Air Staff as misguided, lacking the will to fight for the needs of the RAF, by which he meant primarily Fighter Command.

Dowding's feelings were displayed in February 1939, when he prepared a catalogue of notes of complaint. It is noticeable that what he called 'very cavalier treatment' had begun two years earlier, in the period when he failed to become CAS. He claimed to be dealing with vital matters neglected by them for fifteen years, and accused them of inertia. They had taken decisions about Fighter Command without consulting him, and he finished by hoping that his successor would be *persona grata*, inferring that he was not.[27]

The Air Ministry's opinions present a very different picture. Dowding had never been regarded as the pre-eminent commander by three of the four

Secretaries of State under whom he served. The first of these, the Earl of Swinton, did not think of him as the best, placing Air Vice-Marshal W. Freeman first among air commanders when he took over.[28] Others, also, found difficulties with him. For example, Arthur Harris, subsequently C-in-C Bomber Command, reacted strongly in 1938 on learning that he was to be posted as Dowding's Senior Air Staff Officer. Later he commented, 'My heart went into my boots'. They had disagreed on a number of issues over previous years, when the C-in-C was Air Member for Research and Development and he was in Plans. In Harris's view Dowding was, '... stubborn as a mule, but a nice old boy really. He was just out of touch with flying.' [29] Similar views were held by some in the aircraft industry. Harald Penrose, the manager of Westland Civil Aircraft from 1928 and later the company's chief test pilot, said that Dowding's sobriquet 'Stuffy' was apt, because he was withdrawn and lacked humour, keeping his distance from aircraft designers and directors. Penrose allowed that he was a good and courageous leader, blessed with sound judgement, but said that he lacked the presence of his successor, Wilfrid Freeman, who was a taller, younger man of handsome appearance, to whom the industry responded in a friendly fashion.[30]

An eminent opponent was Air Marshal Sir Philip Joubert, who differed from Dowding over the transmission of information received by RDF to fighter squadrons by way of filter rooms. Joubert wrote that the C-in-C could be 'extremely exacting and tiresome' to subordinates, as well as spending 'too much time on details and less than sufficient on principles'.[31] There was a general view that Dowding could be prickly and difficult, lacking the golden virtue of tact. Even his obituary in *The Times* noted that he was not an easy man, and one to whom 'slackness, hypocrisy and self-seeking were not peccadilloes, but scarlet sins'.[32] These views have been summarized by Denis Richards, author of the official history of the RAF, in referring to Dowding's unclubbable and less than co-operative nature, often displayed to those with whom he disagreed. 'Dowding was really very difficult', in his opinion and, as several opponents appreciated, 'tact was not a weapon in Dowding's armoury'.[33]

The relationship between Dowding and Leigh-Mallory, AOC, No 12 Group, was far from cordial and a factor in the later controversy over tactics. At a conference following an air defence exercise in 1939 Dowding spoke for over an hour on the agenda's 56 items, then allocated only five minutes each to his two Group Commanders. Worse was to follow when Dowding, in front of several other senior officers said, 'The trouble with you, Leigh-Mallory, is that you sometimes cannot see further than the end of your little nose'.

Leigh-Mallory's attitude to his Commander-in-Chief varied, according to eyewitnesses. Sir Kenneth Cross recollected that he never heard Leigh-Mallory make a disparaging remark about Park or any remark at all about Dowding,[34] a point also made by Sir Harry Broadhurst, then a Wing Commander in No 12 Group.[35] Yet Park in 1968 had a different memory. Looking back at an incident that occurred in 1940, when he was Dowding's SASO, he said that Leigh-Mallory came into his office after a meeting with the C-in-C and complained about his obstinacy. 'He said that he would move heaven and earth to get Dowding sacked from his job.' [36] The mutual antipathy between Leigh-Mallory and Dowding on the one hand, and between Park and Leigh-Mallory on the other, came to the surface during the Battle of Britain. This disagreement was destined to play a major part in the changes of leadership, strategy and tactics at Fighter Command.

By the start of the aerial battle, therefore, Dowding's list of friends in the Air Ministry and in some parts of his Command was hardly extensive. His opponents found him to be particularly cantankerous. In assessing some of his differences with the Air Staff it is important to remember that such contests were not unusual, though they were usually less unrelenting. For example, while at Bomber Command, Ludlow-Hewitt disagreed strongly with the Air Ministry over policy as he fought for his corner. Yet Ludlow-Hewitt's sharp comments were generally considered less unacceptable than Dowding's, possibly because the former was easily replaceable. There were more senior staff with the experience to lead Bomber Command than there were to take over from Dowding.[37]

Some of the sharpest differences between the Air Council and the C-in-C, Fighter Command occurred from 1938. In John Terraine's view they consisted of 'a three-pronged argument', which he lists as the question of deployment, the Germans' intentions and the conflicting needs of the RAF.[38] It should be noted also that at the heart of the squabble lay a basic difference of strategic thought on air power in the later 1930s. Most senior officers in the Service were wedded to the Trenchard Bomber Doctrine, while Dowding, especially from the time of the Munich Crisis, endorsed the importance of a Fighter Doctrine.

Lord Trenchard, 'Father of the RAF', had an unequalled influence on the Service from its foundation in 1918. His indomitable and inspiring spirit was fired with ideas of the importance of the offensive, in which aerial bombardment was the nation's prime strategic weapon. His beliefs permeated the Air Ministry, so that until the outbreak of the Second World War roughly two squadrons of bombers were built for each new squadron of fighters.

Trenchard had never enjoyed friendship with Dowding, ever since their old RFC days. When, in 1916, Dowding had asked for squadrons to be relieved periodically, Trenchard sensed weakness, calling him a 'dismal Jimmy' who was 'obsessed by the fear of further casualties'. Dowding was removed from active service and sent back to Britain to command the Southern Training Brigade.[39] Subsequently their relationship improved marginally between the wars, but when the importance of Fighter Command grew after 1937 and, with it, the role of Dowding, Trenchard's Bomber Doctrine was still the linchpin of policy for the majority of the Air Staff.

The first part of the Bomber Doctrine predicted the devastating power of German air attack on Britain, with attendant damage and breakdown of morale. From 1932, when Baldwin glumly confessed that 'the bomber will always get through', the theory grew.[40] Writers foresaw large bomber formations destroying cities, with defending fighters which had less armament and only marginally greater speed unable to stop them.[41] Major-General 'Boney' Fuller suffered morbid fears. London would become 'a raving bedlam', where hospitals would be stormed, traffic halted and the government overthrown 'by an avalanche of terror'. A supporter of Oswald Moseley, he believed the Jews of London's East End would panic.[42] Even the Chiefs of Staff Joint Planning Sub-Committee caught the mood of pessimism in 1936. The Luftwaffe, they reported, would attempt to drive Britain out of a war with a rapid knock-out blow starting on the first day of the conflict.[43] Two years later, when the repercussions of Munich were engaging people's minds, the Cabinet were informed that three weeks of bombing would destroy almost half a million houses and damage a further five million.[44] To add to the gloom, Parliament was told in 1938 that, by the end of the following year, Germany would have a front-line strength of 6,000 aircraft, rising to 8,000; the report added that the RAF's total would not reach 2,700 until mid-1940.[45]

Looking back from the stronghold of hindsight, the distance between fear and reality becomes obvious, but to Service leaders of the time the threat was extreme. No one knew for certain what the effects of mass bombing might be, and, judging from the use of aircraft by the Japanese in China, the Italians in Abyssinia and the Germans in Spain, the auguries were sombre. Fighter defence was an unknown and unproven factor. In Britain the only yardstick was a comparison with what had happened between 1914 and 1918, a sharp memory for many senior officers. They recollected that even in 1925 an Air Staff estimate, based on the earlier German raids, suggested that in London during the first two days of attack some 3,000 people would be killed and 6,000 injured.[46]

Slessor, formerly Director of Plans at the Air Ministry, later commented that if heavy German bombing had taken place, the Air Staff would have been blameworthy if they 'had uttered no warning of the possibility or taken steps to guard against it'.[47] To reinforce this point, Lord Douglas wrote of the degree to which the Air Ministry, along with many others, was affected during the Spanish Civil War both by the bombing of troops and of Guernica. He was sure that this influenced Britain's attitude at the time of Munich.[48]

The public mind was coloured by popular books. Writing for Gollancz, J. B. S. Haldane was, in company with many Socialists and Communists, opposed to rearmament and war. 'This book is intended for the ordinary citizen', he wrote, 'the sort of man and woman who is going to be killed if Britain is raided again from the air.' He predicted that bombers could drop nearly double the 'total weight dropped in Britain during the whole of the last war in half a minute', and that 'the "knock-out" blow might kill 50,000 to 100,000 Londoners'.[49]

The controversy between the bomber and fighter lobbies at the time evolved from selecting the best method of dealing with the menace. The second part of the Trenchard Doctrine clearly stated that threat should be matched with threat, so the aim of the RAF was to retaliate by launching raids on an enemy, especially targeting the economy. In 1939 Trenchard told the House of Lords that the only factor which would stop war-makers was the fear of retaliation.[50] However, it was little appreciated at the time that the bomber was invested with a deterrent power far exceeding its ability to reach, identify and destroy targets.

Dowding's appointment to the newly formed Fighter Command in 1936 was equivalent to receiving captaincy of the Second Eleven, because in military aviation the bomber was supreme, and it was expected that fighters would play an ancillary role. Two factors between 1935 and 1939 altered the balance. First was the development of RDF; second was the revolution in the design, speed and armament of monoplane fighters. These changes increased the importance of Dowding's position. The spotlight fell on his Command, thereby stressing the significance of his relationship with the Air Staff.

Consequently Dowding's Fighter Doctrine was propounded, together with his unwavering belief in the necessity to protect the Home Base. 'The best defence of the country is the Fear of the Fighter', he wrote to the Air Ministry in September 1939. He reasoned that if Britain were strong in fighters she would probably never be attacked in force. Limited strength would draw attacks which would be stopped only after widespread damage had been caused. His most profound worry was that a shortage of fighters would bring unstoppable raids 'and the productive capacity of the country will be virtually destroyed'. In that event, he predicted, other parts of the RAF, and by that he meant Bomber Command particularly, would be wasted and useless. At the end of his homily he suggested, with an argument which failed to persuade the bomber lobby at the Air Ministry, that the future of the nation 'depends upon the Royal Navy and Fighter Command'.[51]

Dowding's strategy was turned to building a complete system of aerial defence for Britain, and in this, by the outbreak of war, he had succeeded to an extent that no other commander probably could have matched. But his concentration upon a laager defence was at variance with those on the Air Staff who believed that fighters were mainly a placebo for the public. An Air Staff note, written shortly after the Munich Crisis had uncovered some of the RAF's deficiencies in fighter strength, stated that it was not enough merely to avoid losing a war. The conflict had to be won, and that could never be achieved by defence alone. Drawing a comparison with the boxing ring, the report said that there would be 'no victory for a boxer who only parried blows'. He needed a big punch of his own, and would have to 'keep on punching until his opponent is out'.[52]

21

In boxing terms Dowding was an astute counter-puncher, learning to husband and employ limited forces in a defensive battle aimed at preventing the Luftwaffe from achieving mastery in British skies. The nature of the task he was set to solve prevented him from taking a direct involvement in the strategy of the bomber lobby, which was firmly entrenched in Whitehall. Yet, of course, their basic argument was sound. Wars cannot be won by fighters; they may be won by bombers.

A second example of Dowding's difficulties with the Air Staff during the later 1930s came from their respective attitudes towards the number of squadrons needed by Fighter Command. In brief, the Air Staff, with their insistence on expanding the number of bombers, were unwilling to provide as many fighters as Dowding claimed he required. He, however, was worried particularly by the limitations of biplane fighters when set against the monoplane bombers being built in Germany. By March 1938 Dowding believed that there should be no fewer than 45 squadrons, yet four months later Slessor, then Deputy Director of Plans at the Air Ministry and thus an officer of great influence, considered that 35 squadrons of fighters – 28 in the line and seven in reserve – should be the minimum home defence strength. Again, Fighter Command, with spreading responsibilities, wanted more.

The minds of politicians and Service officers were concentrated rapidly by the Munich Crisis, after which the needs of the RAF, so long neglected by government policies, received swift relief. On 1 October 1938 Britain's fighter strength was 406 machines. The sobering thought for those who drew a distinction between numbers and quality, however, was that there were only 70 Hurricanes and 14 Spitfires in the total, and the latter at the time were non-operational. The remaining 322 fighters, of which the most effective were 84 Gladiators, could barely catch, let alone shoot down, the contemporary German bombers.[54] Dowding's frustration was shown in a note on 12 October in which he wrote that, to constitute an adequate defence force, 'I should consider 41 squadrons upon the presence of which I could *rely* would be adequate for Home Defence purposes'.[55]

Faced with the twin demands for bombers and fighters, the Air Staff tried to follow a double strategy. Firstly, in forward planning they hoped to create a strike force of heavy bombers capable of devastating an enemy's economic power and of forcing him to deploy much of his own strength in defence. Secondly, through Fighter Command they intended to compel any attacking force to call off an offensive by inflicting unacceptable losses.

After Munich more of the Air Staff appreciated not so much that their bomber creed was over-optimistic, but that more fighters were needed to defend Britain. This was admitted in November 1938 by a document stating that, in the past, the case for the bomber had possibly been overstressed. Later it became obvious that one reason for that belief was the exaggeration of Luftwaffe numbers and capabilities, assumed by RAF Intelligence.[56] What the Air Ministry failed to make adequate allowance for, however, was that developments of monoplane fighters, with great speed and firepower, would affect not only unescorted German bombers over Britain, but also unescorted RAF bombers over Germany.

The Air Staff had no little difficulty in trying to meet the dual needs of the RAF within a short time. The dichotomy can be deduced from statements made by Kingsley Wood, Secretary of State for Air, after Munich. On 2 November 1938 he told the Air Staff that the strong were those whose influence could be backed by force, and 'this we cannot do if we are inferior in air power, which means striking power'.[57] However, eight days later he assured the Commons that he would provide 'the highest priority to the strengthening of our fighter force, that force which is designed to meet the invading bomber in the air'.[58] By March 1939 he was speaking of having 'what I would call a balanced Air Force'. The policy of the counter-offensive, he claimed, had not been abandoned, but 'security of the base is one of the vital principles of war'. Both offensive and defensive operations were needed, and neither would be neglected.[59] It is noteworthy that, even at a time when Dowding's Command was a prime candidate for expansion, much greater financial allocations were given to bombers. Under Scheme M the cost of fighters was estimated at £45 million; bombers were allocated £175 million.[60] The Air Council made efforts to improve the production and provision of monoplane fighters in the months before the outbreak of war and, considering other demands made upon them, deserve credit for that. Dowding, however, did not approve of either their attempts or the results, as may be judged from his Battle of Britain Despatch. Dissatisfaction broke through. He complained that, in a letter written to the Air Ministry at the start of the war, he had reminded the Ministry that the Air Staff estimate of the number of squadrons required for home defence was 52, whereas he had no more than 34 for the task, allowing that some Auxiliary squadrons were only partially ready. The controversy over fighter numbers lasted for the rest of his time at Fighter Command.[61]

Other related differences also divided Dowding from his employers. He did not believe that they appreciated the urgency of providing underground control rooms at headquarters. In his view they were slack in supplying concrete runways for aerodromes. A small, yet telling example of Dowding's care for his pilots – and the occasion of another difference with the Air Staff – was his request for bulletproof glass to be fitted to fighters.[62] Dowding's third area of overall disagreement with the Air Ministry stemmed from their respective ideas of the strategy of employing Fighter Command. The Air Staff were bound by the demands set by government policy, with which they did not always agree. In his view, nonetheless, the squadrons existed exclusively for the air defence of Great Britain.

As war approached, the responsibilities of Fighter Command grew. Originally, Dowding had interpreted its role as the provision of cover for two vital areas lying within the radius of attack from unescorted bombers, which would fly from Germany, cross the North Sea and approach Britain from a mainly easterly direction. The first area was London and south-eastern England, where he deployed No 11 Group. The second was the wider geographical region of East Anglia, the Midlands and parts of the north, particularly industrial centres, where No 12 Group was based. It was anticipated that the burden of battle would be shared by these two Groups, an important factor to be borne in mind when assessing events of the later battle. In Dowding's view his Command would be exercised to the limit in protecting those areas; any further demands could be met only by the provision of greater resources.[63]

During 1939 Fighter Command's expanding role was recognized by the formation of No 13 Group and the planning of No 10 Group. The former covered the wide sweep of coastal Britain lying to the north of No 12 Group, while the latter, in time, would cover south-western England.[64] Further responsibilities were added. The naval base at Scapa Flow needed protection, as did coastal shipping, especially off the east coast. Then the defence of Belfast, a large industrial centre, was included. By the opening of war Dowding was required to protect factories, especially those producing aircraft, and to ensure the safety of the systems of supply and distribution, particularly at major ports. He also had to cover Royal Navy shore bases and guard coastal shipping, in spite of his feeling that this was the Navy's task. He was required to cover Belfast with one squadron, and to provide fighters to protect British forces in France. By September the planned strength of Fighter Command to meet these duties had risen to 57 squadrons, yet the reality was that there were 39, of which 25 were Regular and fourteen Auxiliary. To compound difficulties, four squadrons immediately flew to France, as prearranged.[65]

Dowding sometimes showed an air of paternalism, verging on ownership, towards his men and machines, giving the impression of selecting which duties his Command would undertake. Although possessing an almost messianic sense of mission towards the defence of the Home Base, he was still a servant of the Air Ministry. With the benefit of hindsight, his burning belief in the need to retain fighters to protect Britain has been widely praised.[66] Nevertheless, the burdens laid on the Air Staff at the time should be recognized. They were affected by requirements from the Government and by the needs of the other two Services. Blaming them for the problems and weaknesses of the RAF is easy, but unjust, as they were servants of masters with whose decisions they did not always concur.

PART 3: THE FRENCH CONNECTION

Nowhere were the differences which separated Dowding from the Air Council more marked than over the question of fighters for France. The main *casus belli* was the extent to which Fighter Command should support the British Expeditionary Force in France, and the French themselves. The argument stretched from the aftermath of the Munich Crisis to the end of the French campaign in June 1940.

Dowding's supporters claim that he fought virtually singlehanded to retain squadrons in Britain, an attitude formed by his prescience that they would be required, while the Air Ministry were profligate in preparing to send them to France. There were two phases of disagreement. The first lasted until the eve of the German *Blitzkrieg* in the West on 10 May 1940, and the second followed on until the French collapse in late June. However, the portrayal of Dowding's lone opposition is less than just to some other senior officers.

At the root of the problem lay British mistrust of entanglement in a war on the European mainland and, when such an involvement became inevitable, an unwillingness to commit forces on a large scale. Nevertheless, it was obvious that RAF aircraft would have to be part of the force despatched, both to fulfil the Air Ministry's expectations of the efficacy of bombing targets in Germany and also to protect British forces. As a matter of government policy the planned sending of four squadrons from Fighter Command was far from unreasonable; it was a decision approached by the Air Ministry with guarded charity and towards which Dowding was distinctly hostile.

The protection of Great Britain was ensured by a Fighter Command which depended on RDF, control rooms and the squadrons themselves. By the start of the Second World War no other nation had a system of air defence to equal that established in the United Kingdom. However, this system, of which Dowding was more the builder than the architect, limited the Command's strategic use, although this weakness emanated from the Air Council, which altered the concept of the indivisibility of air power when separate Commands were created in 1936.[67] Hurricanes and Spitfires would not be used fully as weapons against Germany, a point noted by Slessor, an able strategist, in 1939. He suggested that unless they could fly from French bases, some 'five or six hundred good short-range fighters sitting in England' would be unable to influence the result of battles on the Continent which could affect Britain's future. He pointed out that 'our quite natural and proper obsession' with the fear of a 'knock-out' blow could lead to an insular outlook. This would give little help to France, whose defeat could be followed by heavy attacks on Britain.[68]

Newall, as CAS, felt the pressure being exerted on Fighter Command. The four squadrons allocated to the Field Force were no more than a token gesture, and he received urgent requests from the French for support, particularly as their own *Armée de l'Air* was weak. Yet he was aware simultaneously of Fighter Command's prime responsibility for the defence of mainland Britain, a task which could be carried out only through Dowding's controlled system. In May 1939 he resisted undertakings being given in advance to the French to despatch more fighters to them. That, he announced, would be decided by the Cabinet 'in the light of the circumstances at the time'. Yet, as his responsibilities to Government policies weighed on him, he planned for a further six squadrons to be made ready from early 1940, in case they should be needed in France.[69]

Dowding's objections to this policy lasted unremittingly through September and October. 'The secure base must be the foundation for all our war plans', he warned sternly within a fortnight of the outbreak of hostilities, 'and, at the present moment, our base is dangerously insecure.' However, the demands made on the C-in-C, Fighter Command, were at least equalled, if not exceeded, by those aimed at the CAS and the Air Council, as is shown clearly by the correspondence between Dowding and his masters at the time.[70] In this matter, Dowding's reputation for obstinacy and an unwillingness to co-operate fell into sharper focus. Denis Richards has written of the strength of his feelings, but then adds that, although he seemed unaware of it, 'he had the Air Staff with him all the way'.[71] His reaction to other staff could be combative. In his memoirs, Sholto Douglas remembered approaching Dowding over sending fighters to France, 'and almost as I expected, I got a smart rebuff'.[72] This attitude was remembered and not forgiven by some who had suffered from his tongue and pen.

Yet Dowding's supporters have painted a portrait of a lone campaigner, virtually without allies, struggling to ensure the aerial security of Britain. Wright wrote of 'the long and lonely struggle that he was to have to wage during those first eight months of the war to maintain, let alone build up, what he felt to be sufficient forces for the air defence of the country'.[73] Such a claim does not present a balanced view of the feelings of the time.

In reality, both Dowding and the Air Staff were less than prepared to weaken the defensive arm of the RAF; the difference was one of degree. The Air Ministry were, more particularly, servants of military and political demands to give adequate cover to the BEF and to demonstrate that Britain was an ally of France not in words alone.[74]

The different appreciations of the role of Fighter Command, made by those at the heart of Britain's air defences, were sharpened by a cause other than the need to retain in the United Kingdom a basic number of squadrons required for the protection of the Home Base, with no reductions for any other duties. This cause was an awareness, a deeply worrying omen in view of the forthcoming struggle, of the weaknesses of the French Air Force. They mistrusted the abilities of the French to fight a war in the air, disturbed by their pervading pessimism and lack of a system of integrated air defence.[75] For Dowding the mistrust was fuelled by personal experience. In 1939 he flew, with his Personal Assistant, to Lille to examine their defensive system. The meeting was preceded by a long luncheon in a public restaurant, during which Dowding, an abstemious man, drank far less than several French commanders. He was then escorted to a basement where the system was revealed. It consisted of a French airman with a public telephone, taking occasional messages then entering chalked arrows on a squared blackboard. Dowding, anger blended with disappointment, could barely wait to return to his aircraft.[76]

The number of aircraft available to the French in 1940 is not easy to discover, as some totals disguise the inclusion of obsolete machines. This was to prove a crucial factor in battle because, in Terraine's estimate, of the 170 bombers and 614 fighters ready *en ligne* in February 1940, only 37 of the former and 523 of the latter had been built within the previous two years. The probable figures of operational aircraft for early May were 465 fighters and 459 bombers.[77]

The Air Staff were painfully aware of French failings. Factory production, lack of adequate RDF defence, squadron organization, fighter performance and lack of replacements all fell below RAF standards. Consequently an even greater burden was bound to fall on Fighter Command when the main battle opened. The French machines, supported by a small, though valuable, British contingent, were faced by a Luftwaffe of over 4,000 aircraft, of which about 1,700 were fighters or dive-bombers.[78]

When the blow fell, on 10 May, within a few days or, as some would claim, a few hours, the Air Staff's worst fears were realized. In the words of one historian, the French Air Force 'shattered into a thousand pieces at the first blow'. The earlier predictions and fears soon came to pass as the Luftwaffe established battlefield superiority not only in numbers but also through tactical application.[79]

On 10 May the RAF had 45 fighter squadrons in the United Kingdom and six in France. Losses, euphemistically called 'wastage', were soon heavy, and requests for reinforcements arrived without respite. Some came from the French, who could not comprehend Britain's unwillingness to use an under-employed resource.[80] Others came from the British Army in France, and yet others from the RAF component there. The assistance demanded was not only for replacement aircraft, but also for the change in strategy favoured by some of the Air Staff but feared by Dowding, namely a greater 'battlefield presence'. Probably the battle to save Britain was being fought over France and Belgium.[81]

For him, the persistent demands on Fighter Command to send additional aircraft to France, combined with the rate of wastage of squadrons in action, promised doom both for the RAF and the nation. This period has offered, for some, signal proof of Dowding's greatness in retaining his Command for what he saw as its prime purpose. Others, nevertheless, felt the severity of Dowding's strictures; they thought of him increasingly as tetchy and uncooperative, narrow in outlook.[82]

As the crisis developed, Dowding and the Air Staff suggested that, as an alternative to sending more fighters to France, Bomber Command should attack oil targets in Germany. That would bring retaliatory raids on Britain, where Fighter Command was equipped to counter them, over Dowding's territory and under his control. He was also shrewd enough to sense that, as soon as German bombs fell on Britain, fewer voices would ask him to despatch fighters to France. On 14 May he wrote 'the Hurricane tap is now turned full on', and expressed the fear of being 'bled white'. Certainly the Air Staff shared these fears, and there was a corporate unease that few fighters would be left to defend the Home Base.[83]

Dowding was therefore present, although for two items only, at a Cabinet meeting on 15 May when the matter of fighters for France was again raised. In spite of claims to the contrary, he did not speak. This confusion has ensnared several of the eminent, beginning with Beaverbrook, who, Terraine says, 'was never one to let mere facts spoil a good story'. Others at fault include A. J. P. Taylor, Robert Wright, who was misled by Dowding's imperfect memory, and Basil Collier. The C-in-C did speak at an earlier meeting of the Chiefs of Staff Committee, but the RAF's case was laid before the Cabinet by Newall, as CAS. Afterwards, the flow of fighters was staunched, but not stemmed, before several changes of policy occurred. It is important to explore what really happened then, because the myth has grown that Dowding alone saved the nation by struggling to retain squadrons. Others, particularly Newall, played their part.[84]

The next day, Dowding wrote what is generally regarded as his most influential document, a letter comprising ten points, to the Air Ministry. Two of them explain his position clearly. Also, they demonstrate the state of mind in which he approached the forthcoming battle over Britain, and illustrate his need to be sparing with what forces lay at his disposal for fighting a defensive campaign:

'5. I would remind the Air Council that the last estimate which they made as to the force necessary to defend this country was fifty-two squadrons, and my strength has now been reduced to the equivalent of thirty-six squadrons.

'10. I believe that if an adequate fighter force is kept in this country, and if the Fleet remains in being, and if the Home Forces are suitably organised to resist invasion, we should be able to carry on the war single-handed for some time, if not indefinitely. But, if the Home Defence Force is drained away in a desperate attempt to remedy the situation in France, defeat in France will involve the final, complete and irremediable defeat of this country.' [85]

Fighter Command was widely employed in the week of the Dunkirk evacuation. The RAF Component returned to Britain on 21 May and the aerial defence of forces still in France was provided by squadrons under the command of No 11 Group, flying from south-east England. Dowding had the satisfaction of controlling these aircraft, but carried the burden of protecting an army facing disaster and a navy valiantly attempting to save them.

By 3 June most squadrons had seen action over the battle area, flying over 2,700 sorties, and had suffered heavily. In the three weeks from 10 May, 432 Hurricanes and Spitfires were lost, 106 of them during the Dunkirk evacuation. On 1 June Dowding had 321 Hurricanes and Spitfires ready to fight and the battle for France was unfinished. Two days later he again attended a Cabinet meeting and this time he did speak, pointing out the risk of sending fighters abroad now that the French Army was in a parlous condition. He produced a graph showing that, on each of ten days during May, 25 fighters were lost, while only four replacements were received. These were irrefutable facts and overcame contrary arguments, although by then they were few.[86]

At the end of the French campaign the RAF had lost more than 900 aircraft in six weeks, some 450 of them Hurricanes and Spitfires, rubies beyond price in the eyes of Dowding and the Air Staff. His relief at the French surrender was later disclosed to Lord Halifax, the Foreign Secretary, who was told, with emotion, that at the news, 'I went on my knees and thanked God'.[87]

The proving ground of battle had resolved several questions. The Luftwaffe was a formidable adversary, used as an integral component of *Blitzkrieg*, and its fighter tactics were both flexible and effective. For the RAF, the use of unescorted bombers in daylight raids had proved to be suicidal. Bomber Command's attempted intervention by making night raids on German industry was barely noticed. The Bf 109 was an excellent fighter, especially in the dive and climb. On the other side, British fighter pilots had gained valuable, though costly, battle experience, flying against more experienced opponents. Pilots in Hurricanes and Spitfires had shot down all types of enemy bomber and felt confident at taking on Bf 109s, being able to turn inside the German aeroplane.[88] Few people appreciated the extent of German fighter losses in the campaign; they had lost 247 Bf 109s and 108 Bf 110s, together with roughly one-seventh of their pilots, although those who had become prisoners of war were released at the French surrender. The Luftwaffe had received a setback in its first failure of the war.[89]

On 23 May Goering had telephoned Hitler with the offer that the Luftwaffe, single-handed, would destroy British resistance at Dunkirk. 'We have done it!' he told Milch, the Inspector-General of the German Air Force, at headquarters. 'The Luftwaffe is to wipe out the British on the beaches. I have managed to talk the Führer round to halting the army.' Reasons such as poor weather and a lack of forward bases have been advanced to explain the Luftwaffe's subsequent inability to support the confidence of their Commander-in-Chief, but the courage and skill of RAF pilots, flying excellent machines, must not be overlooked among the prime reasons for the German failure.[90]

Dowding's sorest blow was the number of pilots lost in the French campaign, many of whom were experienced airmen, the cream of the pre-war

Fighter Command, with long flying hours to their credit. Had they survived, they would have commanded flights and squadrons in which their skill would have been invaluable. Their loss threw a heavy burden on to the Command, especially for those formations which came to be led by new commanders, lacking the knowledge of their predecessors. The C-in-C felt the greatest sympathy for all of his pilots, and on 2 June wrote a general letter of thanks to all of the squadrons, showing again his care for his men.[91]

PART 4: WHY RETAIN DOWDING?

Hence, on 10 July Dowding's position as Commander-in-Chief was far from firm. Why, then, had he lasted so long in office? There are three main reasons for the anomaly.

First, no other senior officer had acquired such a detailed knowledge of fighter defence before 1939. This was due partly to his length of service, which included, from 1926-29, the position of Director of Training, then, from 1930-36, the position of Air Member for Supply and Development. With such wide experience behind him, Dowding was able to promote rapid changes at Fighter Command after 1936. For example, he encouraged the development of metal monoplane fighters – Hurricanes and Spitfires, their Rolls-Royce engines, eight-gun armament and radio control. Dowding was a pioneer of Operational Research. He deserves much credit for promoting RDF into a defensive system, where information was transmitted to operations rooms and action was controlled.

Second, in spite of the wish of the Air Staff to replace Dowding, a series of emergencies and accidents had occurred which made change either undesirable or impracticable. The Air Ministry's letter of August 1938, informing Dowding that his services would not be required after the following June, was followed in the next month by the Munich Crisis. Subsequently, the significance of Fighter Command increased in the plans for the overall defence of Great Britain, and the role of its Commander-in-Chief grew in importance. The rush to expand the Command demanded continuity of leadership, and Dowding was not replaced. From then until the outbreak of war the political situation in Europe was increasingly unstable, especially after the German occupation of the remainder of Czechoslovakia in the spring of 1939, providing a further reason for maintaining the *status quo*.

In August 1938 Air Vice-Marshal C. L. Courtney was informed by the Air Ministry that he was to succeed Dowding in the following June. However, three days before the proposed take-over Courtney was involved in an air crash, suffering serious injuries, and Dowding was left at his post.[92] Thus the force of events, more than any measured planning by the Air Council, ensured that he was at the head of Fighter Command as the Battle of Britain opened.

A third reason for his retention of command is seldom recognized. It is that he had the support of two eminent politicians who, noting his dedication and skill in fighter defence, believed him to be the best commander available. The first was Lord Beaverbrook, Minister of Aircraft Production, with whom, in spite of their different personalities, Dowding formed a good working relationship. Probably the catalyst of their friendship was their mutual dislike of the Air Ministry, whose occupants Beaverbrook called 'the bloody Air Marshals', and with whom Dowding had already fought running battles. An example of Dowding's more cordial relationship with Beaverbrook was apparent on 5 July, when he was asked by the Minister to provide Spitfires for photographic work. He replied that he begrudged giving up any Spitfire, but then added with a note of charity seldom displayed to the Air Staff, 'but I must take a broad view of the question'. Their mutual friendship lasted until Beaverbrook's death in 1964.[93]

Dowding's second political patron was Churchill, who harboured doubts over the running of the Air Ministry. He approved of Dowding's organization of Home Defence and, as the spotlight turned on Fighter Command after Dunkirk and the demands made on its pilots became more obvious, Churchill warmed both to those young men and, *pari passu*, their Commander-in-Chief.

Under the British system of governmental control of the armed Services, such political support was paramount. In matters of policy Parliament was the final arbiter; in its application, the Services were servants of the Crown, through Parliament. An officer of Dowding's rank and responsibilities, which affected the lives of ordinary people, was compelled to enjoy the confidence of his ultimate masters. In July 1940 he had certainly gained that.

Nonetheless, neither the C-in-C nor the Air Ministry knew at the time that the Prime Minister's support was based on the needs of the moment. Writing to Beaverbrook on 8 July, Churchill spoke of the urgent requirement for fighters 'till we have broken the enemy's attack'. Then he looked to the future with uncanny vision. There was, he said, only one way to win the war. Britain had no army to defeat the military power of Germany, and the blockade was ineffective. If he did not defeat Britain, Hitler would 'recoil Eastward and we will have nothing to stop him'. Only one thing would bring him down, and that was 'an absolutely devastating, exterminating attack by very heavy bombers from this country upon the Nazi homeland'. In this expression of opinion, Churchill had nailed his colours to the mast. He shared the belief of the bomber lobby within the Air Ministry in the power of aerial attack against the Germans' economy and morale. 'We must be able to overwhelm them by this means', he continued, adding significantly, 'without which I do not see a way through.' His final words were, 'We cannot accept any lower aim than air mastery. When can it be obtained?'[94]

As a result, Churchill, while recommending to Sinclair in his letter of 10 July that Dowding should be retained, recognized that fighters would not bring final victory. He was already estimating that the forthcoming air battle would be no more than a holding operation, designed to keep the Germans at bay until Britain had the strength to strike back. His words would have brought solace to those in the Air Ministry who wanted Dowding replaced, preferably by the end of October.

As the contest with the Luftwaffe developed, further reasons to remove Dowding were discovered or developed by his chief critics, who came to appreciate the value of political patronage. Gradually, moves were instituted to change the leadership, strategy and tactics of Fighter Command, but the value of political support for him then has been underestimated. Sinclair, new to the Air Ministry, was unready to resolve the difficulties faced by his predecessors.[95] Beaverbrook and Churchill backed Dowding as the best, or only RAF officer capable of leading Fighter Command into battle. However, within two months they were to see that the commander who had shown clarity and ability in strategic preparation had a less sure touch in its tactical application.

2
THE THREAT FROM THE LUFTWAFFE

The fear of German aerial attack which prevailed in Britain throughout the 1930s was overestimated. Therefore great benefit would have accrued to Sinclair, Dowding and Newall had they enjoyed the luxury of examining the true power of their enemy. On 'the other side of the hill', which was no more than the width of the Dover Strait, was an opponent whose intentions and capabilities were different from those generally believed.[1]

The perception of most British people was that German success on the Continent came from plans of action laid by the Nazis from 1933. Hitler gained the reputation of invincible success in aiming to dominate Europe first, then the rest of the world. The bloodless victories of the Rhineland, the *Anschluss* and Czechoslovakia, followed by the campaigns against Poland, Norway, the Low Countries and France, were regarded as inexorable stages in the timetable. The signing of the Russo-German pact of August 1939 showed Hitler's cynical approach to international politics, and was part of his calculation of German expansion.[2]

In all of this the Luftwaffe had played a prominent part and gained an awesome reputation. Their victories by June 1940, especially over the French Army, were a fearful novelty in war. Stories of the effect of dive-bombing on ground forces were magnified, with vivid descriptions of screaming aircraft and siren bombs.[3] In Britain, the proof of Germany's might was offered by the sight of an exhausted British Expeditionary Force, rescued from Dunkirk but having suffered defeat, and little imagination was required to transfer similar humiliations to the surroundings of southern England in a *furor Teutonicus*.

Although the RAF had fought magnificently over France, especially at Dunkirk, there was trepidation regarding the power of the Luftwaffe even before the air battle over Britain began.[4] However, many of the earlier successes were gained as much through opponents' weaknesses as through the Luftwaffe's strength. Then, when faced with the novel frontier of the Channel, the German Air Force was confronted with unattainable goals. It was fortunate for British leaders who did not appreciate this point that their ignorance was shared by the enemy.

A radical difference between Fighter Command and the Luftwaffe was now demonstrated. The former was called on to meet the role for which it had been created and prepared, namely the defence of the United Kingdom. The latter was charged with achieving an aim for which it had neither adequate resources nor capability, namely the defeat of Britain without help from the German Army and Navy.[5]

Before 1938 the Germans had barely considered the possibility of war with Britain. They believed that the British Government, although suspicious of Hitler's actions, would not intervene against his policy in Central and Eastern Europe. The Führer's powers of diplomacy would avert war.[6]

Even the cooling of friendship during 1938 did not quench the fires of hope. Ernst Udet, head of the Luftwaffe's technical department, opposed the development of the Heinkel He 177 heavy bomber because he foresaw no use for it, and claimed that the Luftwaffe General Staff agreed with him. There might be war with Czechoslovakia or Poland, he argued, but Hitler 'will never let us in for a conflict which might take us beyond the confines of the Continent'.[7]

However, the abandonment of the heavy bomber was a great error from which the Luftwaffe was to suffer later. The change of policy was brought about particularly by German intervention in the Spanish Civil War, which had shown the value of tactical co-operation between air and ground forces. Great store was then set on producing bombers capable of making dive-bombing attacks, a policy which did much to assist the Army in a land-based campaign, but which came to a halt at the Channel coast in 1940.

The potential of the heavy bomber had been foreseen by General Walther Wever, the first Chief of the Luftwaffe General Staff, whose width of vision in strategy encompassed the value of a bomber which could reach targets far from Germany. After Wever's untimely death in a flying accident in 1936 the work was gradually discontinued. What different policies would have been adopted had he lived? His influence was great, and he would undoubtedly have pressed for a strategic air force equipped with heavy bombers. What is less certain is the extent to which he would have been able to influence Hitler and Goering when the Luftwaffe showed its worth as a tactical force.[8]

A cooling of Anglo-German relations began in 1938 with the *Anschluss* with Austria. German leaders disliked the outcry in the British Press, regarding it as interference in a domestic matter. In February Goering ordered some Luftwaffe staff to investigate the feasibility of making attacks on London and southern England, especially on ports and factories, a study which was led by General Felmy, commander of *Luftflotte II*.[9] Nonetheless, the first, and smaller, crisis of 1938 passed without direct confrontation between Britain and Germany, and both air forces continued to expand as rapidly as their governments would allow.

At the next crisis, in August 1938, the unwelcome prospect of war with Britain arose again. On 23 August Felmy was ordered to gather further information on possible targets in the United Kingdom, including armament factories and docks in London. The Channel ports and airfields in eastern England were also selected, the latter showing the current Luftwaffe planning that raids would be made by unescorted bombers flying across the North Sea from aerodromes in western Germany. In September Felmy was appointed to lead *Sonderstab* (Special Unit) *England*, but his report offered small comfort. The Luftwaffe, he suggested, could achieve no more than a 'disruptive effect', and a war against Britain with the resources available 'appears fruitless'. He added a point not lost on his readers by explaining that, for the Luftwaffe to make adequate attacks on the British Isles, airfields would be needed in Belgium and Holland.[10]

The Munich Crisis was a watershed as much for the Luftwaffe as for the RAF. In mid-October Hitler ordered a five-fold expansion for the German Air Force and plans were laid for an air armament programme lasting until autumn 1942. At the same time, discussions were held on the possibility of an air war against Britain, and these showed that German strategy envisaged tackling Britain by two methods. First, the importance of sea trade to the United Kingdom was acknowledged by allocating 13 of the planned 58 *Geschwader* of bombers to attack the Royal Navy and shipping. These *Seekampfgeschwader* were enhanced with the buccaneering title of 'Pirate Formations'. Thirty of the remaining 45 *Geschwader* were to attack the British mainland, and He 177s were requested as the best machines; at least 500 were required by 1942. No more than fifteen Geschwader were required against France. Under the title of 'Concentrated Aircraft Procurement Programme', the document was signed by Jeschonnek on 7 November 1938.[11]

This ambitious plan put faith in two untried types of bomber, the Junkers Ju 88 and the He 177. The subsequent argument over these aircraft brought later relief to Britain because of the Luftwaffe's division of responsibilities. On the one hand an aircraft was needed to offer close support to ground forces, with bombing of extreme accuracy, namely a dive-bomber. Thus early in 1938 both Udet and Jeschonnek supported with enthusiasm an order issued by the General Staff which stated, 'The emphasis in offensive bombardment has clearly shifted from area to pinpoint bombardment. For this reason, the development of a bombsight suitable for use in dive-bombing aircraft is more important than the development of any other aiming device.'[12] On the other hand, a strategic bomber was required to strike at distant enemy targets. The early enthusiasm for the Ju 88 included the view that it would satisfy both criteria, so the need for a heavy four-engined bomber was set aside.

The decision to abandon the building of the large bomber was taken early in 1937, yet in the following year, especially after Felmy's report showed that the contemporary Luftwaffe bombers would have difficulty in making effective raids on Great Britain, attempts were made to press ahead with the He 177. However, this work was bedevilled by the faith pinned in dive-bombing by both Udet and Jeschonnek, who were greatly impressed by the performance of the Condor Legion's Ju 87s in the Spanish Civil War. They now set the requirement that all bombers should have the capacity to be used in diving attacks.

In the case of the Ju 88 the changes necessary in design to meet this and other requirements led to an increase in the aeroplane's weight from seven to twelve tons and a resulting loss in speed. For the He 177 the decision was even more disastrous. There were problems in producing a suitable engine for this bomber, and the additional demands of a dive-bomber role for the 32-ton aircraft seriously delayed its development.[13]

The muddled Luftwaffe strategy of pre-war days proved to be a saving grace when the Battle of Britain opened. In the opinion of Suchenwirth, who discussed the matter with senior German officers after 1945, the possession of a long-range bomber would have made a crucial difference between July and October 1940. He believed that these aircraft would have overwhelmed anti-aircraft defences and would have been important in naval warfare.[14]

There were still hopes in Germany that peace would last until 1942, when plans for the expansion of the German Air Force would be more advanced. However, during 1939 events moved irrevocably towards war. At that stage 'Beppo' Schmid, leader of the Intelligence Branch of the Operations Staff, made one of the incorrect predictions for which he later became renowned. He claimed that the British and French air forces were out of date, that the defences of the United Kingdom were weak and that aircraft production was low. Here, the folly of British overestimation of the Luftwaffe's power to launch a strategic campaign was matched by German underestimation of Britain's capacity to build aeroplanes. In Schmid's view, only Germany had 'an overall view of war in the air'. Schmid's assumptions and predictions were several times wide of the mark both before and during the Battle of Britain. They were a contribution of no small importance to the failure of the Luftwaffe's day campaign in 1940 – and a great boon to Fighter Command.[15]

Preparations for the attack on Poland (*Fall Weiss*) were started in April 1939, with close co-operation between the Army and the Luftwaffe, aiming for a rapid victory. Nonetheless, the spectre of a possible war with Britain lurked nearby, and in May Felmy carried out a three-day exercise based on conflict with the United Kingdom. His subsequent report admitted that the strength of *Luftflotte II* would fail to bring a quick decision in war, a view of disquieting importance for Nazi leaders who were preparing to march.[16]

Such pessimism was not shared by Hitler, especially after his hopes were buoyed with misguided confidence. On 3 July he attended a Luftwaffe display at Rechlin, arranged to impress him, where he was shown aircraft and equipment at the research stage, including the world's first purpose-built rocket-propelled aeroplane, the He 176. However, he saw few aircraft at the operational level. Goering, who accompanied him, was in a position to offer Hitler a balanced assessment of what he was witnessing, but failed to do so. Three years later he complained, 'The Führer reached the most serious decisions as a result of that display. It was a miracle that things worked out as well as they did, and that the consequences were not far worse.' Goering conveniently overlooked his own responsibility for the results of that day. It is therefore easy to agree with Suchenwirth that, had Hitler been better informed of the Luftwaffe's inability to attack Britain effectively, he would have been less willing to invade Poland.[17]

Until the last moment, German leaders believed that France and Britain would refrain from declaring war over Poland. Apart from other reasons, they felt that the geographical position of Poland made Franco-British intervention unlikely, remembering Britain's traditional reluctance to become involved in Eastern Europe.[18] Nevertheless, if war were to occur, Hitler was determined to exercise personal control of any bombing campaign. In his 'Directive No 1 for the Conduct of the War', issued on 31 August, he ordered that the Royal Navy should be a target but added categorically, 'The decision regarding attack on London is reserved to me'.[19]

When hostilities against Poland began on 1 September, the Luftwaffe gained rapid and overwhelming success over an air force smaller in numbers and equipped with relatively outdated machines.[20] After this, Hitler turned his attentions to the West and very soon identified the opponent posing, in his view, the greater danger to Germany. In 'Directive No 6 for the Conduct of the War', issued on 9 October 1939, he spoke of an early offensive, moving through Holland, Belgium and Luxembourg. The purpose of the offensive was to defeat the French and any other armies standing in his path, 'and at the same time to win as much territory as possible in Holland, Belgium and northern France to serve as a base for the successful prosecution of the air and sea war against England and as a wide protective area for the commercially vital Ruhr'. In this, his policy was not only to obtain bases from which Britain could be subjected to a strategical bombing campaign, but also to provide a protective belt of defences against RAF bombing of German industry.[21]

A month later the Intelligence Branch of the Luftwaffe, under 'Beppo' Schmid, described Britain's importance in the war and suggested how action could be taken against her. Schmid noted that British policy foresaw a long war in which she hoped to defeat Germany 'by severing our entire foreign trade, both imports and exports'. He summed up his enemies. Britain was 'the most dangerous of all possible enemies', whereas France was relegated to 'the second class'.

The strategy was clear; all that was lacking was the strategic bomber. Britain should be attacked through her vulnerable trade routes, and although ships in harbour would be legitimate targets, civilians should not be harmed. The British Government would be given 'ample time for evacuation' before attacks began. The retention of the right to reprisal was upheld if the RAF were to bomb German towns, but the report made clear that the prime German aim was not attacks on airfields, which would divert effort, but 'the paralysis of British overseas trade'. The report, written in an optimistic vein, would have been the basis for an excellent strategic plan, had the Luftwaffe possessed adequate and suitable resources. However, the largest aircraft generally available both at this stage and later, in attacks on Britain in 1940, was the Heinkel He 111K, which was no more than a medium bomber.[22]

Another document from Luftwaffe Intelligence, entitled 'Plans for Air Warfare on England', expanded several points, suggesting that continuous attacks should be made by day and night in widely separated areas. The RAF would then have to retain aircraft in the United Kingdom and even withdraw some of those already in France. Dowding would have agreed with this assessment. However, the weakness of the German plan was shown when the targets to be raided by a force which numbered fewer than 400 medium bombers of *Fliegerkorps X* were listed. They included warships at sea and in port, the naval dockyards of the Tyne, Clyde, Birkenhead and Barrow-in-Furness, harbour installations at Liverpool, the Manchester Ship Canal, Avonmouth, Cardiff, Swansea and 'the important military target' of Billingham. The hope that Britain's industrial and trading capacity could be overwhelmed by an air force lacking a heavy bomber shows a mixture of overconfidence and ignorance from Luftwaffe Intelligence, which made no mention of Fighter Command's defensive plans. Had Dowding seen this report, his faith in defeating daylight attacks would have remained undimmed. More ominous for him would have been the planned night raids, which his Command was poorly equipped to meet.[23]

The prophets of doom, as well as RAF Intelligence, were shown to be wide of the mark when the feared and anticipated 'knock-out' blow from the Luftwaffe never materialized at the start of the war. The British people were spared the predicted apocalyptic bombing. The 'Phoney War' on land was matched by desultory aerial attacks on parts of the United Kingdom, particularly daylight raids on naval units at Rosyth and Scapa Flow. At night, magnetic mines were sown in coastal waters. No bomb fell on mainland Britain until 9 May 1940. A particular reason for the Luftwaffe's inactivity was that it was employed elsewhere, first in Poland, then in the Norwegian campaign, before being prepared for the main offensive in the West in May 1940.[24]

Consequently, before the Battle of Britain many German aircrew had gained wide practical experience of fighting in war, particularly in close cooperation with ground forces. However, this experience was counter-productive in that the Luftwaffe concentrated on the type of campaign which could not be used profitably against Britain.[25]

Air fighting tactics for fighters were developed particularly during the Spanish Civil War. Ironically, the fighter tactics, which soon became the best in the world, evolved partly from a shortage of aircraft in the Condor

Legion. Previously, fighters were flown in threes, but the first Bf 109s to be sent to Spain operated in pairs. These flew in line abreast, some 200 yards apart. When larger numbers arrived they operated in fours, usually adopting the incomparable 'finger-four' formation. This brought three benefits which were recognized immediately by German airmen. First, each pilot had a clear field of vision inwards, watching the blind spots behind and below his companion. Secondly, any attacker of one of the pair would be followed by the second aircraft, and thus become a potential victim. Thirdly, the leader of the pair was always reassured, in making an attack, that his own tail was covered by his wingman.[26]

When pilots had gained experience in Spain they returned to Germany as instructors. However, their tactics limited their best use to becoming a type of flying artillery, or flame-gun, co-operating with ground forces, and it was on these lines that the Luftwaffe was developed. The air force became a crucial component of *Blitzkrieg* tactics and, from September 1939 until the fall of France, it was employed with devastating effect. What German leaders failed to appreciate was that different strategy and tactics were needed against an enemy protected by a sea barrier. In addition, in early campaigns bombing onslaughts were made with precision, often uninterrupted by fighter intervention. The reality of what would be experienced in British skies, guarded by the strongest air force the Luftwaffe had encountered, produced different conditions and problems.[27]

PART 2: THE WESTERN CAMPAIGN AND ITS EFFECTS

Much has been made of the heavy casualties suffered by the RAF during the French campaign as a factor affecting Dowding's policy during the Battle of Britain. What is usually overlooked is that by July 1940 the Luftwaffe also had taken heavy losses; the victories won in Poland, Norway, the Low Countries and France were bought at a high cost of machines and experienced crews.

During May the German Air Force had 1,044 aircraft destroyed on operations, 229 of them fighters. This total was made up of 147 Bf 109s and 82 Bf 110s; twelve other fighters were lost, but not on operations. In June the comparable losses were 100 and 26. In that period Bf 109 pilot casualties totalled 169, over 15 per cent of the total available, although those captured were released at the French surrender. During the same two months 643 bombers were lost from all causes.[28]

These figures were brought into sharper focus by the comparative slowness of German aircraft production from the start of the war. A study of the respective figures for fighter production during 1940 is revealing. Luftwaffe records show a total of 3,382 single- and twin-engined aircraft, whereas the British figure was 4,283, all single-engined. Overall, Britain trebled production during the year, while in Germany it was doubled. The weakness of the Luftwaffe position is underlined by the fact that only 2,268 Bf 109s were produced. The difference in building, repair and replacement was accentuated later in the year, but was already important at the start of the battle over the United Kingdom.[29]

Some blame for the Luftwaffe's failure to produce sufficient aircraft has been apportioned to Udet. Nonetheless he, in common with many German leaders, believed that the war was almost ended after the fall of France. He was heard to declare that expansion plans 'are not worth a damn ... we don't need them any longer'. This failure to maintain production, combined with a lack of appreciation of the different mode of strategic warfare needed against Britain, led to weaknesses in the Luftwaffe after June 1940. This carelessness, stemming from overconfidence, was destined to prove expensive for the German Air Force.[30]

At the end of the French campaign only Britain stood between Germany and total victory in the West. Hitler, enjoying the euphoria of a triumph not only over France, but also over the pessimistic predictions of some of his generals, was prepared to wait for Britain. He believed that sooner or later she would have to accept the reality of her position and sue for peace. Lord Bullock suggests that, in the Führer's reckoning, there was no reason for the British Government to adhere to former policy, as their allies had been subjugated and their Army beaten. 'They must now surely accept the impossibility of preventing a German hegemony in Europe, and, like sensible people, come to terms.' [31]

Yet in some ways it was already too late for the Germans, because the three weeks between the evacuation of Dunkirk and the surrender of France gave Britain the opportunity of taking stock and embracing a resolve to continue the war. Winston Churchill, in a series of memorable speeches and wireless broadcasts made during May and June, had already reflected the mood of most British people. His approach, 'rhetorical and cheeky at the same time, Macaulay and contemporary slang mixed together', succeeded in cementing a general public determination to combat Hitler and bring a halt to his run of victories.[32]

Some pessimistic observers regarded this as an insupportable policy, yet it was soundly based. Churchill acknowledged the forthcoming burden of bombing to be borne, yet foresaw the relief that could be brought if the enemy were held off for three months. Then, bearing in mind the faith he shared with the Air Staff in a strategic campaign which would be launched with the new generation of heavy bombers, Britain would strike back. He also put great faith in anticipated help from the USA. Therefore, the British attitude was no show of bravado, but a shrewd assessment of the possible, fortified by confidence in the nation's defensive capabilities by sea and air. Nor should it be forgotten that the British homeland was intact from land invasion and was unlikely to submit, in boxing terms, 'on the stool'. [33]

This might not have happened, nonetheless, had the advice given on 5 June by Milch, the Inspector of the Luftwaffe, been followed. Asked by Goering to suggest steps for ending the war rapidly, Milch, in typically forthright fashion, recommended that Britain should be invaded immediately. He added that if the British were left in peace for four weeks 'it will be too late'. Why was this advice ignored?[34]

First, the British refusal to seek terms, a policy which some outsiders found difficult to comprehend, was a positive, not negative, choice. The onus of response was placed on a surprised and disappointed Hitler, and thus the British forces were given a short period to reorganize. For Fighter Command the time was invaluable. Squadrons were brought back to strength, airfield defences prepared and the Dowding System brought to a state of readiness.[35] Second, the Germans were victims of their own success. Few had dreamed at the outbreak of war that inside nine months the British capital would be within range of Bf 109s. Consequently the suddenness of victory was overshadowed by lack of detailed planning for exploiting the new circumstances.[36] Third, not the least benefit to Britain was Hitler's relaxation of his own efforts; increasingly he turned all attention from the West to his cardinal ambition of overthrowing Bolshevik Russia. He constantly hoped that Britain would seek terms and therefore, when on 21 May Admiral Raeder unveiled a Naval Staff study of the possibilities of invasion, he showed little interest. As late as 17 June the navy were told that the Führer had not expressed an intention to invade.[37]

However, on 24 May he offered new targets for the Luftwaffe. No longer were they limited to bombing trade routes and ports, but were 'authorised to attack the English homeland in the fullest manner'. They were to start with 'an annihilating reprisal' for Bomber Command's attacks on the Ruhr.[38] Yet Hitler's lack of drive towards defeating Britain was noted after the fall of France, when he toured battlefields, visited Paris, and then returned to the Black Forest. Only in early July did he issue orders for preparations to be made. Even these lacked urgency. His Directive of 2 July stated 'the invasion is still only a plan'.[39]

General Jodl's report at the same time claimed that a German victory 'was only a matter of time'. After suggesting terror raids and attacks on food stocks to break public morale, he laid down the precondition understood by all three Services. First, the Luftwaffe had to gain command of the air.[40] However, a grave blow to German hopes was struck on 3 July when the Royal Navy sank units of the French Fleet at Oran. The effect was widely felt, not least in the USA, and those who harboured reservations about British resolve were left in no doubt that battle would come before surrender.[41]

Consequently the German armed forces were confronted with considerable problems. The Army could do nothing unless put ashore. The Navy, after crippling losses in the Norwegian campaign, could not put them ashore. Pressure fell on the Luftwaffe, the only Service capable of making swift contact with the enemy. Basically, the Luftwaffe alone was being asked to defeat Britain, so the German war machine was attempting to work on one cylinder out of three.[42]

At this stage Goering's attitude was ambivalent, and the directive he issued on 30 June was no more than a mixture of hope and ambition. At the close he ordered that the RAF should be attacked constantly, yet the earlier section called for a tentative approach, less in keeping with the Luftwaffe style of *Blitzkrieg*, and spoke of the strength of British defences, ordering that every effort should be made to avoid harming civilians. There was no mention of the Luftwaffe's effort being a preamble to, or major constituent of, a seaborne invasion of the United Kingdom, but Goering, whose light seldom saw the cover of a bushel, was not displeased that his forces were being drawn to the centre of the stage.[43]

There are mixed views on the difficulties of preparation. Werner Kreipe, who served with KG 2 and then became Chief Operations Officer of *Luftflotte III*, wrote of relatively light casualties and claimed that, after the battle for France, the German Air Force was ready 'within a few days'.[44] On the other hand, Kesselring, who commanded *Luftflotte II*, said that the task took several weeks.[45] Bekker, who later interviewed a number of Luftwaffe staff, pointed out that units needed rest and reorganization before being ready to tackle the RAF.[46]

By early July the Luftwaffe had numerical superiority over their adversaries, and much has been made of this to show how a small force of British fighters overcame a larger enemy. What is often ignored, however, is that Fighter Command was comparatively stronger than generally recognized, and that the strategic placing of some Luftwaffe units left that force in a weaker position than it might have enjoyed. The crux of the forthcoming battle was a struggle between two sets of single-seat fighters and, of these, the Germans had about 760 serviceable Bf 109s, while the RAF possessed some 700 Hurricanes and Spitfires. These aircraft were the lords of the skies and, in the subsequent battle, the weaknesses of Bf 110s, Defiants and Blenheims as fighters were quickly uncovered.[47]

Plans were laid for Britain to be assaulted by *Luftflotte II*, stationed in north-eastern France and the Low Countries, and by *Luftflotte III*, flying from north-western France. A smaller force, *Luftflotte V*, was to launch raids from Norway, while *Luftflotten I* and *IV* were to defend the German homeland.[48] The offensive by the three *Luftflotten* was to be launched by about 2,800 aircraft, of which some 1,800 were bombers. This was to be the prime – indeed, apart from submarine and motor torpedo-boat activity, the only – offensive power designed to cause Britain to surrender, or to prepare the way for a successful seaborne invasion. Although most aircraft were dispersed in the Low Countries and France, poor strategy led to insufficient forces being placed from the start close to the narrowest part of the Channel crossing, where the *Schwerpunkt* of attack would take place. The aeroplanes stationed in Norway had little chance of playing an active part in battle. However, they caused the ever-cautious Dowding to retain squadrons in the north against raids which, in the event, came on one day only. This lack of concentration of resources in the main battle area was to cost the Luftwaffe dearly in the long run.[49]

A major contributory factor to weaknesses in the Luftwaffe in July 1940 stemmed from leadership. For this, blame must first be placed at the top. It is not sufficient to state that Hitler took little interest in the aerial campaign against Britain, although there is little evidence to prove his close involvement. What is more important is that the Führer had little understanding of a strategic plan by which Britain could be forced to sue for peace by the employment of air power. He never demonstrated wide awareness of the value of either air fleets or navies; subsequently the waters of the Channel proved too great an obstacle for his land-based, military thinking. The crossing of an unpredictable and boisterous sea was too much for his vision, which therefore travelled elsewhere across the map-table, allowing the impetus of attack on Britain to be lost.[50]

In spite of the German fear of war on two fronts, Hitler's greatest ambition was to attack Russia. In a sense, the defeat of Britain was a sideshow which, ideally but not necessarily, required completion before the *Drang nach Osten* could begin. At this stage his mind was divided between the two objectives, and settling with Britain never held the monopoly of attention required for the success of such a venture. The position became even more uncertain as Hitler vacillated until late July, with a blend of hope and conviction that the British Government would come to the conference table. He also appreciated the difficulties of launching and sustaining a successful invasion.[51] Through his position in the Nazi state, the Führer could be dictatorial in a way that Churchill never was. The Prime Minister was more open to the advice of his Chiefs of Staff and two committees which studied and then reported back in depth on problems. In Germany, however, few men were brave enough to offer honest opinions to Hitler, and preferment went to sycophants. Without the Führer's interest and involvement in a venture there was little chance of sustained progress.[52] Hitler hoped that the air war would be conducted successfully by Goering, whose claims for the Luftwaffe had been constant. Never was faith more misplaced, as the weaknesses of Goering's leadership became apparent.

It is instructive to compare the Reichsmarschall's approach to duties with those, for example, of Sinclair, Newall and Dowding. These were hardly charismatic characters, having no widespread popularity with subordinates, yet at a political or Service level they were constantly close to the action, seldom far from London and always available. Unlike Goering, they did not neglect duties while in pursuit of luxurious living, hunting on estates far from the front line or acquiring art treasures from the conquered. Whatever their weaknesses, they were trying to serve the RAF. In the British State they were more answerable for decisions taken and, from their immediate subordinates, gained loyalty. Few showed this quality to Goering.

The extra burdens thrown on to Luftwaffe commanders by the Reichs-marschall's absence from the battle area were heavy. He was in France from 5-29 June, by which time the air battle over Britain had not started and he might have stayed in an organizing and inspiring role. Instead, a number of conferences were held at Karinhall, his estate in East Prussia and, apart from brief interventions, he did not reappear in the front line until 7 September. The tide of battle was not then running for the Luftwaffe, and he arrived in France to take personal charge.[53]

The weaknesses in the Luftwaffe chain of command stemmed from the Commander-in-Chief himself. Murray says that Goering's 'mental frame-work' did not exceed that of an ordinary fighter pilot (which he had once been), and goes on to refer to his ignorance of 'logistics, strategy, aircraft capabilities, technology and engineering – in other words, just about every-thing to do with air power'.[54] The veneer of bonhomie, charm and cama-raderie produced socially acceptable graces unmatched by other Nazi leaders and made 'The Iron Man' a most popular figure with the public. Yet it concealed flaws of character which were, in the long run, to cost the Luft-waffe heavily. The results of this lack of ability and control in a man who often referred to the air force as if it were his personal possession were felt by senior officers. Milch, Udet and Jeschonnek carried out their duties with-out the necessary close support of their Commander-in-Chief.

According to some authorities, several of these leaders were not entirely suited to their responsibilities. For example, it is suggested that Udet, a bril-liant pilot, lacked the ability and temperament to serve as chief technical officer, a task involving much desk work.[55] Possibly Jeschonnek, an admin-istrator of great potential, was too young and inexperienced to carry the bur-dens as Chief of the Operational Staff.[56] It is known that Milch, the Reich's State Secretary for Aviation, was disliked by some officers, who contrasted the slimness of his Service background with his overbearing style and width of ambition.[57]

Kesselring and Sperrle, commanding the two *Luftflotten* closest to action, were not drawn into a carefully planned and co-ordinated campaign. The former, in his memoirs, reflected bitterly on the aimlessness of his posi-tion just before the Battle of Britain began. 'In contrast to our previous cam-paigns', he wrote, 'there was not one conference within the Luftwaffe at which details were discussed with group commanders and other services, let alone with the High Command or Hitler himself.' Kesselring continued by claiming that he had no more than informal talks with Goering, rather than 'binding discussions'. He had been given no instructions for tactical assign-ments or co-operation with either the army or navy.[58]

An Operational Order on 12 July offered some objectives for the Luft-waffe, pointing out that a seaborne landing would be possible only along the

Channel coast, where German air supremacy would counteract British naval power. This was obviously written by a High Command which lacked an understanding of the intricacies of strategic air power. For the Luftwaffe to gain supremacy over the Channel coast, a campaign was required against fighter and bomber airfields deep inland. The German Army, grateful for the Luftwaffe's contribution to land victories, failed to realize that a different approach was now required to defeat an enemy protected both by the sea and by the strongest air force yet encountered.[59]

When Hitler's Directive No 16 was issued on 16 July it was still couched in tentative terms. He announced that a landing operation against Britain was being prepared and that he had decided 'if necessary to carry it out'. The Luftwaffe was ordered to overcome the RAF and operate against ground targets and ships of the Royal Navy, but to assess the lateness of decision here, it should be remembered that the air battle over the Channel, with growing forces, had begun six days earlier. Even at that stage the Directive still demanded proposals and detailed plans 'as soon as possible'. Only eight or nine weeks remained before the weather could deteriorate, which throws the extent of the task facing the Luftwaffe, the only Service really involved, into sharper focus.[60]

The following day, Luftwaffe units were placed on maximum readiness, while on 19 July Hitler played his last diplomatic card in a comparatively conciliatory speech made in Berlin. His invitation to the British Government to come to an agreement was clear.[61] Churchill would not reply to Hitler's speech, 'not being on speaking terms with him'. When the offer was rejected by Lord Halifax, the Foreign Secretary, three days later, the Germans at last – and too late – realized that action would have to follow.[62]

It was not until this late stage that Goering finally called a conference of his commanders to make detailed plans in unison. Needless to say, it was held at Karinhall, hundreds of miles from the action. The destruction of the RAF, especially Fighter Command, was high on the agenda, together with attacks on the aircraft industry. Goering asked Kesselring and Sperrle to let him know how aerial supremacy could be achieved, hardly an inspiring opening to a battle which had already started.[63]

When a number of features of German leadership are taken into account, therefore, clues are offered for the reasons why the Luftwaffe entered the Battle of Britain at some disadvantage. This alone throws doubt on any view that it was in a position of overwhelming superiority in July 1940.

One cause of weakness in leadership came from faults in German Intelligence. Unlike its British counterpart, the Intelligence Branch of the Luftwaffe lacked independence and was held in comparatively low esteem. For example, an Intelligence officer might have extra duties, such as propaganda and censorship. Another difference from the RAF was that, in 1940, no Intelligence officer was stationed at any unit below a *Fliegerkorps*.[64]

A sharp rivalry between various Intelligence agencies brought no sharing of material. This failing was particularly evident between the *5th Abteilung*, the Air Intelligence Department of the Luftwaffe General Staff under 'Beppo' Schmid, and the *3rd Abteilung*, the Luftwaffe Signals and Cypher Service led by General Wolfgang Martini. German Intelligence agencies were victims of the German political system, where knowledge brought power, to be retained and withheld from opponents. On air matters, Intelligence was gathered by eight, and radar information by ten, agencies.[65]

Those in Intelligence told their superiors what they wanted to hear, rather than confront them with realities. For example, Schmid had the reputation of failing to give unvarnished reports both before and during the battle. Had German leaders had a more accurate realization of the power and potential of the RAF, their strategy would have followed a different course. The Intelligence branches served the Luftwaffe badly in three vital areas, and these proved critical in the main battle.

The first was ignorance of the wide use of RDF in British defences. On 16 July the *5th Abteilung* produced a summary of the RAF, without any mention of RDF, although Martini's *3rd Abteilung* was aware of its exis-

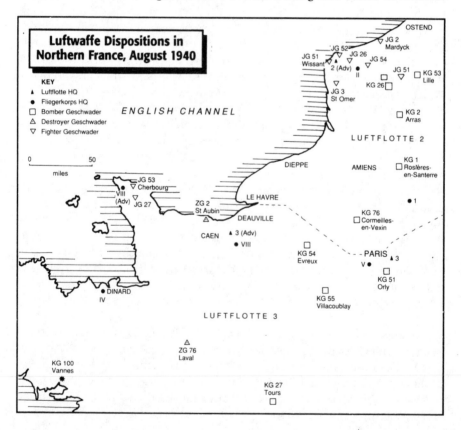

tence and had attempted before the war to determine the frequencies used. The oversight, caused either by ignorance or rivalry, was to prove expensive to the Luftwaffe.[66]

Dowding's carefully planned system of fighter intervention was misunderstood. 'The command at high level (i.e., Command/Air Staff),' wrote Schmid, 'is inflexible in its organization and strategy. As formations are rigidly attached to their home bases,' he continued, 'command at medium level (i.e., Group/station) suffers mainly from operations being controlled in most cases by officers no longer accustomed to flying (station commanders).' Possibly Schmid's conclusions were based on signals interception of Fighter Command's radio telephone messages, which he falsely believed would make the British defence system inflexible.

His estimates of British fighter performance and production were also awry. He said, for example, that the Bf 110 was superior to the Hurricane, no doubt to please Goering, who had pinned great faith in the German machine. This evasion of the truth proved very costly soon after the start of the battle, when the twin-engined fighter had to be protected by Bf 109s. The figures given for British fighter production were equally wrong, estimating between 180 and 300 aircraft per month, a total likely, in his reckoning, to fall under the pressure of bombing and shortages of materials. In reality, the figure, which had grown steadily from April, averaged between 450 and 500 aeroplanes monthly from July to September.[67] 'The Luftwaffe is clearly superior to the RAF as regards strength, equipment, training, command and location of bases', the report claimed. The German Air Force would be able 'to achieve a decisive result this year', if allowed to take advantage of the period of better weather from July to early October.[68]

Such errors of judgement contributed strongly and crucially to the policy of German leaders at the time. Hitler was encouraged to believe that weaknesses in the RAF would force the British Government to the conference table. Goering anticipated that Fighter Command would be crushed speedily and the remainder of the RAF within succeeding weeks. These misinterpretations of Britain's position help to explain why, at first, Hitler did not maintain the momentum of war after the defeat of France. They also underline the value to British defences of the slow start to the Luftwaffe's campaign.[69]

Dowding, his Group Commanders and his pilots were in a stronger position than many believed when the main German attacks began on 10 July. The fact of the matter was that the Luftwaffe had never been prepared adequately from pre-war days to defeat the RAF and compel Britain to sue for peace through a bombing campaign. Their best chance of success, immediately after the evacuation from Dunkirk, had been allowed to pass. In many respects they had lost the Battle of Britain even before it began, and any assessment of the strategy, tactics and leadership of Fighter Command is incomplete unless this point is taken into account.

3

THE OPENING PHASE OF BATTLE
10 JULY TO 18 AUGUST

PART 1: DOWDING'S DEFENSIVE STRATEGY

The period from 10 July to 18 August marked the opening of the first stage of what is generally known as the Battle of Britain, but what should be called, in the opinion of some participants, the Battle *for* Britain. This opening phase did much to prove wrong several impressions of the contest which have been widely held since, and which, unfortunately, have clouded the issues of leadership during the battle.

The first was that only a handful of young pilots of Fighter Command were available to face the juggernaut of the Luftwaffe and prevent total Nazi victory. The impression of 'The Few' as a small band of British fighter pilots engaging German formations of overwhelming strength was caused not so much by an overall shortage of RAF aircraft as by Dowding's strategy of defence. At this stage he chose to keep as many Spitfire and Hurricane squadrons outside the main battle area as were retained in No 11 Group, where the main blows were bound to fall.[1]

Secondly, there were misconceptions regarding the resources available to Fighter Command. The reality was that, while the German Air Force had more aircraft at its disposal than did the British, the advantage was considerably offset by the quality of the British defensive system. Fighter Command's squadrons fought a carefully prepared battle, using RDF and radio control, while the *Luftflotten* were engaged in bludgeoning attacks with no comprehensive strategy.[2] Numbers alone gave the Germans little advantage.

Even here, if the root of the battle is accepted as a contest between two sets of single-seat fighters, then the sides were not so unevenly balanced. In addition, the German lack of a heavy bomber seriously weakened the effects of attacks.

Thirdly, it is important to appreciate that, in this phase, Dowding received more support from the Air Ministry than he was later prepared to acknowledge. Officers there have been awarded less recognition than deserved for their efforts.[3]

Fourthly, Fighter Command's tactics in action were patently inferior to those of the Luftwaffe. Although the recommendations made by pilots who had been in battle generally suggested the employment of larger or differently arranged formations, the C-in-C was not prepared to approve them. Consequently, losses sustained in this period were unnecessarily high.

Fifthly, both sides suffered from poor Intelligence. However, this affected the German Air Force more than the RAF, especially because plans for a seaborne invasion were still vague and indefinite, bringing greater pressure on the Luftwaffe as the number of possible landing dates declined.

The final factor during this period, and one the importance of which should not be underestimated, was the value to Dowding of continuing political support. At the time, both Churchill and Beaverbrook, although not examining the tactics of battle closely, were content that Dowding's strategy was enabling Fighter Command to hold off German attacks.

The inherent weaknesses of the Luftwaffe on 10 July were either unknown or not fully appreciated in Britain. There, the sense of foreboding was great, although tempered by a grim determination not to allow the enemy an easy passage to victory. Nevertheless, the shield afforded by the sea, which had prevented the Germans from turning the land attack on to Britain immediately after the defeat of the French, had enabled British leaders to take stock on two vital issues over the preceding six weeks. These issues marked the outline of the Government's overall aims, which the strategy of the RAF, and in particular that of Fighter Command, had to attempt to implement.

They were summarized by Air Commodore Slessor, Director of Plans at the Air Ministry, when referring to a Joint Planning Committee paper produced on 24 May. 'We had been asked,' he recollected, 'whether Britain could hold out until help from the Empire and the United States became effective, and whether we had any chance of defeating Germany.' In his view the crux of the answer to the first question was the capacity to replace fighter wastage, which would bring – or lose – air superiority. On the second point, he believed that Germany might be defeated by three factors – attack from the air, economic pressure, and revolt in the defeated countries.[4]

In reporting to the Prime Minister on 25 May the Chiefs of Staff, whose RAF representative was Sir Cyril Newall, reached a number of conclusions. The main one was that, while the RAF was in existence, the Royal Navy and Air Force in unison probably had the power to prevent seaborne invasion. If, however, the Germans gained air superiority, the navy would not be able to stop landings 'for an indefinite period'. Then, German land forces would get ashore and the British Army would be 'insufficient to deal with a serious invasion'.[5]

The next point underlined the burden laid on the RAF, and especially on Fighter Command under Dowding's leadership. The crux of the problem, they suggested, was air superiority, and if the Germans gained that they could attempt to win by aerial attack alone. They then showed a resurgence of the fears that had lurked since pre-war days, namely that the morale of civilian populations could be broken by bombing. In their ninth paragraph they referred to the 'moral effect on the work people' of 'wholesale havoc and destruction', while in the tenth they mentioned 'moral damage within the industrial area' resulting from attacks on the aircraft industry. To under-line the belief that the fears of the working class knew no national frontiers, the Chiefs of Staff stated that a British bomber force could attack German industrial centres and 'by moral and material effect' disrupt or destroy them. Their summary defined the real test as being whether Service and civilian morale would be able to withstand the advantages possessed by Germany.

The onus thrown on to the RAF was double-edged. Fighter Command was not only to hold off enemy attacks on Service positions and establish-ments, but also was required to guard civilians whose will to continue the war might well be broken by enemy bombardment. In view of what had happened in Spain, Poland, the Low Countries and France, the view was understandable.[6]

Yet, even at this crucial moment, with the strong possibility of German landings, the basic difference in strategic thought between the Air Staff and a number of politicians on the one side, and the Commander-in-Chief, Fighter Command, on the other, were demonstrated. For the latter, the for-mers' earlier neglect of the importance of ensuring the safety of the Home Base through the agency of his Command verged on the criminal. They, nevertheless, had a wider view of strategy, realizing that attack is often the best means of defence.

At this stage, Churchill's determination to blend offence with defence was shown. Writing to General Ismay on 4 June, with the disaster of Dunkirk barely passed, he was already suggesting that raiding forces might be used to attack German-occupied coasts, and announced that the 'defen-sive habit of mind' which had ruined the French should not be allowed to have a similar effect on Britain. This thread of aggression ran through his early premiership, and a month later he was asking Herbert Morrison, the Minister of Supply, whether vessels were being designed to transport tanks across the sea to attack enemy countries.[7]

Within the RAF, thinking was still at two levels. By early June it was obvious that Fighter Command held the key to Britain's immediate survival, and as many machines and pilots as possible were required to hold off the Luftwaffe. Nevertheless, the Air Ministry still had faith in the Trenchard Doctrine of strategic bombing and believed that Bomber Command raids would make a significant contribution to the defence of the United King-dom.[8] The view was summarized by the Director of Home Operations, Group Captain Stevenson, on 28 June, when he wrote that there was no hope of winning the war 'without hitting and hitting hard'. Increases in the number of bombers were 'absolutely essential,' he added, while acknowl-edging the contemporary need for fighters.[9] To compound difficulties, at the time there were growing differences over policy and its application between the Air Ministry, under Sinclair, and the Ministry of Aircraft Production, led by Beaverbrook. These differences, exacerbated by Beaverbrook's highly individual approach to the achievement of aims and targets, caused a controversy which lasted throughout the Battle of Britain. The uneasy relationship was a stong undercurrent in the story of Dowding's handling of resources during the battle, and played some part in his subsequent dismissal.[10]

The nation's strategic need was summarized by the Chiefs of Staff on 19 June. They showed an awareness of the importance of the immediate future by writing that the issue of the war would 'almost certainly turn upon our ability to hold out during the next three months'. Their next words reinforced the importance of Fighter Command, whose efforts, they claimed, should be 'concentrated on taking all steps necessary to meet the imminent threat with which we are now confronted'.[11]

Such statements of policy focused attention on the importance of Dowding's responsibilities. A factor magnifying his difficulties at the start of the battle was the increased number of directions from which the enemy could now launch attacks. Pre-war planning had anticipated raids by unescorted bombers, coming from a generally easterly or north-easterly quarter.[12] On 10 July, however, Luftwaffe aircraft were dispersed on airfields stretching round Britain in a great arc from Norway to north-west France. The closest of these airfields were in the Pas de Calais, enabling fighter protection to be given to German formations raiding south-east England.

At this stage, one of Dowding's greatest problems was to decide on the disposition of forces to meet responsibilities for the defence of targets varying from naval bases in northern Scotland to London, and from convoys sailing in the Western Approaches to East Anglian aerodromes. As he recollected less than a year after the battle, German objectives 'might be Convoys, Radio-Location Stations, Fighter Aerodromes, Seaports, Aircraft Factories, or London itself'. He went on to explain that the enemy's policy was to engage Fighter Command continuously, thus weakening it until the Luftwaffe had gained air supremacy.[13]

Although the fall of France brought a form of respite for the RAF, this was no more than an interval. In particular, German occupation of western France provided opportunities of attack on lightly defended targets on the western side of Britain which had not, in pre-war days, been considered especially vulnerable. The coastal area from Portsmouth round to Bristol was now at particular risk. There was also the thought that a German invasion of Eire might be carried out as a forerunner to landings on the British mainland.[14]

These worries added to Dowding's burden, but all too often the impression has been given that he carried it alone. Certainly, his was the particular responsibility for the fighter defence of Great Britain, yet the support afforded by officers in the Air Ministry is overlooked, or at best, neglected. They, in turn, were pressed by requirements from the Chiefs of Staff, who had a broad view of what was needed from each Service, taking their instructions from the Cabinet.[15]

Thus Group Captain Stevenson wrote several times to Dowding in June, stating the Air Council's policy and decisions. For example, on 11 June he sought information on Fighter Command's intentions for extending defences in the west of England. Seventeen days later the DHO wrote a review of fighter organization resulting from the German occupation of France, including the prediction that Britain would 'lose the war unless we are able to secure our ocean convoys and our shipping in the Irish Sea'. On the following day Dowding was notified of his Command's role in the event of invasion. First, troop-carrying aeroplanes should be attacked, and then bombers. Cover should be offered to RAF bombers raiding enemy ground targets. Diversionary sweeps made by the Luftwaffe should not be met by too great a strength because 'the main objective of the fighters is to assist in repelling the invasion'.[16]

It was, nonetheless, a grim irony for Dowding that Stevenson's estimate of fighter numbers needed to meet the anticipated strength of the Luftwaffe and its potential growth, now that the aircraft industries of several European nations had fallen under German control, was 120 squadrons. These would constitute a first-line strength of 1,920 machines, between two and three times what was actually available to Fighter Command that day. At the same time plans were being pressed forward to form three new fighter Groups. No 10 would cover the West Country, No 14 the north coast of Scotland, and No 9 would defend the north-west of England.[17]

It is obvious that the C-in-C was greatly influenced by the width and variety of duties which had been pointed out to him by the Air Staff, the onset of which, he would claim, they had failed to discern in good time. Also he had to bear in mind the strategic advantages which lay with the Luftwaffe in their position as an attacking force with many airfields at their disposal from Norway to France. There was the possibility at this stage that a seaborne invasion might be launched from any one or more of three general directions. Firstly, ships might cross the North Sea from Norway or the Baltic, to land forces on the east coast. Secondly, the Germans could use French or Belgian ports as bases for an attack on the south coast of England. Thirdly, they might sail from Brittany to invade Eire or the south-west of England.[18]

Therefore, the disposition of the forces at Dowding's disposal at the start of the battle is of interest in demonstrating his anticipation of German intentions. An airman who flew under his command at that time pointed out that the C-in-C's freedom in this matter was extensive because 'no power on earth could have disputed his order without undermining his command responsibility, with all the implications inferred thereby'.[19]

On 8 July Fighter Command had 58 squadrons, although eight at the time were non-operational, either forming or re-forming. The table opposite[20] shows how they were dispersed.

The dilemma facing Dowding at that stage is pointed out in the Official Narrative. Although the bulk of the German Air Force was stationed opposite No 11 Group – 'no less than one thousand bombers and 400 fighters directly threatened the No 11 Group area' – the Luftwaffe could, by menacing other parts of Britain, cause the C-in-C to hold back forces from 'the main zone of operations'.[21] He had to keep his Command together as a composite force, even if at times it would be unable to prevent enemy

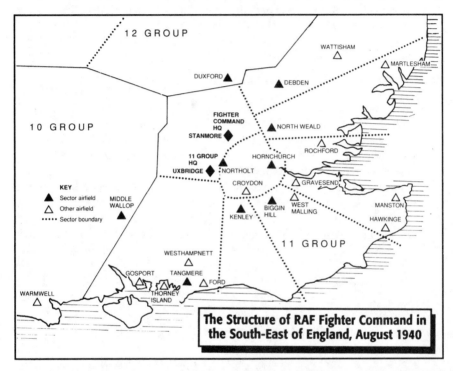

The Structure of RAF Fighter Command in the South-East of England, August 1940

Group	Hurricane	Spitfire	Defiant	Blenheim	Total opnl	Total non-opnl	Grand total
10	2 (2)	2	–	–	4	2	6
11	12 (1)	6	–	4	22	1	23
12	5 (1)	5	1	2	13	1	14
+ FIU Unit							
13	3 (4)	6	1	1	11	4	15
Total	22 (8)	19	2	7	50	8	58

Fighter Command Strength at 8 July 1940

bombers from reaching targets. 'The destruction or paralysis of the Fighter Command,' he wrote, 'was therefore an essential prerequisite to the invasion of these Islands.' His prime task was to prevent that.[22]

For Dowding, a great problem was the shortage of pilots. The production or repair of aircraft was advancing at a satisfactory and improving rate by July 1940,[23] but the training of men to fly them was a far slower process. In addition, the depredations of the French campaign had reduced not only the total of pilots, but more especially the number of experienced airmen.

On 1 July there were available, for all first-line squadrons, including those that were non-operational, a total of 1,103 fighter pilots. Their allocations were: No 11 Group – 553; No 12 Group – 228; No 13 Group – 322.[24] At this stage, in Dowding's reckoning, the fate of the nation depended on the skill and courage of about a thousand men. He was not alone in regretting the tardiness of the Air Ministry in supplying sufficient aircrew. Churchill noted in a Minute to Sinclair on 27 June, 'the proved failure to provide a proper supply of pilots when they have so long been crying out about a plethora of pilots'. He hoped that Sinclair would reform 'a most cumbersome and ill-working machine'.[25]

Some help came from the Admiralty, who immediately searched units of the Fleet Air Arm for pilots. By July they were able to provide 58 airmen who then served under Dowding's command.[26] He, believing that deficiencies of men and *matériel* precluded him from an aggressive use of resources, deployed squadrons in a conservative manner. Obviously he, as much as Jellicoe in the First World War, saw the importance of his Command to the nation's survival. Another naval analogy, seen from the German side, is that Dowding valued Fighter Command as a 'Fleet in Being'. He wished to avoid a Jutland which would demolish his strength in one blow. His aircraft were therefore arranged with a balance of types of machine maintained among all Groups.

His strategy in this respect has been open to some, though generally muted, criticism. Yet it led in part to the development of the Big Wing controversy and to accusations that Dowding should have displayed more flair and aggression in opposing the Luftwaffe. He was implementing the policy of response planned before the war to meet raids from unescorted bombers coming from the east. Now, conditions were crucially changed, with German fighter bases only 30 miles from southern England.

The weakness of his position is underscored by examining the advantages stemming from the Germans' choice of assault.[27] Most writers and authorities therefore accept that the C-in-C had little option in this matter, and fail to question his strategy. However, his policy led to extreme pressure being laid on No 11 Group even before the battle started.

Park's 22 squadrons, comprising about 350 aircraft, were faced by some 1,400 fighters and bombers. This strain, particularly in August, led to dissension over tactics.

One of the chief criticisms of Dowding's strategy comes from a former Battle of Britain pilot, Wing Commander R. Allen. While allowing that the C-in-C was influenced in his decision by others, for example the Chiefs of Staff Committee, he says that the deployment of the fighter force 'was to invite disaster'. In Allen's view, Blenheim squadrons should have been moved north from No 11 Group and replaced by the eleven Spitfire squadrons available to Nos 12 and 13 Groups. 'Every Spitfire squadron in Fighter Command should have been based in the 11 Group area,' according to Allen, who believed that Dowding would then have been meeting the principle of concentration of force with his best fighters.

Rather than agree that Dowding had to retain forces in the north to meet a possible attack, Allen argues that this emphasis 'shows no military logic of any kind'. In support of this view it has to be remembered that no raids on the north could have been escorted by Bf 109s, so fighters other than Spitfires could have been deployed there.[28]

This leads to a salient point in the general criticism of Dowding's strategy, and one which has grown in recent years. It is that the C-in-C failed to respond when the battle with which he was confronted proved not to be the one for which he had planned, and he thus allowed No 11 Group to bear too heavy a burden. In the opinions of two eminent officers who flew in the battle, pilots who were trained to meet raids by unescorted bombers coming across the North Sea never anticipated having to compete with escorted bombers flying from the south. One of the officers believed that Dowding should certainly have appreciated this by September and taken appropriate steps; in his view, there was a place for Big Wings.[29]

If Dowding had realigned his Groups to meet the new threat from France, and if he had entrusted the immediate control of action to one commander, instead of leaving it to two men who had little wish to collaborate, much of the strain could have been removed from No 11 Group. However, even after it became obvious that the *Schwerpunkt* of the German attack was falling on the south-east and would continue to do so, Dowding was unwilling to reinforce that area adequately. His fear of German onslaughts on other Groups was unfounded and, in reality, occurred on one day only, when it was repulsed.

The fact that authorities at the time and many writers since believed Fighter Command to be heavily outnumbered and no more than a thin blue line clouds two important factors. The first is that Britain's defensive system was not composed solely of RAF fighters, but also contained anti-aircraft guns and barrage balloons. The second is that Fighter Command, using RDF and the Observer Corps, was far more effective in defence than the Luftwaffe was in attack. The RAF had a singular purpose; the German Air Force lacked clear objectives and failed to maintain a constant and undivided aim. Taken together, these two factors went some way to redress the apparent imbalance between the two sides. They also show that, if the David and

Goliath analogy is accepted, the former was better prepared and the latter less fearsome than customarily believed.[30]

The value of a well-equipped anti-aircraft arm had been demonstrated during the German campaign in the West. The *Flak* arm of the Luftwaffe was concerned to provide defence of home targets and also of the Army in the field. Heavy casualties were inflicted on RAF bombers in the early days of the offensive, when low-level attacks were attempted.[31]

In Britain, anti-aircraft defences were part of the Royal Artillery, an Army Command, yet the need for co-operation between them and Fighter Command had long been recognized. The relationship between General Sir Frederick Pile, GOC-in-C, AA Command, and Dowding was both cordial and fruitful, lacking the controversy which soured the latter's relations with the Air Ministry. As Dowding pointed out in his Despatch, he had the nominal responsibility for guns employed in the air defence of Great Britain, but 'this was little more than a convenient fiction'. He paid tribute to Pile's 'tact, patience and loyalty'.[32]

Both commanders made much of the shortage of guns, and such complaints give an impression that lack of resources led to ineffectiveness. This was certainly not true of AA Command at the time. In addition, it should be borne in mind that the number of guns estimated as vital to Britain's defence covered all areas of the United Kingdom, and these would have proved totally inadequate had German daylight attacks been launched nationwide. However the aerial battles by day between July and November were fought almost exclusively south of a line from London to Bristol, so wide areas of Britain had no occasion to employ guns by day.

Pile later recalled that the public mind appreciated that the RAF played the predominant part in the battle and that the lesser role taken by ground defences would fade from memory. Yet, in his reckoning, fighter pilots needed the help of AA Command just as, two years later, the infantry and tanks at Alamein would have won no victory without assistance from the gunners.[33] Dowding summarized the value of anti-aircraft fire under four headings. It could destroy or disable enemy aircraft; bomber formations could be broken up, to the benefit of waiting fighters; the accuracy of enemy bombing could be dislocated; and shellbursts were good indicators of the enemy's position. He could also have underlined the boost given to public morale by AA gunfire, because civilians, regardless of the guns' accuracy, felt reassured in defence. Considering the fears over public morale, the value of AA Command should not be overlooked.[34]

The seven AA Divisions employed were intended particularly to protect the aircraft industry. At the same time they were deployed to support Fighter Command, and Dowding acknowledged their success in shooting down enemy aircraft. It is immaterial whether or not the figures he gave are accepted; their immense contribution underscores the point that Britain's air defences were not so weak as often claimed.[35]

A further and often disregarded defence was offered by Balloon Command. Under the leadership of Air Vice-Marshal O. T. Boyd, the Command controlled about 1,400 balloons in July 1940, of which some 450 were placed to defend the capital. Their particular value as a deterrent to low-flying aircraft, especially dive-bombers, is not apparent from the negligible number of enemy aeroplanes they destroyed, but rather from the number of attacks which their presence prevented. In addition, they were a visible boost to civilian morale.[36]

The second underestimated factor in Fighter Command's favour at the start of the battle was the planned efficiency of response to raids. Many books note that the employment of RDF interception and sector control of squadrons, together with the accuracy of reports from the Observer Corps, came as a surprise to the Luftwaffe. Few, however, have pointed out that the 'Dowding System' went far to alleviate the imbalance of numbers between the two sides. British plans were worth many squadrons to the RAF and, in the opinion of the Chief Operations Officer of *Luftflotte III*, 'Radar at least doubled the efficacy of their fighter force'. This under-praised area of the organization helped to give Britain in 1940 the world's best system of aerial defence, unmatched by Germany, France, Russia or the USA.[37]

The system depended on the acceptance and transfer of information by radio, telephone and telegraph. Although there were delays in obtaining equipment and some weaknesses in practice before and during the battle, pioneer work carried out over the previous fifteen years gave Fighter Command a considerable advantage over the German Air Force. The Luftwaffe still had all the advantages of the aggressor, being able to choose the time and place to strike, yet this superiority was considerably offset by the efficiency of British communications. In essence, the system offered RAF fighters the greatest blessing, speed of response, which was crucial to a defence unable to afford wasteful standing patrols. It was of particular assistance to No 11 Group, where there was short warning of the enemy's approach.[38]

Consequently, a new assessment is needed of the relative strengths of the two sides. It shows that, as so often in history, numbers alone were of no more extensive value than a prepared plan. The pilots of Fighter Command were generally well rehearsed and supported in aims and duties, while those of the Luftwaffe were not. Terraine has referred to the British scheme as 'a delicately interlocking net of communications and responsibilities, comprising a carefully tuned instrument of war'.[39] Overy has pointed out that only massive bombing raids carried out by vastly superior numbers could have defeated 'the technical and organisational advantages enjoyed by the RAF'.[40] Even before the main fighting began, weaknesses in leadership and deficiencies in controlling aircraft in action ensured that the Luftwaffe was unable to meet the criteria demanded for success.

British strategy, no less than German, relied heavily on Intelligence reports and assessments. It is enlightening to explore briefly the resources of knowledge of the enemy that were open to the Air Ministry at that time. Evidence was available from four types of German signals traffic. First came high-grade cyphers, the Enigma; second were low-grade wireless telegraphy messages, usually from aircraft; the third consisted of low-grade R/T traffic; and the last was more general traffic, such as navigational beacons.[41] The RAF's main interception station at Cheadle was well experienced by this stage, having listened to low-grade Luftwaffe W/T traffic, whose security was not strong, since 1935. The RAF radio Intelligence service (the 'Y' service) was able to build a composite picture of the strength of Luftwaffe units.[42]

However, Air Intelligence, a separate Directorate within the Air Ministry,[43] had from pre-war days overestimated the power of the German Air Force.

They gave reports frankly, without the constraints experienced by their rivals in the Luftwaffe; yet although their figures and recommendations were sometimes treated with scepticism by some senior officers, their predictions helped to reinforce the Air Staff's belief that the Germans were capable of launching a 'knock-out' blow by means of a concentrated bombing campaign. This fear had also occupied Dowding's mind from his earliest days at Fighter Command, and affected his prepared strategy of response.[44] A crucial revision of their estimates was not made until a few days before the air battle began. By the time the information reached Dowding it was late for him to revise strategy, even if the unlikely assumption is accepted that he would have been prepared for last-minute, radical alterations.

During an investigation made from June, Professor Lindemann, the Prime Minister's close confidant and scientific adviser, was suspicious of the Air Ministry's estimates of German bombing capabilities, which reckoned that 2,500 bombers could deliver 4,800 tons of bombs daily.[45] Lindemann's enquiries brought realism to a world of fantasy when, on 5 July, he met the head of AI3, the German Section, who explained the hypotheses on which the figures were based. Having been compelled to examine their theories more vigorously, Air Intelligence produced revisions reducing the number of bombers to 1,250 and the daily load to 1,800 tons.[46] It was little wonder that the new totals, emanating from Enigma interpretations, enabled the Air Staff to 'view the situation much more confidently than was possible a month ago'. The great pity was that exaggerated figures had remained for so long, bolstering fears within the Air Ministry and affecting Dowding's arrangement of forces.[47]

Air Intelligence was closer to the mark in two other fields. First, they were convinced that no landing would be attempted before air superiority had been gained. Second, Enigma decrypts provided good advance warning of the impending battle, helping the C-in-C to plan his general response.[48]

Nonetheless, in assessing Dowding's contribution to both strategy and tactics in his Command, one issue needs to be resolved, because of several incorrect descriptions and the magnification of the error owing to the authority of the writers. Did Dowding receive information directly from Enigma? The fallacy, based first on Group Captain Winterbotham's claim, was that a soundproof cubicle was installed at Headquarters, Fighter Command and that the C-in-C had immediate information. According to Winterbotham, who was a senior Air Intelligence officer, both Dowding and Park benefited from a foreknowledge of German intentions, a claim supported by historians as eminent as Ronald Lewin and John Terraine.[49] However, the record was set straight by Martin Gilbert, who showed that not until 16 October 1940 was the C-in-C added to the list of those privy to Enigma.[50] Hinsley states of Enigma, 'the deductions were of no operational value to the C-in-C, Fighter Command,' and that Dowding had to depend on 'his own strategic judgement,' without help.[51]

Wing Commander H. Ironside, Dowding's Personal Assistant in October and November, can recollect no soundproof cubicle, although he was close to the C-in-C every day.[52] Yet Lewin, relying on Winterbotham's fallible memory, claims that Dowding received advance warning of German attacks on the north of England on 15 August. This is highly improbable. Sir Kenneth Cross, then on the staff of No 12 Group, remembers that, on that day, Leigh-Mallory was not at his headquarters, but was visiting an aerodrome when the raids took place. It is difficult to believe that, if Dowding had received forewarning of these raids, he would not have advised his Group Commander, who then would have stayed at his headquarters.[53] Similarly, on 7 September Park was in conference with Dowding when the first heavy daylight raids were made on London. It is unlikely that the meeting would have been held if they had known the Luftwaffe's intentions. Edward Thomas suggests that Winterbotham's fabrications stemmed from a lack of access to papers, to his poor memory, as 'he was over 70 years old', and the fact that 'he made up a good deal'.[54]

Therefore, the importance of Air Intelligence's exaggerated predictions of German capabilities must be borne in mind when assessing Dowding's deployment of forces. Their effect on his caution as a 'counter-puncher' may then be recognized, leading to a conservation of resources destined to bring No 11 Group under extreme pressure by late August.

PART 2: TACTICS IN BATTLE

At the start of the Battle of Britain, German tactics of fighter warfare were superior to those of the RAF. This point has been made by a number of Luftwaffe pilots and by many who served in Fighter Command. As the responsibility for tactical preparation of airmen lay with the Air Ministry, and particularly with Dowding, it is revealing to examine the steps taken to provide pilots with the best advice.

The tactics used by Fighter Command were written in its Bible of warfare, the Training Manual. The lines for engaging in combat were laid down, yet some pilots found difficulty in allowing for rapid changes to the design and performance of machines during the later 1930s. This is not surprising. They had learned to fly on biplanes with performances inferior to those of the Hurricanes and Spitfires introduced not long before the opening of war. Their conception of air tactics came from aircraft which took longer to climb and reach the enemy, and had smaller firepower when engaging. Having no actual experience in action, unless they had taken part, for example, in operations against tribesmen in distant parts of the Empire, their approach was a parade-ground exercise unrelated to the reality shortly awaiting them. For example, the Royal Air Force Training Manual of 1933 set out a series of principles to which no aspiring pilot could take exception. Air superiority is gained 'by the pursuit of a policy of relentless and incessant offensive against the enemy's air forces in the air and on the ground', and 'the importance of accurate marksmanship cannot be over-estimated'. Again, 'Altitude confers a tactical advantage upon the attacker', and 'an attack should be delivered with caution, but once attempted should be driven home with resolute determination to destroy the enemy'.[55]

However, these instructions were provided for men whose aircraft were in design and performance little more than updated versions of First World War biplanes. The Hawker Demon, a two-seat version of the Hart bomber, entered service in April 1933. At its ceiling of 15,000ft its maximum speed was 181mph, with an armament of three machine-guns. The Gloster Gladiator, best of the pre-war biplanes, which came into the RAF as late as 1937 (by which time it was already obsolescent), could manage 250mph and carried four machine-guns.[56]

On such machines the drill of flying a close 'vic-three' formation was an immutable law, with the two wing pilots giving undivided attention to holding a correct position in relation to their leader. Some airmen complained that such practice equipped them well for the annual RAF Display at Hendon, but was totally unrelated to modern war.[57] The writers of the Manual, themselves without experience of air combat in fast monoplanes, were at a loss when the accepted wisdom had to be updated. There was little time before the outbreak of war either for tutors to compile new advice, or for squadrons to practise the suggested tactics, or even evolve their own. Hurricanes did not come into squadron service until December 1937, and No 19 Squadron received the first Spitfires in August 1938.[58]

The section on 'Air Fighting Tactics' in the 1938 Manual made several suggestions unproven by experience. Manoeuvre at high speed was not possible because the effect of gravity 'causes a temporary loss of consciousness', so fighter attacks were to be made 'from the general direction of astern'. To carry out the recommended attacks, sections of three fighters were expected to maintain a 'vic' formation and fly into action. As an example, Attack No

1 was planned for the interception of a single bomber by three fighters. Attack No 2 was for two Sections of fighters intercepting an enemy bomber formation. Both attacks came from dead astern, with no deflection shots, and were adequate for dealing with the circumstances which Dowding had anticipated and for which he had prepared, namely attacks by formations of unescorted bombers coming mainly from the east. They were poor preparation for the reality of August 1940, when combat involved tackling enemy fighters flying from the south, with the advantages of height and sun, protecting bombers in an aerial screen.[59]

A further point lacking general recognition in subsequent controversies over leadership is that, throughout the French campaign and over the following month, efforts were made by Headquarters, Fighter Command, to learn some lessons about tactics and to disseminate information received. Some was of great practical value, and demonstrates that attempts were made to formulate the best methods of attack and defence. Dowding and Park showed, in certain directions, more initiative than some of their adversaries later gave them credit for. What was disappointing was that some recommendations were not advocated strongly to squadrons.

For example, a signal sent to all Groups on 19 May, based on the experience of a squadron just returned from France, suggested avoiding close formation on the way to rendezvous, never flying straight, and keeping an above guard when attacking. Two days later, Groups were told to expect visits from two Wing Commanders who had seen recent action, to discuss tactics 'with Sector and Squadron Commanders'.[60]

Subsequently, great interest was shown at Headquarters, Fighter Command. On 25 May a minute for Dowding reported 'the unanimous opinion that larger formations are essential'. It was better to fight in 'large numbers less frequently than in small numbers more often,' which would damage German morale and shoot down more bombers. Dowding's desire to spread information was shown when he asked all Groups to forward 'constructive ideas as to tactical methods' from pilots who had been in action.[61] A small piece in the jigsaw of Dowding's later dismissal fell in place at this time when Harold Balfour, Under-Secretary of State for Air, visited No 601 Squadron, which was led by Beaverbrook's son. He came away with the opinion, offered by many pilots, that larger formations were essential, a policy of which he approved during the later controversy over Wings.[62]

In June, Fighter Command Tactical Memorandum No 8 was issued. It was important as an attempt to provide guidance for squadrons now that German bombers could fly over parts of Britain with fighter escorts, a new dimension for RAF pilots. The document started optimistically, claiming that 'under conditions of Home Defence, where a highly organized system exists, the task of our Air Force should be simplified'. This reinforced belief in the Dowding System, carefully prepared, calling for a disciplined riposte to attacks, a response made strictly under orders.

Under 'THE AIM', the Memorandum stated that Britain's ability to continue the war depended on the success of fighters in protecting 'vital centres, and especially those concerned with aircraft and food production'. Dowding crossed out those last three words. Then came his main aim. 'It must, therefore, be constantly borne in mind that our aim is THE DESTRUCTION OF ENEMY BOMBERS, and that action against fighters is only a means towards this end.'

Further details laid down conditions of attack. Fighters should patrol higher than enemy aeroplanes, and an upper squadron should draw off escorts while a lower unit attacked the bombers. In protecting aerodromes it might be necessary not to engage enemy fighters 'who are in the nature of a decoy', but to wait for the following bombers. The 'Summary' contained eight points, seven of which offered excellent practical advice, such as keeping a constant watch behind and conserving ammunition. The final point contained the overall policy. 'Always remember that your objective is the ENEMY BOMBER.'[63]

Memorandum No 8 was a useful document, within the limitations of contemporary experience, laying down principles which enforced Fighter Command's planning, and was not revised until November. However, it quoted ideal circumstances, and when the battle developed these did not always obtain, as, for example, when Luftwaffe fighters flew close by their bombers. Some pilots then had to devise their own tactics.

Throughout June and July, Dowding wanted instructions which were passed on to squadrons to come only from his headquarters, fearing that otherwise his ideas would not be followed. Nonetheless, it should be remembered that, in reality, the C-in-C left the fighting of the battle to his Group Commanders, so his influence was only marginal, as he had no tactical command. Information was passed to him, but he was in no position to use it directly; he watched while it was passed forward to his four subordinates in command of Groups, who bore the immediate responsibility for engaging the enemy.[64]

It is interesting to note the dates and content of replies to the Memo of 3 June received from the three Groups involved, remembering that intensive German air activity built up from early July. The first response came from Air Vice-Marshal Saul, AOC, No 13 Group, on 7 July. Two sources had recommended that squadrons be organized into three Sections, each of four aircraft, rather than the RAF's traditional pattern of four Sections of three. The four aircraft could split into pairs for attacks against opponents. 'In several combats against enemy fighters the second aircraft of the pair was instrumental in shooting down Messerschmitt 109s, which were on the tails of the first aircraft.' No finer advice could have been offered to the pilots of Fighter Command. In essence, the Luftwaffe system of the *Rotte* (pair) was being advocated, with a wingman guarding the leader's tail.[65] Dowding was slow to adopt the suggestion. In his Despatch he stated that the organization should allow for pairs to operate, with one pilot guarding the second, yet this crucial point was never pressed strongly to squadrons. 'It was of course undesirable to make any sweeping change during the Battle,' he wrote guardedly, although the change would have saved many lives. Writing of the suggestion that squadrons might have been split into two Flights of eight aircraft, each comprising two Sections of four, he commented unimaginatively that it 'would upset standard arrangements for accommodation'.[66]

The value of the advice offered often depended upon the acumen of the squadron leaders receiving it. Some changed tactical formation quickly, but others stuck to the traditional 'vic-three' throughout the battle; the difference between such squadrons was, unfortunately, all too often reflected in their casualty rates. For example, the then Squadron Leader H. Darley, OC No 609 Squadron, was a resilient leader who altered tactics by introducing four Sections of three, all in line astern, with the fourth Section above and behind, preferably 1,000ft higher. As a pre-war instructor he believed that squadron discipline was essential, and that a collective force had to fight cohesively. By early October his squadron's results vindicated his tactics, and his men stayed in the front line of No 10 Group throughout the battle.[67] This may be compared with the experience of a pilot officer with No 145 Squadron, who recollected that they stayed 'by the book', in vics, from Dunkirk onwards, and by August were 'virtually destroyed' and had to be re-formed.[68]

Park's reply to the Memo, sent from his headquarters on 12 July, also made the point of rearranging squadrons and named Nos 54 and 74 Squadrons as the source of the idea. They had suggested breaking into six pairs, which in dogfights could operate as one attacker and one wingman.[69] No reply had come from No 12 Group by 17 July, so a reminder was sent to Leigh-Mallory, who then promised suggestions within a week.

Their response arrived on 25 July, and is remarkable in view of No 12 Group's later advocacy of Big Wings.[70] For example, the opinion of the OC No 264 Squadron was enclosed, strongly opposing those formations. 'It is improbable that any three squadrons would be able to take off, form up and set off on a course in under twelve minutes. In which time an enemy formation would have covered 40 miles.' The slow speeds of the formation would give the enemy time to reach a target before being engaged. If new raids appeared, the Controller would have to split up the Wing to counter them. 'However good the ground direction and R/T may be I do not feel that such methods would give the best results.'

Another note enclosed with No 12 Group's reports was a paper, 'Single Seater Fighter Tactics', submitted by the OC No 19 Squadron, Duxford, on 22 June. He was a further convert to the use of pairs in combat. The pilots should maintain line astern, which had proved to be successful and 'in point of fact, two pilots who adhered to this system throughout the patrols met with considerable success and were themselves unscathed'.

It is noteworthy that, at this stage, No 12 Group were making no strong recommendations on the advisability of employing Wings of at least three squadrons to meet German attacks. Over the following month, however, as raids grew in intensity and the pilots of No 11 Group came under increasing strain, those on the fringes of battle examined the role of squadrons stationed in their Groups.

At the start of the Battle of Britain the RAF officer with the greatest experience of the tactical employment of fighters was Park, who had commanded No 11 Group during the French campaign. Through controlling squadrons under battle conditions over the main fighting area he learned lessons that served him well during subsequent months. It is not generally recognized that he appreciated the value of employing Wings when circumstances were appropriate and that that was his policy during the later stages of the Dunkirk evacuation.

On 8 July he wrote No 11 Group's report on action during the French campaign and sent it to Dowding who, a fortnight later, passed the document on to the Air Ministry, with the comment that, although the paper was of interest, 'I cannot endorse all the opinions expressed'.[71] The report explained how squadrons had been organized. While operating from French bases, on escort duty or flying patrols, squadrons were employed in Flights, or singly. When the Allied armies were retreating, however, and the Germans were operating large formations of aircraft, RAF squadrons were employed in pairs. Park then underlined the dilemma of this policy, because cover could not be maintained continuously over the Allied troops. 'It seriously reduced the number of hours that our fighters could be on patrol.'

In the following paragraph he claimed that at the start of the Dunkirk evacuation 'the Air Ministry ordered continuous weak fighter patrols throughout the 18 hours of daylight', a comment beside which Dowding pencilled a cross on his copy of the report. Park added, 'As forecast, this resulted in our squadrons suffering heavy casualties for small casualties in combat'. He went on to express clearly the merits of Big Wings when used under favourable circumstances. After representations had been made to what he termed 'Higher Authority',[72] 'the Group was permitted to employ offensive fighter patrols at 2-squadron strength, leaving a few hours of daylight in which there were no patrols on the line'. Dowding made a pencil mark in the margin by the last point. The report continued, 'This resulted in less casualties to our fighters, and a marked increase in the number of successes in combat. When enemy formations were from thirty to sixty bombers, closely escorted by formations of fifteen to thirty fighters, permission was obtained to employ offensive sweeps of four squadrons working in two pairs. Whenever possible, the upper pair of squadrons consisted of Spitfires and the lower pair of either Hurricanes, or Hurricanes and Defiants.' The paragraph finished by explaining that this policy led to more Luftwaffe, and fewer RAF aircraft, being shot down.[73]

Park criticized the lack of pre-war training in Fighter Command in seven important items, ranging from fighter v fighter tactics to deflection shooting. Dowding, who had the habit of pencilling in the margin with blue crayon, placed question marks beside three of the items, either because he did not comprehend the point or, more likely, that he disagreed with Park's criticism. Yet however much Park criticized the training of squadrons, and however well Dowding tried to avoid the blame, the fact remains that here was a duty of Fighter Command for which both had special responsibility.

The C-in-C had a field day with paragraph 46 of the report, marking each side in a double line of blue crayon, his standard procedure for reinforcing a strongly held belief. Here he was applauding Park's tilt at Dowding's own adversaries on the Air Staff. They failed to appreciate his difficulties, claimed Park in a style guaranteed to gain no friends among them, by constantly badgering his headquarters for patrol and combat reports. The flow of enquiries was a great embarrassment to his staff, blocked land lines, and sometimes hindered operations orders.

In the light of what was to follow from late August, Park's report is instructive. He was the only senior commander involved to have experience of using Wings in action. He, not Dowding, exercised tactical control of the fighter force. Of the two main disciples of Big Wings, Douglas was at the Air Ministry, an interested and involved observer, yet without direct command. Leigh-Mallory, even when the Duxford Wing flew in September, never controlled them to a set pattern over an area for which he had responsibility. From the point of view of practice as opposed to theory, no one had a more legitimate right than Park to express opinions on the matter.

In addition, it should be remembered that the French campaign had far-reaching effects on the subsequent attitudes of both Park and Dowding. Fighter Command's losses had been heavy and, to ensure the safety of the Home Base, both men feared profligacy with such a limited resource as the RAF's fighters. In their view, ill-chosen forays over the homeland with fighters flying *en masse* could have incurred disastrous casualties at the level the Germans were seeking to inflict. Such an approach was especially far removed from the nature of the conservatively-minded Dowding.

PART 3: LUFTWAFFE ATTACKS AND FIGHTER COMMAND'S RESPONSE

Authorities differ over the particular dates of various phases of the Battle of Britain. Did it begin in late June, at the fall of France? Was Dowding's later selection of 10 July an apt choice? Were some Germans correct in believing that it did not start until early August?[74]

The usual selection of 10 July is capricious, doing less than justice to those airmen involved in action after the fall of France but before that day, who were shot down, killed or wounded, and consequently regarded in some quarters as not having taken part.[75] Probably the view held by some German writers that the battle was an indivisible part of the general Western campaign is a more accurate assessment.[76] It is possible, nevertheless, to choose 18 August as the end of the opening phase, because on that day the Luftwaffe made an extensive effort to destroy what their Intelligence believed to be the small residue of fighters left in the RAF. The resulting aerial fighting brought heavier combined losses than those suffered by the Luftwaffe and the RAF on any other day of the battle. The Germans discovered that Fighter Command was stronger than they had estimated and, at a conference the next day, Goering told commanders of changes in strategy and tactics which, in reality, helped the British defences.[77] Additionally, the events of that day and the results of the conference led to a growth of the uneasy relationship between Nos 11 and 12 Groups, Fighter Command, as attitudes were sharpened in the Big Wing controversy.

From the end of the French campaign the German Air Force held as its main strategic aim the destruction or neutralizing of the RAF, especially Fighter Command. They intended to achieve this mainly over southern England. 'First of all success is to be achieved in the target areas of *Luftflotten 2* and *3*,' Goering ordered at a conference on 21 July. 'Only a complete victory over the RAF in southern England can give us the possibility of further attacks on enemy forces stationed in the depth of the country.'[78]

The first raids were therefore made against Channel shipping. Werner Kreipe, who took part in several of these onslaughts, recollected the Luftwaffe's double task. Hand in hand with the destruction of the RAF was to go 'the interdiction of the Channel to merchant shipping', which, he claimed, the British were still sending 'with characteristic imperturbability'. In this way the Germans hoped to clear the Straits of all British ships, both naval and merchant, to control the crossing area for their own forces when the time came.[79]

The protection of shipping became, for the RAF, a matter of controversy because of the commitment demanded of Fighter Command. On average, twelve convoys needed cover every day and roughly one-third were attacked. An immediate burden was laid, especially on No 11 Group, at a time when they were faced with 'the bulk of the German Air Force'. The employment of convoys in the general area from the Suffolk coast to Lyme Bay negated the value of using the sea as a protective shield, because fighting conditions there nearly always favoured the attacker, as RDF could give little advance warning of raids. Far more goods could have been moved by rail over a mainland better protected by fighters.[80]

On 3 July Dowding asked for convoys to be redirected round the north of Scotland, appreciating that not all could be adequately protected, yet almost four weeks later, after heavy German raids on Dover and the Straits, the Air Ministry instructed him to meet the enemy with large formations and superior forces.[81] Shipping suffered regular losses, but by 9 August Churchill still wanted them used as 'bait', leading to greater casualties than Fighter Command should have been asked to bear.[82]

Several deductions can be made of this phase, in which both sides had gains and losses. The German effort was hampered by cloudy weather, which was shown as 'Fine' on four days only from 10-31 July,[83] yet a heavier burden was the indecision displayed by their leadership. Not until 1 August did Hitler order, in Directive No 17, 'the final conquest of England', decreeing that the RAF was to be rapidly defeated, preparatory to an invasion date set for 15 September.[84] In addition, Goering's plans were slow. He did not issue the final directive for *Adlerangriff* until 2 August, with the aim of overwhelming the RAF in the way that had been employed against the air forces of Poland and France.[85]

In air combat, German tactics were generally superior. Not only did RAF fighters protecting convoys find the enemy at greater height and in larger numbers, but also the employment of vic-formations and Fighter Command attacks by the book brought considerable casualties.[86] The Germans also discovered that the Bf 109, especially flown by an experienced pilot, was a most competent aircraft, and proved finally the superiority of single-seat fighters over other types by taking a heavy toll of the RAF's Defiants, especially on 19 July, when these machines were encountered near Folkestone and six destroyed in one battle.[87]

Several results surprised the Luftwaffe, counting to their disadvantage. The quality of Hurricanes and Spitfires, flown by spirited pilots, reinforced the opinions formed of these machines during the battle in France. Far from reassuring was the proof gained over the Channel that the Bf 110 and Ju 87 were extremely vulnerable in combat, and would be able to play a lesser part in the fighting over Britain than had been anticipated.[88]

Probably the greatest surprise for the Luftwaffe was the discovery that British aircraft were being controlled by a sophisticated system of communication, enabling fighters to be directed to targets. The RAF during this period were able to 'work some bugs out of their radar systems',[89] and learn about Luftwaffe tactics, showing that German strategy was at fault. The fighting took place over Channel shipping because the general plan of assault on Britain had not been formulated in July, yet the Luftwaffe had to show itself capable of action.

The surprising effect of British RDF on the Luftwaffe High Command was recollected by Galland, who flew Bf 109s during the early sorties.[90] The unpreparedness demonstrates the weaknesses of the Luftwaffe Intelligence services. As late as 7 August 'Beppo' Schmid expressed the view that Fighter Command aircraft were 'tied to their respective ground stations and are thereby restricted in mobility'. Consequently he believed that a mass attack on a target by German bombers would meet only 'light fighter opposition' and that there would be 'considerable confusion in the defensive networks'.[91]

The slow start to preparations for a possible invasion, stemming particularly from Hitler's disinclination and lack of drive, made matters more difficult for the Luftwaffe, who were virtually the sole contributors to action from the German side. Apart from other considerations, the number of days suitable for landings in Britain was limited by such ungovernable factors as the weather and by the more predictable one of tides. As detailed plans for an offensive against the mainland were not laid before the end of the month, the possible dates for July were lost. The ideal form of invasion, by a combined operation of land, sea and air forces, was limited to seven 'best days' in August or fewer in September, by which time adverse conditions could be expected. Together with other difficulties facing German plans, this compression of opportunities for landings obviously affected the outlook of the German navy and forced the Luftwaffe into a much narrower time-scale of operations than its commanders would have chosen.

Various branches of British Intelligence, which appear not to have recovered fully from their failures in the Norwegian campaign, issued sets of wary predictions of invasion throughout the summer and early autumn. Other reports brought more hope, and are proof of the pressure of time placed particularly on the Luftwaffe. On 1 August Churchill told the War Cabinet that Britain's position 'was now considerably more secure than in May'. On 9 August he said that Britain was winning the air battle. Three days later a spy from within German military Intelligence informed London that two or three weeks would elapse before invasion forces were ready. The RAF's role, and particularly Fighter Command's part, must be viewed in relation to German capabilities. Only September was available realistically for Operation 'Sealion', a late and hazardous time. The Luftwaffe's main offensive then appeared as little more than a forlorn hope.[92]

To assess the effect of this period of German attacks, before heavy raids moved to the mainland, it is necessary to explore the strengths of the two air forces in early August. The RAF had grown relatively stronger. On 10 July Fighter Command had 52 squadrons ready for operations; by 8 August there were 55 squadrons, with six others under training, including three 'foreign' squadrons, two Polish and one Czech, formed during the month and containing some very experienced pilots. Overall, the total of pilots rose by 175 between 6 July and 3 August, in spite of the loss of 74, plus 48 wounded.[93]

On 3 August the Luftwaffe, according to figures issued by the Quartermaster-General, had 878 single-engined and 320 twin-engined fighters listed as 'serviceable', although Suchenwirth estimates the figures of these categories which were 'combat-ready' on 8 August as 760 and 230 respectively. German Air Force losses for July were given as 53 Bf 109s and 22 Bf 110s.[94]

Additionally, British economic power, a factor on which some leaders had pinned their faith for some time, was showing in figures of aircraft production. Fighter deliveries to the RAF in June, July and August were significantly greater than those to the Luftwaffe, and certainly covered losses. The planned British figures for those three months, 292, 329 and 282, became in reality 446, 496 and 476 respectively, as Beaverbrook's Ministry of Aircraft Production built on the framework laid particularly by the efforts of Wilfrid Freeman.[95] In comparison, the German aircraft industry produced only 274 Bf 109s and Bf 110s in August.[96] Blame for this situation, later directed towards Udet and Jeschonnek, can also be laid at Hitler's door. He was already planning the campaign against Russia, and placed air armament fifth in line for allocation of raw materials.[97]

At the start of the second phase of the air assault, Goering was attempting to overcome Fighter Command in the south of England before extending the offensive until the Luftwaffe controlled all skies over Britain. In grand fashion he intended to open, and virtually close, the campaign with a massive attack, *Adlertag*, which would demolish resistance within a few days. This phase actually lasted from the beginning of August until the 18th of the month. The period witnessed many demands on both the Luftwaffe and Fighter Command, and by its close the strategy, tactics and leadership of both air forces were being examined closely and critically. Evidence shows that by mid-August, although No 11 Group were under increasing pressure, the German Air Force had gone far to denying themselves victory.

On the German side there was frustration over this stage, which had opened with a strong air of confidence among Luftwaffe leaders and crews.[98] At Goering's conference held at the Hague on 1 August, plans were formulated for attacks from the south and west, moving closer to London, with the intention of forcing Fighter Command into a battle of attrition.[99] However, a combination of slow preparation, poor reconnaissance and unfavourable weather led to insignificant major action before 8 August. In retrospect, such delays made small difference in the long run to part of a general battle to which little strategic thought had been devoted. Even before the main 'Eagle' attacks opened, the German lack of a direct and concentrated aim was a relief to Dowding, and more particularly to Park, who carried the immediate responsibility for defending London and the south. Strategy demanded undivided purpose, and there were three basic possibilities. First, Britain could be forced to surrender by the effects of blockade; second, victory could come from the power of air attack alone; and third, the Luftwaffe could create conditions under which a seaborne invasion would be successfully launched. The weakness stemming from Goering and his planning staff was the dissipation of effort among all three.[100]

Basic faults in strategy led to tactical errors. Heavy attacks were launched on 8, 12, 13 and 15 August and Fighter Command, especially No 11 Group, was greatly stretched.[101] However, no sustained and concentrated raids were launched on the Chain Home Link radar stations, without which the Dowding System could barely operate. Temporary damage was done, but once again German Intelligence failed to recognize the importance of

RDF to Fighter Command. Proof of this ignorance was displayed at Goering's Karinhall conference on the 15th, when the Reichsmarschall announced that there was little point in maintaining attacks on RDF sites 'in view of the fact that not one of those attacked has so far been put out of action'.[102]

A scattering of effort resulted from several raids being made on airfields not vital to Fighter Command, such as Eastchurch and Detling. The importance of Sector stations to No 11 Group went unrecognized, and no prolonged bombing of these took place.[103] In a small, yet significant way, the weakness of Luftwaffe communications was demonstrated on the 15th. Dornier Do 17s of *KG 2*, escorted by Bf 110s, were already airborne when their operation was postponed, but only the escorts received the radio message and they had no means of communication with the bombers, which carried on in ignorance.[104]

The failure of wide-ranging onslaughts on the 15th, involving all three *Luftflotten*, has been well documented as an example of Dowding's wisdom in maintaining squadrons in the north to meet any German assault there, and as a defeat for the German Air Force. On the other hand, the Germans gained one benefit, appreciating the difficulties of using *Luftflotte V* in attacks across the North Sea. Many of its aircraft were later moved south to reinforce the main area of combat, but Fighter Command's strategic policy was not changed. Partly from British Intelligence fears that the enemy were retaining aeroplanes for further raids in the north, and partly from his own cautious nature, Dowding held about half of his fighter strength outside the main fighting area, allowing the heaviest burden to fall on the other half. On 8 August, 26 of his squadrons of best fighters, i.e. Hurricanes and Spitfires, were in Nos 10 and 11 Groups, while 21 'best' squadrons were in Nos 12 and 13 Groups. Nine out of nineteen squadrons of Spitfires were stationed outside what was and obviously would continue to be the main battle zone. Ten days later, when the German campaign was building in intensity, there were still 24 squadrons of Hurricanes and Spitfires to the north of the Thames. This was a major factor in the developing controversy over tactics.[105]

Luftwaffe incursions added to the burdens of Nos 10 and 11 Groups over the next few days, pressing at all levels from commanders to groundcrew, and from pilots to WAAF plotters, who worked virtually without respite. Assaults were launched particularly on airfields, with bombers used as bait to draw RAF fighters into battle. Naturally such an offensive also taxed the Luftwaffe, which flew 1,485 sorties on the 13th and 1,786 two days later.[106] The climax of this phase of battle was reached on Sunday 18 August when, with unfounded optimism, aircraft from *Luftflotten II* and *III* were dispatched to administer a final, crushing blow to Fighter Command. Nonetheless, the result was a day on which the combined casualties of both sides in numbers of aircraft destroyed exceeded those of any other day in the battle. Luftwaffe pilots discovered that the RAF was able to counter almost every move.[107] A prime reason was bad Intelligence, which was in some respects the Luftwaffe's heaviest casualty. Schmid's survey of British losses over the previous fortnight, written on 17 August, was a flight of fancy set out mainly as a subtraction sum. The figure of 900 RAF fighters was given for 1 July. Of those, 574 were claimed to have been shot down in the period, with 196 lost from other causes. Taking replacements as numbering 300, this gave an overall loss of 470. Of the remaining 430 fighters presumed, 70 per cent were reckoned to be serviceable, i.e. 300 machines. Schmid estimated that 200 were in the south, 70 in 'Central England' and 30 in the north and Scotland. The Intelligence service's damage to the cause was shown in the figures issued for 8 August. The loss of 14 German aircraft was admitted, while in reply, 42 Hurricanes and Spitfires were claimed as destroyed 'over the Channel'.[108]

On the British side, Nos 10 and 11 Groups, and especially the latter, bore the heaviest burden.[109] The Dowding System worked satisfactorily, although RDF was not always accurate, as mass formations sometimes jammed radars. Also, on cloudy days the Observer Corps had obvious difficulty in tracking aircraft inland. Yet Park had to rely implicitly on information fed to his headquarters and always feared that his Sector stations would be attacked, telling one pilot that without signals the only thing he commanded was his desk.[110] He later noted that at this stage German fighters often flew higher than their bombers, which gave them an advantage in interception but did not always offer the best protection to their charges. His aim, following the policy which he and Dowding had set as their credo, was to engage the enemy as soon as possible.[111]

Fighter Command's greatest problem was a shortage of experienced pilots, although one clear advantage for the RAF over the Luftwaffe was that German aircrew who baled out over England were lost to further action, whereas British pilots might live to fight another day. In July and August the Command lost 222 men killed or missing, with 205 others wounded, the great majority in the south, the centre of battle.[112] By the end of August the air defences were holding, but at great cost, not the least cause of strain being Dowding's policy of reinforcement, planned from pre-war days. The C-in-C later referred to this policy in his report on the battle,[113] but weaknesses showed during early August, even before the concentrated offensive against Fighter Command's aerodromes began. Some squadrons suffered exhaustion from persistent combat and heavy losses, and were far from efficient before being withdrawn to a quieter sector. This factor, together with the odds confronting them in almost every action, caused No 11 Group to enter the next phase of battle at a considerable disadvantage. For example, one pilot later noted that, during the turmoil of 18 August, 'The Hardest Day', no aircraft from Nos 12 or 13 Groups were damaged and only two from No 10 Group were hit.[114]

PART 4: GROWING POLITICAL INTEREST

Almost every account of the Battle of Britain fails to explore the continuing saga of Dowding's appointment and the response of politicians to him during August. However, an examination of his leadership is incomplete without this, and can be opened with a summary of the Prime Minister's attitude. The extreme bravery of the pilots of Fighter Command, and the conduct of the battle by their leader, gained Churchill's approval during the month. Realizing that, in spite of Britain's growing power of defence, much depended upon the actions being fought by the RAF, the Prime Minister kept in close touch with the events of combat. On 3 August he visited Headquarters, Fighter Command during the afternoon, and that evening entertained Dowding with several others, including Lindemann, to dinner at Chequers. Four days later Lindemann asked Churchill to approve of experiments which Dowding wanted, relating to RDF with night defence. The Prime Minister was therefore well aware of the work being carried out by Dowding and of his role within the RAF.[115]

Churchill's approval of Dowding at that stage is shown by a letter which he sent to Sinclair on the 10th. The tone displays definite displeasure with the Secretary of State, yet great sympathy with the leader of Fighter Command. 'I certainly understood from our conversation a month ago that you were going to give Dowding an indefinite war-time extension,' he began, adding peremptorily, 'and were going to do it at once'. He could not understand how any contrary impression had been gained 'about my wishes'. Churchill then urged Sinclair to take 'the step I have so long desired,' adding how wrong it was to keep the C-in-C in uncertainty over his appointment. That was not fair, 'least of all to the nation'. Churchill added strongly that he could not approve, and finished by asking that 'you will be able to set my mind at rest'.[116]

There is one piece of direct evidence as to what prompted the Prime Minister to send the letter and resurrect the question of Dowding's future. Undoubtedly the C-in-C's handling of the battle had been under review, so possibly the matter had arisen in conversation with Dowding himself, or even with Lindemann, who was deeply interested in night defence and whose judgement and opinions Churchill trusted. The Prime Minister had evidently discussed Dowding with Sinclair on the day before writing the letter because, in his reply, dated 12 August, the Secretary of State noted that 'after our talk on Friday I spoke at once to the CAS'. The letter was noticeably apologetic in tone, expressing sorrow over any misunderstanding and claiming not to have deliberately ignored the Prime Minister's wishes. That was 'the last thing I should want to do'. He added that Newall had written to the C-in-C, withdrawing the earlier time limit.[117]

On 12 August Newall's letter informed Dowding of the new conclusion and commented that he realized the disadvantages involved of the decision taken in July. He hoped that the news 'will be agreeable to you'.[118] Dowding replied formally to the letter, whose contents 'I have noted with pleasure'.[119] The brevity of response is understandable, having been written on a day when the Luftwaffe flew 1,485 sorties over Britain. Official notification of the cancellation of the time limit came from the Air Ministry eight days later.[120]

Churchill showed further evidence of interest in the air war on 15 August. Eden recalled how he and the Prime Minister sat in the Cabinet Room as reports arrived, then Churchill went to Headquarters, Fighter Command to watch the defensive effort.[121] Colville noted that on his return the Prime Minister was 'consumed with excitement' and, after sending news to Chamberlain, claimed it as one of history's greatest days. An undoubted reason for this was the factor, common to both sides, of exaggerated claims, because Churchill believed that more than a hundred German aircraft had been destroyed, when in reality the total was 76.[122] Churchill's interest was maintained on the following day when, with an example of leadership significantly lacking on the other side of the Channel, he visited the headquarters of No 11 Group at Uxbridge, seeing the Operations Room in action. During the evening he told General Ismay that he had never been so moved, then uttered the quotation beginning 'Never in the field of human conflict ...' which became famous when repeated in his parliamentary speech five days later.[123]

Yet Churchill showed altogether greater realism over air losses on the 16th, when he minuted Newall, reminding him of Bomber Command's losses on the ground the previous day, making the point that these deductions considerably altered the balance of success between the two air forces.[124] His praise for the pilots of Fighter Command was clear from his speech to Parliament on 20 August, yet it is often unnoticed that his words included great praise for Bomber Command, whose contribution to Britain's defence at the time is usually overlooked. As well as mentioning fighter pilots 'whose brilliant actions we see with our own eyes', he showed a judgement of what would happen to the enemy. Hitler, he predicted, would have no gain if the economic and scientific background to German war power was devastated at home. Churchill's clarity of purpose in seeking to hit back aggressively was never far absent, and marks an important difference between him and Dowding.[125]

Three days later, W. P. Crozier, editor of the *Manchester Guardian*, interviewed the Prime Minister. His report summarized the guarded optimism being felt even at the height of battle. Churchill said that between 8 and 18 August Britain had done well in the air battle, 'But I don't think it's over. Some people do.' He added that a German invasion could not be attempted without air superiority – '*that* he must have' – and that over England, apart from in the sea, the bodies of 150 German airmen had been recovered in the period.[126]

It is not easy to assess Sinclair's sentiments towards the leadership of Fighter Command, because his personal papers from that period were later destroyed, yet certain deductions can be drawn from the recollections of those who knew him.[127] First, he disliked offending Churchill who, according to Colville, sometimes treated him 'with a half serious levity'.[128] He was held in low esteem by several politicians, including Stanley Bruce, the Australian High Commissioner, who did not think he was 'much good or has any particular force and drive'. 'Chips' Channon disliked his parliamentary style, which made the 'exploits of our airmen sound dull and trite'.[129] Beaverbrook, with whom he regularly crossed swords, believed him to be easily swayed by his Air Marshals.[130] 'Chubby' Power, a Canadian politician, claimed that Sinclair addressed him 'in speeches such as he would make in the House of Commons'.[131]

Nonetheless, some thought better of his contribution. Douglas, perhaps unsurprisingly, referred to his 'vigour and great ability and success',[132] while Saundby, who served in the Air Ministry at the time, remembered his 'perfect manners, integrity and personal charm'.[133]

Sinclair's passage within the Government was made less easy because of Churchill's reservations over the abilities of the Air Ministry, and also through the power struggle between that ministry and the Ministry of Aircraft Production, under Beaverbrook. Beaverbrook appeared to carry more weight with the Prime Minister, and his pungent style led to frequent controversy with Sinclair. According to Colville, Beaverbrook 'exerted an infallible fascination' on Churchill and his opinions and interventions were of considerable importance.[134]

Partly because he recognized Dowding as a fellow sufferer from the machinations of the Air Ministry, and partly through his respect for the C-in-C's work, Beaverbrook held Dowding in high regard. He could agree with Pile's assessment on 19 August that 'thanks to Sir Hugh Dowding, an invasion of this country is not practical'.[135] Beaverbrook's appreciation of him was transmitted to Churchill, influencing his opinion of the RAF's leadership. This appreciative enthusiasm was displayed during an interview between Beaverbrook and the ubiquitous and inquisitive Crozier, when the Minister of Aircraft Production referred to Dowding as 'coming to the front in everything that relates to the war'. He added optimistically that there was no idea Dowding would not try, an assertion that a number of the Air Staff would have disputed.[136]

Yet, ironically, although he was the C-in-C's champion, Beaverbrook's dislike of Newall led to a disclosure of some of the Air Ministry's reservations over Dowding. This emanated from a five-page typed document of undeclared origin, entitled *A Weak Link in the Nation's Defences*, which was circulated among several members of the Conservative Party and was basically a swingeing attack on the Chief of the Air Staff. Unfortunately for Dowding, one section of the paper was critical of him, calling Fighter Command 'a one man show', commenting on his 'inadequate mental ability and very slow brain' and calling him a 'complete non-co-operator with authority' who treated his staff deplorably.[137]

Irene Ward, a Conservative MP, sent a copy of the paper to Churchill on 21 August and he, in turn, passed it to Sinclair with the request to have it returned. Its importance was that the Air Ministry's case for Dowding to be replaced was carried closer to politicians, a side-effect never intended by Beaverbrook. Possibly the author was Wing Commander Kingston-McCloughry, who worked at the Air Ministry and, for reasons of his own, wished Newall to be removed. Irene Ward's unlikely involvement appears to have started when she was approached by RAF officers who had no confidence in Newall, who was shortly to retire, believed that Dowding's appointment to succeed him as CAS would be a disaster, and wanted Portal to have the position. She espoused their cause with determination, sending a copy not only to the Prime Minister but also to his confidant, Brendan Bracken. Sinclair met her in September and, after Portal had gained the promotion in October, wrote to Bracken, who had already sent a note to Churchill, calling her 'a rather ferocious female'. Sinclair's letter referred to her as a 'your virago' who probably believed that her intervention had ensured Portal's appointment and that 'not for the first time, a goose had saved the Capitol'. Certainly the episode proved the power held by politicians over Service appointments, a manifestation that was to recur for Dowding.[138]

Another politician who saw weaknesses in Newall was Hugh Dalton, at the Ministry of Economic Warfare. In discussions with him, an RAF officer regretted the Air Force's lack of 'power over the port'. Old generals and admirals could meet with Cabinet ministers who had been at school with them and exert their influence, but the officer feared that Newall had not been at school 'with anyone that mattered'. Dalton, unusually both an Old Etonian and a Labour MP, offered to help.[139]

Consequently it may be deduced that Dowding's efforts in August were generally well received, but the undercurrent of latent dislike emanating from the Air Ministry was reaching a wider audience. This happened at the stage, late in the month, when changes in Luftwaffe strategy and tactics led to Fighter Command's most difficult days – and brought the pilots of No 11 Group close to being overwhelmed.

4

THE DEVELOPMENT OF
THE BIG WING CONTROVERSY
19 AUGUST TO 7 SEPTEMBER

PART 1: PRE-WAR BACKGROUND TO FIGHTER COMMAND TACTICS

The period from 19 August to 7 September was marked by a growing intensity of German raids on the mainland of southern Britain. Their prime purpose was the destruction, or neutralizing, of Fighter Command, which had responded so vigorously to earlier attacks. At that stage RAF pilots, especially those of No 11 Group, were subjected to greater strain than they had experienced since the start of the war.

The resulting pressure led to the deepeing of divisions within Fighter Command, with Park on the one hand and Leigh-Mallory on the other at growing odds over the most effective tactics to be employed in defence. Park, following the agreed policy of early response to bombers before they reached their targets, despatched fighters in single, or double squadron strength. In his view there was insufficient warning to organize larger groups and, anyway, he did not believe that Wings of three or more squadrons were the most effective formations in defence. On the other side, Leigh-Mallory, especially towards the end of this period, was convinced that Wing tactics brought greater casualties to the attackers and fewer to the defenders. He wanted the Duxford Wing to be used in conjunction with Park's squadrons.

By 7 September, when this phase of the battle ended, the rift between the two Group commanders was wide. Park surmised that No 12 Group aircraft were to provide a source of reinforcement for him, when he requested; Leigh-Mallory believed that his squadrons should be allowed to operate in their own right over No 11 Group's area. The different interpretations may be traced back to the vagueness of pre-war arrangements, and Dowding, as C-in-C, was in a unique position to exercise authority and resolve the developing quarrel at this stage. However, he failed to intervene. In this way, it is true to say that he lost control of the tactical fighting of the battle and allowed an inordinate and unnecessary burden to fall on Park and the pilots of No 11 Group.

In view of the later criticism of Dowding's tactical handling of the battle, it is important to appreciate a point seldom noted. This is that the seeds of a cardinal difference of opinion over tactics, between staff in the Air Ministry and those at Headquarters, Fighter Command, were sown before the war and were to have great effect on the Command's leadership as the daylight battle progressed. At issue was the division of responsibilities between

Groups and the tactics to be employed against German bomber formations attacking Great Britain.

Within the limits of his planning for defence, Dowding gave considerable independent power to his commanders of Groups, believing that they, as experienced and loyal colleagues, would follow his policy to the letter. In September 1939 he wrote to Leigh-Mallory, 'I have delegated tactical control almost completely to Groups and Sectors, but I have not delegated strategical control and the threat to the line must be regarded as a whole and not parochially'. He finished, 'and I would only ask you to remember that the Fighter Command has to operate as a whole'. [1] Yet although each Group was responsible for its own defensive position, there would be times of interdependence when the need for help and reinforcement arose. Different interpretations of orders and tactics could then become thorny problems, partly through Dowding's failure to plan completely for the synchronization of the actions of his Groups and to predict the result of divergent tactics. Therein lay the main fault in a flawed system which was to lead directly to the Big Wing controversy.

The fault was underlined after the Air Defence Exercises of 1939, when a conference was held at Bentley Priory to discuss results and lessons learned. A particular difficulty was the procedure for handing raids from one Group to another, or between Sectors. A memo from the Home Defence Committee on 7 July 1939 said that it had been necessary 'to provide a sufficiently elastic ground organisation to permit of reinforcement by squadrons from one area to another'. However, the details of who was to control the aircraft and the form in which the assistance would be despatched were not resolved. The problem was never adequately solved then, nor, as events were to prove, a year later. [2] The root of the subsequent Big Wing controversy in August 1940 was that Leigh-Mallory's belief in using fighter Wings of three or more squadrons was taken up by a cabal within the Air Staff who had believed in that policy since pre-war days. They used it against Dowding and Park, who asserted that Wings were, for the conditions at that time, both unwieldy and inefficient.

The tactical use of RAF fighters had exercised the minds of the Air Staff before 1939. For several of them, estimates of the effective disposition of squadrons were based on their own experiences as pilots during the First World War, flying biplanes. Harold Balfour, then Under-Secretary of State for Air, later described the early wartime Air Council. 'Air Marshals, World War One, no doubt in their day were active and gallant pilots. But they'd none of them flown modern aircraft at all. I think I was the only member of the Air Council when I joined the Air Council as Vice-President in 1938 who could really fly Service aircraft.'[3] Among Dowding's principal opponents in the Air Ministry who were covered by this description during the period July to December 1940 were Saundby, Slessor, Joubert, Douglas, Harris and Newall himself.

Little had been learned about employing modern fighters in war, either from the campaign of the Japanese Air Force fighting against China and Russia during 1937-8, or from the Luftwaffe during the Spanish Civil War. The air forces of Britain, the USA and France, which had not taken part in campaigns, had to learn their lessons expensively after 1939. [4]

In 1936 a report by the Joint Planning Committee anticipated that German air raids would be deterred through heavy losses, because if a sufficient percentage of bombers failed to return there would be 'a cumulative effect on the morale of pilots'. The report, written before the introduction of Hurricanes and Spitfires, was a sanguine hope, yet underscored a conception of Fighter Command being employed in an aggressive role. [5]

By 1938 more members of the Air Staff accepted the limitations of the RAF's ability to settle a European war through the power of bombing, yet Trenchard's spirit of attack died hard. In August 1938 they examined a document on plans to meet German raids of 1,000 bombers a day[6] and Douglas, then Assistant Chief of the Air Staff, commented to Stevenson, Deputy Director of Operations, in a style guaranteed to gladden Trenchard's heart. Douglas expressed the opinion, from which he later never deviated, that it was 'immaterial in the long view' whether bombers were shot down before or after they had dropped their bombs. It would be 'very nice' if the Germans could be intercepted before reaching their targets, but the prime need was to cause the enemy such heavy casualties that their attacks 'will dwindle rapidly to bearable proportions'. He went on to say that Stevenson had implied this in his minute, 'but I think it ought to be clearly stated on the file'. [7]

Dowding was critical of these plans for defence, but his opponents believed that he offered no better policy. His letter to the Deputy Chief of the Air Staff of 12 October 1938 was seen by Stevenson, who noted that 'the general criticism of C-in-C's remarks on our plan at Enclosure 18A is that while it aims at exploding the basis of our calculation and plan it makes no constructive suggestion for an alternative'. Stevenson then stated categorically that the object underlying the Air Ministry's plan was to destroy the enemy's scale of attack, as opposed to inflicting a possibly low rate of casualties. Further, he suggested that 'in default of a constructive alternative from the C-in-C, I should be very sorry to see the main principle of the plan go. I suggest, therefore, that we should proceed to implement the plan.'[8]

At this time Dowding felt confident that, no matter which tactics were employed against bomber formations, the Luftwaffe could be prevented from sustaining attacks over Britain. The Hurricanes and Spitfires under his command, growing in numbers, albeit too slowly for his liking, had every advantage over unescorted bombers such as the Heinkel He 111 or the Dornier Do 17 which would form the mainstays of an enemy campaign. In this vein he wrote to Newall, the CAS, on 24 February 1939, predicting heavy German casualties which would bring attacks to a rapid halt. [9]

None the less, the question of tactics was raised again a month later when Air Vice-Marshal Gossage, AOC, No 11 Group, wrote to seek Dowding's advice over a crucial query that had been put to him during a lecture. The questioner had suggested that the 'annihilation of a few raids' was preferable to attempting to intercept them all, and Gossage was forced to agree, although existing resources were insufficient and a compromise had to be reached. What did the C-in-C think?[10]

Dowding's reply agreed on the importance of the question and stated that his principle was 'to match machine with machine'. He warned against sending too many fighters to intercept, lest the enemy employed a small attack to draw the defences before launching a heavier raid when British aeroplanes were grounded for refuelling and rearming. Nevertheless, using small forces to 'nibble' at opponents was bad tactics. The letter ended by restating his basic belief in employing the individual squadron as 'the largest tactical unit', although two or more squadrons might be gathered to meet large raids. On this matter his thinking obviously diverged from that of Douglas and a number of the Air Staff. [11]

The question of air tactics resurfaced in August 1939, when the Director of Staff Studies enquired about Dowding's policy towards engaging large raids. Were trials to be held to decide the best method? The Director recognized that there were two views. Either formations 'exceeding squadron strength' would meet Luftwaffe aircraft arriving in waves, in quick succession, or several squadrons, working as a tactical unit, would have to fight German formations of more than 100 aircraft. [12] Two officers on Dowding's staff examined the problem and reported unfavourably on Wings. In their view they were inefficient, wasted time and lacked the most effective firepower. They suggested that time in interception was more important than a slow concentration of strength. One of the officers claimed that time would be wasted experimenting with larger formations, as 'we have not yet fully studied and practised squadron attacks'. Of particular relevance to the later Big Wing controversy is the fact that this opinion was offered by Air Commodore Keith Park, then Dowding's SASO, and later AOC, No 11 Group. [13]

Dowding's reply made his case against Big Wings, ranging from the argument that pilots might collide or shoot at each other, to the reason that squadrons were untrained for such tactics. In his view, although there might be mass deployment in the future, such work 'would be premature at present', and he reiterated his opinion that individual squadrons would always be 'the largest practical unit' in action. He envisaged unescorted bombers arriving in formations each of about 30 aircraft, and these would be met by a succession of attacks from Flights, then squadrons, of fighters whose aim was to gain superiority of fire. He added that the situation was satisfactory and that the speed, flexibility and safety of Fighter Command's plans should not be exchanged for apparent advantages which would probably be 'illusory in practice'. [14]

These tenets, discussed in peacetime, bolstered the Air Ministry's opinion of Dowding as a less than co-operative commander. By late August 1940 the realities of war showed him still employing a defensive plan designed to meet a challenge that no longer existed, but whose nature and style had changed. In the eyes of his opponents he was then doubly at fault. Firstly, he was resting too great a burden on No 11 Group's squadrons, allowing them to be continually outnumbered, and, secondly, he was not concentrating his fighter force tactically in large formations to cause the Luftwaffe unacceptable losses. Inevitably, the blame they attached to Dowding expanded, by association, to Park. He had helped to institute the system and was attempting loyally to implement it. Herein lies the parting of the ways between the admirers and critics of Dowding. To the former he was showing tenacity of purpose in operating a system which was successfully holding off the Luftwaffe. To the latter better tactics would have achieved the target earlier and at lower cost. [15]

PART 2: GROWING PRESSURE ON BOTH SIDES

Matters came to a head between 24 August and 7 September, when the concentration of German effort, especially against south-eastern airfields, was so great that squadrons of No 11 Group were brought close to defeat. [16] The weather, which was mainly cloudy from 19 to 23 August, improved next day, enabling the Luftwaffe to launch a series of sustained attacks.

In most of these, bomber formations, in accordance with Goering's new ruling, were closely escorted by fighters. Inevitably the interception of bombers, laid down as Fighter Command's chief target, became more difficult. In addition, the pilots of Nos 10 and 11 Groups continually found themselves up against superior numbers of the enemy. [17] Another disadvantage for British airmen, and one seldom assessed in relation to the battle, was that the Luftwaffe customarily sent fighters into action in larger formations than those used by the RAF; through reasons of organization alone, Fighter Command pilots found themselves outnumbered even before combat began, a wearying prospect. The insistence on maintaining the squadron as the prime fighting unit resulted in formations of twelve to sixteen aircraft flying into action. For the Germans the *Gruppe*, consisting of 30 aircraft and occupying one aerodrome, was 'the basic flying unit for operational and administrative purposes'. [18]

The change in German policy was primarily due to the Luftwaffe's failure thus far to destroy sufficient British fighters, which had caused depredations to bombers. On 18 August the German naval war diary reported 'The units report zeal by enemy fighters has fallen off but not stubbornness of attacks on bombers and their pursuit after attack . . . Air Operations Staff sticks by continuation of the battle against enemy fighters under all circumstances.' [19] Goering's conference at Karinhall next day laid down the specific aim of defeating Fighter Command, especially by attacking No 11 Group's airfields, with the aircraft industry listed as a second target. There were to be constant raids, drawing Hurricanes and Spitfires into unrelenting defensive action. However, in attempting this aim, Luftwaffe commanders took a decision that went some way to impede the superiority of their own tactics. Fighter pilots were ordered to stay close to bombers in immediate escort, a policy to which many objected because it prevented the 'free-hunt' techniques they considered essential for success in combat. [20]

None the less, Luftwaffe commanders showed themselves more aware than their counterparts in Fighter Command of the tactical benefits of concentration of force. Many of *Luftflotte III*'s fighters were moved into the Pas de Calais, under Kesselring's command, as close as possible to southern England. The scene was set for a *guerre à outrance* over the approaches to London, with the perimeter of action drawn at the extreme range of the Luftwaffe's single-seat fighters, so Britain's air defences had faced no more daunting a threat. [21]

In that fortnight Park's resources were heavily taxed, for not only were the fighter aerodromes attacked, but also – and more important to the Dowding System – his Sector stations. For example, Hornchurch, Essex, was bombed on the 24th, 25th and twice on the 31st. Biggin Hill, Kent, was raided on the 26th, twice on the 30th, a day of intense fighting, and twice on each of the succeeding days, while Kenley was hit on the 26th and the 30th. A fuller appreciation of the stress on No 11 Group comes from a detailed examination of raids on the 31st. At 8am North Weald and Debden were attacked, followed by Eastchurch and Detling about an hour later. Croydon and Biggin Hill were hit at 12.55pm, Hornchurch at 1.15pm, and the last two were raided again at 5.30pm. [22]

One of Park's greatest problems had its roots in the system which he and Dowding had established. He viewed the main battle as his fight taking place over his area and involving his squadrons, whereas No 12 Group, in his opinion, were to be called for when needed to cover his aerodromes while his squadrons were fighting further south. As late as November Douglas wrote, 'Park still has a sub-conscious aversion to another Group coming down and fighting in his area'. Consequently he and Dowding lost the opportunity of using the power of Leigh-Mallory's Big Wing to the best advantage, as an aggressive, supporting force fighting between London and the south coast. [23]

The extreme pressure placed on No 11 Group thereby provided a second problem for Park. For example, No 85 Squadron moved to Croydon on the 19th and into heavy action, being involved in combat three times on the 31st. In a fortnight four pilots, including two Flight commanders, were killed in battle and six others, including the CO, wounded. By 2 September patrols could be put up at only half strength. By 30 August No 111

Squadron could operate only nine Hurricanes out of its complement of twelve. [24] The effect on individual pilots in the Group varied, although all suffered from tiredness following constant strain. One pilot wrote later that at the age of 21 'you were an old man'. [25] By 6 September No 11 Group was 'a wasting asset',[26] yet Britain's fate in resistance, as well as German strategy in attack, depended on its ability to survive.

What is often overlooked by those who remember the burden laid on Fighter Command is that the pilots of the German Air Force were also under great strain, especially from mid-August to early September. They understood their role as forerunners of a seaborne invasion, yet the stubbornness of the RAF's defence provided them with the biggest problem ever faced by the Luftwaffe. None of the Luftwaffe's previous campaigns, from the Spanish Civil War to the defeat of France, had been against an air force as large, as well equipped or as carefully organized as the RAF. There were specific disadvantages. First, they had to make a double crossing of the Channel, a natural and formidable hazard, and second, if they baled out over Britain, safety would be exchanged for freedom. They were particularly constrained by having to remain close to the bombers, giving up the greatly favoured 'free-hunt' tactics and, as the battle moved inland, the vulnerability of Bf 109s increased through their short range. On that point, Galland later commented that, with auxiliary fuel tanks, 'their endurance would have been increased by 30 to 40 minutes'. [27]

Yet by the early days of September they felt the closeness of success as the pressure grew on Fighter Command. The Luftwaffe flew 1,345 sorties on 30 August and 1,450 the next day, when 39 British fighters were lost, straining a defence that had greater need of pilots than of machines. During August 260 RAF pilots finished training, while 304 were either killed or wounded in action. [28] Nonetheless, the same factor affected the Luftwaffe, which had been in action continually since May, and suffered heavier losses of aircrew because of the number of bombers involved. Peter Stahl, a Ju 88 pilot, wrote on 25 August, 'It is being said that the British are already on their last legs, but when one hears what the operational pilots – and in particular bombers' crews – have to report, we're obviously still a long way from victory. The losses suffered by our bomber units must be terrible.'[29]

A major difference in the styles of leadership of the two combatant nations was shown at this stage. While Hitler did not venture to the area from which the Luftwaffe were attempting to subjugate Britain, Churchill maintained a keen and searching interest in the air fighting, particularly from 19 August until the first large daylight raids on London. His remarkable vision saw the present and future of the war in the widest terms, but also evinced what some found to be a disconcerting eye for detail.

He had to adjudicate between the ministries of Beaverbrook and Sinclair over the question of sending aircrew to Canada for training, and in this he supported the Air Ministry's view. Of particular importance to Dowding's later fate was Churchill's ruling over the power to be given to a department of government. In a private letter to Beaverbrook he showed his belief that a ministry should have freedom to make decisions, pointing out that 'it is not usual to override Service Departments' over policy for which they were responsible. [30]

Yet on 25 August Churchill pressed Sinclair to strengthen fighting squadrons at the expense of communications squadrons. 'Ought you not every day to call into question in your own mind every non-military aspect of the Air Force?', he wrote briskly, implying that Sinclair had shown insufficient dominance in his Ministry. He added the balm that he hoped the Secretary of State would be able to agree to the wishes 'of your old friend'. [31] Nevertheless, Churchill's restless spirit manifested itself four days later. He had been 'much concerned' the previous day at Manston aerodrome to notice unfilled craters. There followed a detailed account of how to complete a task which he obviously felt had been neglected by the Air Ministry. [32]

The growing intensity of the onslaught on No 11 Group occupied the Prime Minister's mind when, on 30 August, he informed the War Cabinet that RAF and Luftwaffe losses were roughly equal, with British reserves disappearing 'at a dangerous rate'. [33] The next day he visited Park's headquarters at Uxbridge to view the battle, and that evening Dowding dined with him at Chequers. Among matters discussed over dinner was the morality of shooting at enemy pilots descending by parachute and, surprisingly, Dowding approved, while Churchill thought it wrong. Afterwards Colville wrote, 'Dowding is splendid; he stands up to the PM'. [34]

Churchill returned to Uxbridge on 1 September, taking Park back to Chequers afterwards. Nonetheless, there was no evidence at this stage that the Prime Minister was aware of the conflict over tactics building within Fighter Command, or of the mutual frustrations between Park and Leigh-Mallory. In fact, after his second visit Churchill showed comparative satisfaction with the RAF by claiming that the Admiralty 'is now the weak spot. The Air is all right.'[35]

PART 3: THE GROWTH OF DISSENT

During late August the warning of impending attack was short for No 11 Group. As German formations gathered over northern France they were detected by RDF, which was more accurate in locating bearings than in assessing height and numbers. Fighter Command failed to implement a recommended scheme to meet 'difficulties if the enemy resorted to mass raids', and consequently on 7 September some of the RDF tubes were swamped by large numbers of German aircraft. [36] Nor, obviously, could RDF predict where and when enemy sorties would develop. Kesselring, with *Luftflotte II*, enjoyed the luxury of moving aircraft on feint raids, or altering the direction of a thrust, having the advantage of an attacker to whom a defender must respond.

Time was No 11 Group's greatest disadvantage because the Germans were so near their targets. For example, the Pas de Calais lay only 95 miles from an inland station such as Kenley, so the strain on Controllers was exceptional. Two of the closest Luftwaffe formations were JG 51 and JG 52, stationed at Wissant and Coquelles respectively. [37] By August, RDF stations in Kent, nearest to the enemy, could give about 20 minutes advance warning of action. To be set against this, however, because of the nature of the defensive system, four minutes often elapsed before the RDF contact appeared as a plot on the table of the Operations Room at Stanmore or Uxbridge. In that time an enemy formation flying at 200mph would have advanced more than 13 miles. German aircraft gained height while assembling over France, or when crossing the Channel, and RAF fighters, having to react to their initiative, were pressed for time.

Following the order to 'Scramble', Spitfires needed 13 minutes to climb to 20,000ft; Hurricanes needed 16 minutes. [38] Then a screen of Bf 109s almost invariably flew above the bombers which, on Dowding's and Park's insistence, were the prime targets, so, as RAF fighters attacked, they in turn were assaulted from above. Soon some squadron leaders, when ordered to fly at a given height, used their initiative and added two or three thousand feet in an attempt to meet the enemy on equal terms. Others used alternative methods to avoid being 'bounced' from above; for example, they flew on the reciprocal of the Controller's course until height had been attained. [39]

The sun, one of a pilot's greatest allies – or enemies – usually favoured the Germans who, progressing from a generally southerly direction, had it behind them, a distinct advantage before combat began. One Spitfire pilot wrote, 'We hated these clear days and always prayed for some high cloud to cover the sun'. [40]

A further stress on squadrons during August came when they were rearming or refuelling, operations which had to be carried out at high speed, as pilots were in action several times each day. Hurricanes and Spitfires on the ground became vulnerable targets as the Germans turned their attention to aerodromes. The Prime Minister's eagle eye for detail had been directed towards this process late in June, after talking to Flight Lieutenant Malan of No 74 Squadron, who said that more refuelling tankers were required. General Ismay, the Prime Minister's personal representative on the Chiefs of Staff Committee, was asked to investigate, and discovered that the real bottleneck was rearming, not refuelling, because three fighters could be refuelled in the time taken to rearm one aircraft. [41]

Dowding's policy of allowing No 11 Group to shoulder the main burden of defence resulted in great hardship to squadrons, and the knowledge that action was always close lay heavily on pilots. Temporary relaxation came when a squadron was 'Released', a short dispensation before being called to the 20 minutes warning of 'Available'. 'Readiness' was ordered as a 5 minute warning, followed by 'Stand-by', which gave the pilots 2 minutes. At 'Scramble' there was a frenetic rush to get the squadron airborne and turned towards the enemy. In reality, for many men the movement into action was a relief after the psychological drain of waiting. Overall, the strain was enormous. [42]

According to the report on the battle which Park rapidly provided for Headquarters, Fighter Command, after a request was made to him on 6 September, the second phase lasted from 19 August to 5 September. This proved to be the period of greatest difficulty for the command, and particularly for No 11 Group. After the report was submitted to the Air Ministry there was a distinct division of opinion over the quality of his tactics. [43]

The battle changed course in his reckoning on 19 August, when German attacks, which had hitherto been directed particularly against coastal shipping, were launched on mainland targets, primarily aerodromes, aircraft factories and RDF stations. On the same day Park issued a further set of Instructions to Controllers, informing them of the new phase and laying down guidelines to be followed. 'Against enemy attacks inland,' he wrote, 'despatch a minimum number of squadrons to engage enemy fighters.' The main object, he declared, was to engage bombers. [44] In this he was following Dowding's policy that combats between fighters would be costly and play into the hands of the Germans. The role of Fighter Command was to prevent Luftwaffe bombers from reaching their targets. If possible, every enemy raid should be interrupted before reaching its objective, an aim certainly not shared by all officers at the Air Ministry.

Nevertheless, Park appreciated the danger facing No 11 Group's airfields when his fighters were airborne. Therefore he instructed that, if all his squadrons near London were engaged, No 12 Group or the Command Controller should be asked to provide cover for Hornchurch, Debden and North Weald, enabling his pilots to be reassured that their stations were protected. He displayed an anxiety that such cover should be given, telling his Controllers if necessary to 'put a Squadron, or even the Sector Training Flight to patrol under clouds over each Sector aerodrome'.

This demonstrated Dowding's view that No 11 Group would be the prime contestants of the battle, calling on assistance when needed from Nos 10 and 12 Groups. Park was asking Leigh-Mallory to despatch some squadrons from the southern sector of No 12 Group to patrol three vital Sector stations in the northern area of No 11 Group. Park's fears for his aerodromes were not unfounded, because on the previous day bombers had reached Biggin Hill, Croydon and West Malling, albeit with little success, but at Kenley considerable damage was caused, and for a short period the Sector Operations Room was put out of action. [45] In his encyclopaedic study of the events of 18 August, Dr Alfred Price stated that the Controllers of Nos 11 and 12 Groups worked well together, and that the latter 'put up 45 fight-

ers to cover the former's airfields'. This, however, was a co-operative part-
nership destined to fade as fighting grew in intensity over the next fortnight.
[46]

Dowding had planned for the replacement of exhausted squadrons, and
that was done generally by moving complete units. Usually a fresh squadron
would comprise sixteen aircraft and about twenty pilots, who would fight
until only nine aircraft were left before they themselves were relieved. Some
lasted in the line for a month to six weeks, but others had to be replaced
after only a week or ten days. The dilemma by early September was that
fresh squadrons could be exhausted before any of the resting forces were
ready to return. [47]

A further difficulty now confronted Park. As German formations came
inland, some broke away to raid separate targets, bringing confusion to
ground defences. Sometimes No 11 Group Controllers were inundated by
reports from, for example, the Observer Corps, listing enemy aircraft in
many places. To solve the problem, Park issued an Instruction to Controllers on 26 August. [48] A number of failures had occurred, he suggested,
through inaccuracies of plotting, or too much cloud, so he asked for leaders
of Flights or Squadrons to report on the rough strength of enemy formations, their height, course and approximate position as soon as they were
located. He offered a specimen message of the kind he required: 'Tally Ho!
Thirty bombers and forty fighters Angels 20 proceeding North Guildford',
and explained that such help would enable the enemy to be engaged on
more equal terms.

The deterioration in collaboration between the two Groups now became
marked. On 26 August Park wrote to Stanmore with a strong, though indi-
rect, complaint about No 12 Group. He was most unhappy about the quality
of squadrons sent to him by Leigh-Mallory, comparing them unfavourably
with those posted by Saul, AOC, No 13 Group, and suggested that 'only
highly trained and experienced eight-gun fighter squadrons' should be
despatched to him. To make his point, Park compared the fortunes of five
squadrons sent to reinforce his area, three of which had come from No 13
Group and two from No 12. According to his figures, Saul's squadrons,
while with No 11 Group, had destroyed 43 German aircraft at the cost of
four of their own; Leigh-Mallory's squadrons, however, had shot down seventeen but had lost thirteen.

Park contended that these relative figures resulted from the fact that No
13 Group had always made a practice of sending 'their most experienced
squadrons, because of the appreciation of the heavy fighting up to date in
the South of England'. Although no explanation of No 12 Group's failures
was added, his omission of comment was full of implication. A similar
approach was employed in his fourth paragraph, where he merely noted that
his Sector Commanders had made favourable comments about 'the high
standard of flying and fighting efficiency of the several squadrons of No 13

Group'. Again, the lack of comment on Leigh-Mallory's squadrons was not without importance. [49]

Next day the disagreement deepened. Park issued a document headed 'Reinforcement from 10 and 12 Groups' to his Controllers, in which he praised 'the friendly co-operation afforded by 10 Group' before laying down guidelines. Then he openly criticized No 12 Group, claiming that when their squadrons were asked recently to patrol his aerodromes, they had failed to do so, resulting in bombing because No 11 Group squadrons were 'not strong enough to turn the enemy back'. [50] Here he was referring to the bombing of North Weald on 24 August, and of Debden two days later. Then the former was raided by twenty bombers, with considerable damage done to buildings and stores, though the operational efficiency of the aerodrome was largely unimpaired. The latter was attacked by about half a dozen unescorted Do 17s which damaged buildings as well as the landing area. It is noticeable here that Park was not reticent to lay out his troubles before the staff of his own Group. [51]

In fact, on the first occasion Leigh-Mallory had attempted to assemble a Wing formation over Duxford, but only the Spitfires of No 19 Squadron managed to engage the enemy, his other aircraft arriving late and discovering the result of German bombing on the ground below. On the 26th the same squadron patrolled above cloud while the enemy were below it, although Hurricanes of the Free Czech Squadron, No 310, also from Duxford, saw action against the main Luftwaffe formation. [52] Was Leigh-Mallory to blame? His constant reply to criticisms made of late arrival was to advance the unanswerable argument that if his squadrons had been called earlier they would have been in time to strike the enemy severe blows.

Park felt frustration at what he considered to be Leigh-Mallory's tardy reaction to policy laid down, especially as Duxford and Debden are only seven miles apart, so he added two new Directives. In future his Controllers were to bypass No 12 Group and put their requests directly to the Controller, Fighter Command, stating 'when and where reinforcing Squadrons from the north are required to patrol'. Such requests should be made only when enemy formations numbered at least 160 aircraft and could not be coped with by No 11 Group squadrons. In this way, argued Park, assistance might arrive later, but it would be in the right place. His last sentence showed an expectation that No 12 Group squadrons would be subsidiary to his own because 'their obvious task is to patrol aerodromes or other inland objectives'. [53] The lack of co-ordination between the two Groups showed the need for a strong, single and centralized leadership at this stage of the battle.

On the same day and in similar vein Park wrote to Air Vice-Marshal Evill, Dowding's SASO, and asked him to instruct his staff accordingly, which Evill did on the 28th. At the same time Evill minuted Dowding, enclosing copies of all of Park's submissions, so, in spite of later disclaimers, the C-in-C was kept fully informed of the relationships existing among various Groups. [54]

What had happened to the scale of co-operation between Nos 11 and 12 Groups during the eight days following 19 August to cause complaints from Park's pen? To unravel the answer, several factors must be explained. Park's Instruction No 7 claimed directly that Leigh-Mallory's squadrons failed to protect aerodromes, an accusation the latter rebutted at a later date in a letter to Dowding. Leigh-Mallory stated that the request for one squadron to patrol each airfield was made too late for his pilots 'to reach the area of the attack at the height of the enemy formation', and consequently the bombing occurred. Two points were being made here. First, he referred to only one squadron being called for, a policy of which he disapproved, and strengthened his case by claiming that the aerodromes had not been bombed 'when the Wing has been operating'. Second, he was supporting the opinion of a number of his pilots that they were given far too short notice to enable them to take off, gain height and establish a good attacking position. [55]

Each commander saw the battle from a different viewpoint. The time factor always constrained Park, who had no opportunity of organizing large formations before German aeroplanes arrived. Leigh-Mallory, on the other hand, had the advantage of observing events from some distance and believed that, with time to gather Wings of fighters, he could provide help for the hard-pressed squadrons to the south. Dowding's task and responsibility was to co-ordinate the abilities of both commanders into an integrated system for holding off the Luftwaffe from what obviously was, and would continue to be, the main area of operations, namely England south of the Thames.

Yet there was an additional and deeper facet of the controversy not far below the surface, and in this Park and Leigh-Mallory were, through force of circumstances, no more than spokesmen or targets. Within the senior ranks of the RAF as the battle developed there were two conflicting theories on the employment of fighters to counter raids. The long-standing disagreements between Dowding and the Air Staff sharpened the differences.

The conservatively and defensively minded C-in-C, ever aware that by reckless use of his limited resources he could, like Jellicoe, lose the war in an afternoon, believed the squadron to be the basic flying unit. His close staff agreed, none more than the ever loyal Park. In the other camp sat such officers as Douglas, Saundby, Stevenson and Crowe, and Leigh-Mallory certainly represented their view that aggressively employed fighter Wings were more effective in dealing with large enemy bomber formations, especially when they were being escorted well inland by fighters.

Little guidance or intervention came from Headquarters, Fighter Command, and this compounded the differences between the two Groups. A resolution of their difficulties at that early stage could have been instituted by Dowding, but he remained detached on the issue. The matter of controversy must have been known to him, because Park's Instruction No 7 of 27 August, instructing his Controllers to appeal to Stanmore when needing help from No 12 Group, was a clear breach of the system so meticulously laid down by the C-in-C himself. That Instruction was also a *cri de coeur* from a frustrated man, and its importance cannot have escaped Dowding, who, however, did not become involved.

On 1 September Park, tenacious for his own cause, aimed another complaint at Leigh-Mallory in a cable to Headquarters, Fighter Command. One of No 12 Group's squadrons which he had criticised in his letter of 26 August, No 616 Squadron, had now made a second application to return to their own Group. The Sector Commander at Kenley recommended this 'because of their low fighting efficiency'. Park remarked on their heavy losses for small returns and requested in their place a squadron from Nos 10 or 13 Groups 'if 12 Group is unable to spare an experienced squadron'. The message was clearly set out for Dowding to see. [56]

PART 4: DOWDING'S RESPONSE TO CRISIS

A further worrying feature of this period of battle was that aircraft factories were hit, causing alarm at the Ministry of Aircraft Production, especially to its ebullient leader, Beaverbrook. During an interview with Crozier, the editor of the *Manchester Guardian*, on 24 August, Beaverbrook disclosed some of his apprehensions, suggesting that production would have to be dispersed because 'they are beginning to find our works now'. There is no doubt that Beaverbrook still held Dowding in the highest esteem, telling Crozier in a later interview that he was 'the man whom I regard as coming to the front in everything that relates to the war'. Nonetheless, his fears of the raids being launched against factories led to him making strong representations for their defence to the Air Ministry. Not surprisingly, Sinclair and the air marshals passed these to Dowding. In this way, inadvertently, Beaverbrook increased the stress brought upon Fighter Command and its C-in-C at a very difficult moment. [57]

Park's frustration with the reinforcement from Leigh-Mallory surfaced again on 4 September and, in an attempt to provide a remedy, he sent a Cypher to Stanmore. As information had been received that the Germans were sending about 160 long-range bombers from Norway to France and Belgium, and that 400 dive-bombers were being drawn up opposite Kent, could not his Group be allocated two extra fighter squadrons?[58] His true motive for the request was contained in the final sentence, 'This would obviate necessity for 12 Group also 10 Group to send Squadrons to operate near the centre of 11 Group'. Then came the inevitable veiled, yet definite, knock at Leigh-Mallory, when he claimed that these squadrons were frequently out of Radio Telephone range and could not be co-ordinated with his own formations, as well as causing 'confusion to Observer Corps and AA Gun Defences who cannot be informed of their movements'. [59]

His request found some fertile ground because, after both Dowding and Evill had read the Cypher, action was taken on the following day. No 504 Squadron was brought down from Catterick to Hendon, while No 73 Squadron from Church Fenton was exchanged with No 85 Squadron, which had suffered severe losses at Debden. These moves alleviated No 11 Group's desperate position, but did not solve Park's great burden of attempting to live in harmony with No 12 Group. Over the following days, because of increasing Luftwaffe attacks, Leigh-Mallory's squadrons had further reason to be called south into No 11 Group's area.

On 5 September Park issued Instruction No 10 to Controllers, and its opening point shows that Beaverbrook's complaints were taking effect. He announced Dowding's decision that certain aircraft factories were to be given 'maximum fighter cover' and named them. His fifth point comprised tactical advice and restatement of his basic tenet of defence, ordering that the enemy's attack must be met 'between the coast and our line of sector aerodromes'. Spitfires should engage German fighters at 20,000ft and above, while Hurricanes, 'because of their inferior performance' should tackle bombers, which rarely exceeded 16,000ft by day. Finally, Park reminded his Controllers that, when aerodrome protection was needed north of the Thames, No 12 Group squadrons were to be requested through Stanmore, to offer cover to North Weald, Stapleford, Hornchurch and Debden. The imputation that they might be late was then added, because Controllers were told to protect Sector aerodromes with their own aircraft 'pending arrival of 12 Group squadrons'. The conclusion restated his view of the relative roles of the two Groups, stating that as soon as Leigh-Mallory's aircraft arrived, No 11 Group's squadrons should be sent forward 'into the main battle'. [60]

Dowding's policy of exchanging complete squadrons was causing a dilemma by 1 September, and he rethought strategy over the following days. Some imported squadrons were inexperienced, certainly unused to the new German tactics, and therefore suffered heavy initial losses on arrival in the firing line. The problem was whether to use them in preference to experienced but exhausted squadrons which sometimes were reduced to eight or ten aircraft. For example, although No 11 Group had been reinforced by two squadrons on the previous day, Park reported on 2 September that seven of his squadrons had been reduced to half strength after the morning's first engagement 'though they operated in pairs', a phrase that proves awareness of criticisms being levelled at his tactics. [61]

Dowding determined to alter his system even when the battle was at its height, and called a small conference on 7 September. Present that afternoon was Douglas, from the Air Ministry, a protagonist of Big Wings. He expressed surprise when Dowding announced that the meeting had been called to plan for Fighter Command to 'go downhill'. Faced with the over-whelming difficulty of pilot shortage and depleted squadrons, Dowding had decided to create three classes. The minutes of the meeting demonstrate the widening gulf between Dowding and Douglas, who represented the Air Ministry. Minute 22 showed the difficulty of persuading Douglas that 'the situation is extremely grave'. A month later, Dowding referred to this gravity in a letter to Park. 'I resisted your request to be made up in your strength of operational pilots from squadrons in other Groups as long as I could and I finally had to give way, not because I liked the system, but because it was becoming impossible to change squadrons quickly enough as their strength in operational pilots ran down'. A revealing insight into the breadth of Dowding's responsibilities is found in Minute 37. 'The thing which gave him the greatest anxiety was the night flying aspect; however, that was one of the things that had to be accepted.' [62]

Dowding's arrangements for the three classes of squadron were trans-mitted next day in a note headed 'Policy for Maintenance of Fighter Squadrons in Pilots'. The classes were listed in order of priority. First were Class A Squadrons of No 11 Group, 'to be maintained constantly at mini-mum strength of sixteen operational pilots'. Next were Class A Squadrons of Nos 10 and 12 Groups, kept to a 'minimum of sixteen operational plus non-operational as convenient'. Class B Squadrons were required to have 'a min-imum strength of sixteen operational pilots with up to six more non-operational'. Blenheim and Defiant squadrons were to remain unaffected. The last category, Class C Squadrons, would retain 'a minimum of three operational pilots to act as leaders', except for three named squadrons which would have eight.

The second point reinforced Dowding's belief in the importance of No 11 Group by stipulating that all pilots posted to its squadrons were to be operational and drawn from Class C squadrons. Each day, Stanmore would inform Nos 10, 12 and 13 Groups of the number of operational pilots required from them to serve under Park. In conclusion, he announced that the commanders of Groups would be allowed to post operational pilots to Classes A and B squadrons at their discretion, but added that these squadrons, 'except in No 11 Group, shall whenever possible maintain their minimum strength of operational pilots by training of non-operational pilots from the usual sources'. [63]

The following day, a minute from Dowding to Evill showed how serious the position of No 11 Group's squadrons had grown under the previous fortnight's attrition of Luftwaffe attacks. 'It is now apparent,' he stated, 'that the scheme must be implemented immediately and that it will only be possi-ble to maintain a few squadrons, outside the battle, in a condition to effect interchange of units.' By using the phrase 'outside the battle', Dowding was acknowledging that the main area of fighting was in the south-east; as depleted and exhausted squadrons were being sent north, his policy of sharing good squadrons among all Groups had, by force of circumstances, gone by the wayside. This adds weight to the argument that No 11 Group should have been reinforced earlier. One critic of Dowding's new arrangements, nonetheless, has questioned why, when Park's men were under such pressure, 'it was justifiable for No 12 Group to maintain five "A" Class squadrons – 130 pilots whom Leigh-Mallory had no intention should ever reinforce No 11 Group?'[64]

Douglas was far from content with the meeting and its outcome. On receiving a copy of the new arrangements he wrote to Evill, suggesting that there were too many Class C squadrons. He also referred to the draft minutes of the meeting, claiming that he had been placed in the role of the music-hall comedian, 'usually called "Mutt"', who asked foolish questions of his partner, 'which call down upon his devoted head laughter-making sallies from his more quick-witted partner . . . frankly, I consider the minutes were drafted by someone with a distinct bias in favour of everything said by a member of Fighter Command'. This statement in itself shows that there were two 'camps' at the meeting, and that he was in the opposite one to Dowding and Park. 'However,' he added, 'life is too strenuous in these days to bother about the wording of minutes', an interesting omen of what was to happen on 17 October, after the Air Ministry meeting on tactics. In the matter of running the battle there was no doubting his belief that better use could and should be made of Leigh-Mallory's squadrons. [65]

A move to strengthen his case was made by the Germans themselves even while the meeting at Stanmore was still in progress. The pilots of No 11 Group had anticipated yet another day of onslaught on aerodromes, aircraft factories and themselves, but there was a seductive calm until late afternoon. Then, with a change of plan, some 300 bombers, escorted by twice that number of fighters, advanced as an armada to launch the heaviest raids thus far experienced. The new target was London, and for over an hour they brushed aside opposition to bomb areas of Dockland in the east of the city, killing over 300 civilians and starting the largest fires seen in Britain since 1666. [66]

For the Luftwaffe, victory over the RAF was not coming quickly enough by the early days of September, with time before a seaborne invasion drifting relentlessly away. This was the prime reason for a change in strategy. Many writers have suggested that the attacks on London were launched as a retaliation for Bomber Command raids on Berlin,[67] but a German Air Force lecture given in 1944 was categorical that, with the new target, 'economic war from the air could be embarked upon with full fury, and the morale of the civilian population subjected at the same time to a heavy strain'. [68]

General Deichmann of the Luftwaffe, when questioned later on the matter, was adamant that military reasons for the change were predominant, although allowing that there were also political implications, as 'the chief aim was to make Great Britain ripe for peace negotiations'. He added that

Luftflotte II believed the mass attacks to be necessary 'if a decisive victory was to be won'. [69]

Yet the motive of retaliation was not far from Hitler's mind as he demanded attacks by night, not by day. That thought can be deduced from his speech of 4 September, when he clearly threatened reprisal for RAF bombing of Berlin. 'When they declare that they will attack our cities in great strength,' he announced, 'then we will eradicate their cities.' [70]

However, at a tactical level the Luftwaffe believed that the attacks on London would cause the remaining RAF fighters to be committed into action more surely than by any other means. This would afford the best opportunity of overwhelming Fighter Command.

At a stroke, although the raids had an electrifying propaganda effect, some degree of burden was lifted from Fighter Command's aerodromes. During the evening, Park flew over the city in his own Hurricane and realized that the devastation below offered a small intermission for his men. There was, however, an expectation that the striking of the new target presaged seaborne invasion. [71]

Strategically, the Germans placed themselves at a disadvantage by raiding so far inland. Although there was an eminent attraction in attacking what was then the world's largest city, and the heart of their enemy's empire, their fighter formations were subjected to risk. No superiority of numbers could compensate for the limited range of the Bf 109, one of whose pilots, Adolf Galland, later commented on the aircraft's reserve of only ten minutes' combat time over London. Apart from dissipating the effect of the loads of their medium bombers on the world's broadest target, the Germans, at a stroke, neutralized the value of their best fighter. [72]

For both sides, the large daylight raid on the capital was a watershed in the battle. Within the RAF it brought to the surface the undercurrents of dissension and controversy over strategy and tactics that had festered in Fighter Command for some time. It was also to have a lasting effect on German intentions of using the Luftwaffe's effort as a forerunner to seaborne invasion, because the raid was the last option, other than covering landings, which remained in their attempts to overwhelm Dowding's squadrons. Since late June they had attacked Channel shipping and coastal ports, aircraft factories and aerodromes, without resolving the trial of strength. With the dates available for successful landings fast running out, and with Hitler's mind divided between 'Sealion' and preparing for an eastern campaign, an early decision was vital. To a large extent this depended upon the effectiveness of bombing the new target, so, after his claims and promises, Goering's prestige was at stake.

However, the attack on London was also important for Dowding's reputation. Ironically, on the previous Saturday, he had told Colville that 'he could not understand why the Germans kept on coming in waves instead of concentrating on one mass raid which could not be effectively parried'. This raid led to the destruction of residential areas on a scale not seen earlier in the battle. It brought an increase in civilian casualties, raising again, especially in the minds of politicians, the question of how the morale of the general population would respond to heavy bombing. Consequently the responsibility of Dowding and his Command was open to scrutiny, and as the start of the new phase was accompanied that evening by raids which continued through the night, again with heavy damage and casualties, the question became more urgent. In a sense, as Collier comments, the daylight raid was a victory for the German bombers; by the next morning 306 civilians were dead and 1,337 badly injured. [73]

Much has been made of the relief brought to Park's squadrons by the change of German target. [74] On seeing the fires from London, Park reflected 'that he would have time to repair his control systems and so maintain an effective daylight challenge to enemy attack'. Churchill later wrote that the new German raids provided a 'breathing-space of which we had the utmost need', but it is infrequently stressed that one of the main benefits offered was a restoration of No 11 Group's morale. Pilots were still drawn into heavy action over the following week but, with the pressure mainly lifted from airfield defence, and the opportunities presented for new pilots to be posted to depleted squadrons, spirits rose. Thus, when a further great challenge arrived on the 15th, No 11 Group was better able to respond. For a few days the noise of battle did not cease, but the volume of strain was reduced.

The main importance of 7 September for Fighter Command's leadership was as a turning point in the Big Wing controversy. Those in the Air Ministry and No 12 Group who believed that poor tactics were being employed south of the Thames felt a certain justification of their criticisms when the enemy was able to reach and bomb the capital with the intervention of comparatively small numbers of RAF fighters. If, as appeared likely, German attacks on London were to be sustained, the importance of No 12 Group's squadrons would increase. In the first place, the Luftwaffe were now flying closer to their territory, and secondly, by employing large Wings of fighters they anticipated taking a heavier toll of the raiders.

It is noticeable that, with the opening of the new onslaught on the capital, those who believed that Dowding had served his time as C-in-C, and that there should be a replacement, gained in strength. The Air Ministry had always hoped that his appointment would end in October, in spite of the Prime Minister's interventions on his behalf. Over the subsequent month Churchill himself was to be confronted with further criticisms of Dowding, this time not emanating from the Air Ministry, and was to experience, through committee meetings, how intransigent the C-in-C could be.

The period from mid-August to the opening of the offensive against London had proved very difficult for Dowding, whose men were under greater pressure from Luftwaffe attacks aimed at eliminating or neutralizing

Fighter Command. By 7 September the Germans had gone some way to achieving superiority over No 11 Group, where Park fought what he considered to be his battle 'by the book' and deployed squadrons as well as he was able. Nevertheless, Dowding, with overall command, failed to introduce the relief that the squadrons of No 12 Group would undoubtedly have brought to the south. As a result he failed to resolve the burgeoning disagreement between his two chief Group commanders.

In one way, the Luftwaffe's poor strategic decision offered some respite to Fighter Command. Their change of target did not alter Dowding's overall responsibility for defence, yet it enabled his hardest-pressed squadrons to prepare for the next phase of battle.

5

THE BATTLE WITHIN A BATTLE
7 SEPTEMBER TO 16 OCTOBER

PART 1: BADER'S INFLUENCE ON TACTICS

From 7 September to 16 October the controversy over tactics, especially between Park and Leigh-Mallory, grew more intense and, as Dowding took no firm action to intervene, the question came under increasing scrutiny at the Air Ministry. Eventually the decision was taken there to hold a conference aimed at resolving methods of air defence by day. [1]

Because the opinion is held, albeit mistakenly, that the fate of Dowding and Park was linked almost solely with the Big Wing controversy,[2] it is worthwhile examining some of the opinions of Park and Leigh-Mallory, the two chief antagonists. These views, offered by men who came to know them well, help to redress a balance. In general, books dealing with the controversy have painted Park as an affable, quietly suffering hero and victim, while Leigh-Mallory has been portrayed as a pompous, self-seeking saboteur. Such works rely heavily on the post-war opinions of Dowding and Park, who had many opportunities of presenting their views, either directly or indirectly, or on assessments made without reference to documents.

Leigh-Mallory did not survive the war and left no record to explain his policy. He has, therefore, become a scapegoat with a damaged reputation. His critics have presented him as unco-operative and scheming, placing him centrally in a plot to unseat Dowding and Park by using political influence. Among other writers, Terraine, Orange, Wright, Wood and Dempster, Collier and Deighton all have no approving word to say of him. Park's obituary referred to the conference of 17 October 1940 as being, 'instigated primarily by the AOC No 12 Group'. Such opinions are unsupported by evidence and do injustice to his memory. [3]

Park was a highly competent leader who has received full and deserved praise for the part he played in the battle, being quick-thinking and decisive in running the system which he had helped to establish. [4] Few details escaped his shrewd eye. [5] There are some doubts, nonetheless, of his abilities as an innovative commander, because although his biographer has commended him because he 'actually listened to what he was told',[6] others have suggested that he borrowed ideas and proposed them as his own. He was, in the view of one former Battle of Britain pilot, 'a vain man . . . he loved to be the centre of attention', and this led to some unpopularity. [7]

Joubert, an opponent of Dowding, believed that Park was not a great commander, yet was successful, highly strung and 'suffered from a sensitive ego'. He judged that Leigh-Mallory, '"could run rings round Park" intellectually'. [8] In the view of an officer who worked daily with him throughout the battle, Park ran his Group well but 'was an unlovable man' who could be unnecessarily harsh on those he felt were not up to scratch, and was somewhat temperamental. [9]

In spite of the avalanche of criticism later levelled at him, there was a better side to Leigh-Mallory. Various officers who worked closely with him found him industrious, caring for his pilots, loyal to his friends and ready to take advice. He built up No 12 Group from nothing in pre-war days by dint of hard work,[10] and was known to go into a Mess to talk directly to young pilots and hear their views. [11] When faced with problems, he liked to have near him men on whose experience he could draw directly. What some regarded as pomposity or vanity was seen by others as a cover for shyness, and his kindness and thoughtfulness were remembered, together with his sense of humour. [12] Several have wondered whether part of his ambitious drive stemmed from a wish not to be in the shadow of his half-brother, George Mallory, the mountaineer who had died on Mount Everest in 1924. Professor R. V. Jones recalls that Leigh-Mallory could be pompous, yet 'on the two occasions when I myself met him I gained the very opposite impression from pomposity'. The first was in November 1940, when Leigh-Mallory visited Jones, seeking information on German beams, and was 'completely unassuming and courteous'. [13]

Leigh-Mallory generally approved of employing fighters in large numbers as a combined force during combat, and was closer to Air Ministry policy than to the Dowding system of immediate, forward response with small numbers, employed by Park south of the Thames. He had a variety of reasons, both professional and personal, for this, not the least being his genuine belief that the employment of Wings would bring fewer casualties to his pilots. Now he was taking a keen interest in a battle drawing closer to his area, therefore in No 12 Group he had moved two squadrons to Duxford one week before the great Luftwaffe raid on London. The aerodrome's Operations Record Book for 31 August shows 'am 611 and 242 arrived to reinforce sector'. [14] He was ready to play a full part in the action.

There were four main reasons for that. Firstly he believed that insufficient use was being made of the potential of his squadrons, a judgement shared by the Air Ministry. The single considerable attack on his Group area on 15 August had been easily repulsed and thereafter, in his opinion, his squadrons were underemployed. An examination of No 12 Group Operations Record Book for July and August shows that regularly only little enemy activity by day was reported in Leigh-Mallory's area. Some of the feelings of his pilots at the time were recorded by Noel Monks, who visited several fighter squadrons in the Midlands and found that 'pilots were cursing the ill-luck that kept them up there, away from the scrapping that was going on down south'. These forces were No 11 Group's main tactical reserve, and it was high time to introduce them, taking pressure from formations to the south. The Official Narrative comments that 'the bulk of the German Air Force was opposed by little more than half the squadrons of the Command'. Dowding's supporters claim this to be wishful thinking, principally as his Group and Sector control was not organized to take additional squadrons. Yet considering Park's desperate situation, this could have been overcome, and Leigh-Mallory's opposite view was legitimate. [15]

Secondly, Leigh-Mallory's ambition was frustrated earlier in the year when Park, junior to him in both rank and seniority, received the command of No 11 Group. There is no doubt in the minds of those who served close to him that, as senior Group commander, Leigh-Mallory considered that he should have received the appointment. He was eager and wanted to play an active part in a battle crucial to the nation's future, which he honestly believed was being allowed to slip away from the RAF. Leigh-Mallory became an Air Vice-Marshal on 1 November 1938, whereas Park held the rank of Air Commodore from 1 July 1938. The latter had taken over No 11 Group on 20 April 1940, and his rank as Air Vice-Marshal was confirmed in July. A strong reason for appointing Park, in Dowding's eyes, was that he had helped to prepare the defensive system and, as SASO, had agreed with the C-in-C. [16]

Thirdly, by forming a Wing of fighters at Duxford, Leigh-Mallory would guarantee the chance, when asked by the Controllers at Uxbridge or Stanmore, of moving squadrons swiftly into action. The customary riposte offered to the complaint of the slow arrival of his aircraft was that they were invariably called too late. Posting squadrons at Duxford, very close to No 11 Group's northern boundary, was partly an attempt to overcome this criticism. [17]

But overall in the opinions of both men was the fact that Leigh-Mallory was strongly influenced by one of his squadron leaders, Douglas Bader, whose charismatic direction, lack of fear and insatiably pugnacious desire to wrestle with the enemy were matched by few other Service leaders. These qualities, combined with freely expressed views and an unvarying confidence, brought him first the command of No 242 Squadron, then the ear of his Group commander, when he preached with evangelistic ardour the virtues of employing Big Wing tactics. Bader took command of No 242 Squadron on 26 June, after having been a flight commander with No 222 Squadron. A number of pilots who served with him believed him to be a leader of unique merit. 'He possessed in greater degree than any other officer known to me personally,' wrote Sir Hugh Dundas, who flew with No 616 Squadron, 'the characteristics which can raise the courage and performance of followers far above their natural level.' Bader's part in the Big Wing controversy was considerable, not because he intervened personally and intentionally in the various disagreements over Fighter Command's leadership, as he had no deliberate wish to remove Dowding or have Park replaced, but because his ideas and enthusiasms soon became the focal point for those who did. [18]

Therefore it is important to recognise that there were in 1940 *two* Big Wing controversies, not one. The first was over the view, held primarily by Leigh-Mallory and Bader, that squadrons of No 12 Group stationed closest to London should be employed over the No 11 Group area, giving support to their hard-pressed pilots. Although he believed that formations of at least three squadrons flying as a Wing were more effective than three squadrons entering action separately, Bader appreciated that No 11 Group lacked time to implement this tactic. His position is made clear in notes he wrote in 1969, when angered at accusations made in Wright's uneven book on Dowding. He made the point that only one of the authors of books on the Battle of Britain had troubled to discuss matters with him and find his views before stating with emphasis that the suggestion that Park should have operated Wings of squadrons was nonsense. 'You cannot operate large formations from close to an attacking enemy' he asserted, and added that Leigh-Mallory shared this opinion. 'At no time, and I say this with certainty, was it in Leigh-Mallory's mind.' [19]

The second Big Wing controversy was the disagreement, dating from pre-war days, between the Air Ministry and Fighter Command over the most effective way to counter attacks made by large formations. Dowding's opponents there, who considered him to be unco-operative and unsuited to his Command, seized eagerly on others who disagreed with his policies. In this way Leigh-Mallory and Bader were drawn into controversy and used by those who saw No 12 Group's theories as a useful lever to discredit Dowding and Park. Prominent among these opponents was Douglas, and one of No 12 Group's staff officers recalled that during the Battle of Britain there was little telephone conversation between either Leigh-Mallory and Dowding or Leigh-Mallory and Park, though there was 'plenty between Leigh-Mallory and Sholto Douglas'. He believed that Douglas was an *éminence grise* behind the scenes of the Big Wing controversy. [20]

To understand Bader's appeal to senior officers who were wedded to a more aggressive approach in fighter defence, it should be remembered that his heroes were those fighter pilots of the First World War who had achieved success in combat, for example Ball, McCudden, Mannock and Bishop. From them he had learned the value of height, sun and close proximity in air fighting. [21] His persistence in seeking to return to the RAF after an accident which would have left most men in a wheelchair for the rest of their lives was an example of formidable spirit overcoming adversity, and was helped in two ways. Firstly, because he was a graduate of Cranwell, a number of his contemporaries who had gained advancement in the Service were able to assist. Secondly, his custom of treading on official toes and of seeking help from those in authority brought results and he was readmitted to the Service. [22] However, some believe that Bader's period outside the RAF from 1931 to 1939 left him out of touch with the theory and practice of flying in Fighter Command, as his ideas on combat had been overtaken by rapid developments in fighters and defence systems. His supporters, nonetheless, would claim that basic principles of fighter combat never change and that Bader was maintaining them.

What his brother-in-law, Wing Commander 'Laddie' Lucas, termed 'the three basic articles of a First World War fighter pilot's faith' were set in Bader's mind. First, he who has the height controls the battle; second, he who has the sun achieves surprise; and third, he who gets in close shoots them down. At 30 years of age he was older than many other pilots, and this added to the air of confident authority with which he led his men. Some found him conceited and loud of voice, but his complete lack of fear and his relentless aggression in air fighting were an inspiration to his squadrons. [23]

Within the Air Ministry the protagonists of Big Wings judged success in terms of figures, because their criterion from pre-war days had been to destroy so many aircraft that the enemy's offensive would be rapidly reduced or abandoned. It is important to note, in judging the actions of various leaders involved, that from the moment of Bader's entry into the main battle at the end of August his claims were excessive, yet were accepted by his superiors at the Air Ministry as accurate and proof positive of the validity of their theories. As post-war research has shown, both sides made excessive claims against enemy aircraft, an understandable result of pilots' reactions to the maelstrom of combat. Such assertions are an obvious propaganda ploy, but dangerous when used as the basis for a change in strategy. [24]

For example, on 30 August No 242 Squadron was scrambled at 4.45pm. Bader's log book for the day stated, 'August 30th. Hurricane D 1 hour, 30 minutes. Intercepted 100 E/A with Squadron. Shot down 12. Self two Bf 110s'. A note added, 'Met about 100 E/A bombers at 15,000 feet just west of Enfield. Was up-sun and above them. Dived the whole squadron into attack from above and behind. Squadrons destroyed 12 E/A for loss of none. No bullet holes in any aeroplane. '[25] If these claims are compared with the known casualties of the day, discrepancies appear. For example, one authority offers two prizes, both He 111s, to No 242 Squadron and lists four Bf 110s shot down that day as victims of other squadrons which, however, destroyed them before noon. [26] The second authority allocates no German losses specifically to No 242 Squadron, but shows two Bf 110s, both shot down at 4.55pm, near Ponders End, although Bader's claims are unsubstantiated. [27] A third account confirms the shooting down of two Bf 110s at about that time, but then mistakenly adds a He 111 as a 'possible'; this aircraft, however, was shot down at 4.35pm, before No 242 Squadron had taken off. [28]

But soon after the action, when Leigh-Mallory telephoned Bader, he was told, 'If I had had more fighters we would have shot down more of the enemy'. The AOC No 12 Group was impressed, and a few days later the Duxford Wing of three squadrons was formed. [29]

On 2 September Leigh-Mallory wrote to Headquarters, Fighter Command, in connection with their letter of 26 June, regarding the provision of Tactical Memoranda. He claimed that insufficient information about fighter tactics had been produced by Nos 10 and 11 Groups. The only information so far received had come from combat reports and Intelligence summaries which did not 'go sufficiently deeply into the tactics employed by our own fighters'. He recommended, therefore, that an experienced officer who had seen action, yet was now unfit for flying, should visit stations, giving lectures and holding discussions. [30]

In this, Leigh-Mallory gave the impression that No 12 Group had been neglected. He felt a great loyalty for his squadrons and wanted them to have the best possible preparation for combat. An obvious difficulty in this respect was that the course of battle was so intense that there was little opportunity to organize such visits, yet it is also apparent that pilots on the edges of the main battle were very keen, for not altogether altruistic reasons, to learn the lessons gleaned from combat.

To make the point more strongly, Leigh-Mallory wrote again to Headquarters, Fighter Command, on 8 September, this time enclosing a copy of the type of advice which he believed should be given to squadrons. It was, he said, written by the 'OC, No 242 Squadron in connection with the tactics they employed on the 30th August, which proved to be very successful'. He added that copies had been sent to all No 12 Group squadrons for their information. [31]

This document is of some importance. It had been written by Squadron Leader Bader six days earlier 'at the suggestion of the Intelligence Officer', and was addressed in the first place to the OC, Coltishall. At that time Bader wished fervently to be drawn into action in the south, was critical of the lateness of the call from No 11 Group, and used the opportunity for setting out his ideas of the tactics to be used against escorted bomber formations. In the opening paragraph he suggested that his report might be of use because of 'the warning signal from 11 Group of increased casualties suffered in that Group due to enemy tactics of tight formation with bombers and escort fighters intermingled'.

The report, nine paragraphs and nearly 1,000 words in length, then described his squadron's action, supporting his basic beliefs in principles to be followed, all of which would have been approved by any first-rate fighter pilot. At the start 'it was decided to attack down sun'. Green Section engaged the enemy top aircraft, while his other three sections tackled the main formation. The severity of the attack broke up the enemy formations and 'the result of all this was a general shambles which it had been the original intention of 242 Squadron to create'. After that, the disorganized Germans were at the mercy of the Hurricanes. He mentioned the need for height advantage and spoke of 'point blank shots'.

Many pilots of No 11 Group would have smiled ruefully at one sentence in his seventh paragraph. 'It was anticipated (and the fight in question proved it) that if a squadron of Hurricanes or Spitfires met a large enemy bomber and fighter formation (provided there were no single-seat escorts) the Hurricanes or Spitfires would have the advantage (in spite of numerical inferiority) if the enemy formation could be broken up and provided the Squadron started with the height advantage.' Time and again in their combats south of the Thames, there had been no opportunity of meeting the two crucial criteria which Bader stipulated. First, there *were* Bf 109 escorts and, second, there *was not* time to gain height advantage. Nevertheless, had Bader's precepts been followed, some relief would have been brought to the sorely pressed No 11 Group. His aircraft could have entered the battle with height advantage.

The report was modest in explaining that, for this particular action, fighting conditions were very favourable and that, for No 242 Squadron, 'luck definitely played a part'. It added that the squadron enjoyed 'complete immunity from damage to aeroplanes or personnel', and made no mention at all of the number of enemy aircraft claimed as shot down or damaged.

In the long run the report served a double purpose. It gave Leigh-Mallory an opportunity of becoming more closely involved with the battle, showing that he was lacking neither in opinions nor in care for the interests of his Group. Also it brought the name of Douglas Bader to those senior officers who did not already know it, proving that he had definite views on the tactics of battle and no fear either in expressing or practising them. A vital result of the report for the antagonists in the Big Wing controversy was that some officers in the Air Ministry seized upon Bader's claims and employed them as a weapon in their struggle with Dowding.

PART 2: DISAGREEMENT OVER TACTICS

On 9 September Headquarters No 11 Group sent a message to Stanmore which began, 'Reference visit of C-in-C here 7/9 HQ 12 Group state it will take twenty-five minutes from time of request to provide fighter formation to patrol line of aerodromes North Weald, Stapleford Abbots, Hornchurch in event of mass attacks'. Obviously, during Dowding's visit the question of co-operation between the two Groups had been raised and Park had been making some subsequent investigation. The AOC No 11 Group continued by restating his views and thus setting out explicitly the difference of policy between him and Leigh-Mallory. He would rather, he said, have one squadron arriving on the patrol line within 15 minutes than more squadrons

appearing after aerodromes had been bombed. 'If No 12 Group cannot reinforce by less than a whole wing then we would suggest for your consideration that their first and second squadrons proceed direct to the line of
aerodromes mentioned and form Wing there instead of in the North outside
the battle area.' This, claimed Park, would enable the enemy to be met
before they reached the Sector aerodromes. [32]

The note was read by Evill, SASO at Stanmore, who then minuted
Dowding. What he wrote was in favour of No 12 Group and obviously influenced the C-in-C. He opened by mentioning the importance of the time factor for No 11 Group, but said that he believed that Leigh-Mallory's Wing
had been successful 'on the two occasions when it has been used as such',
and doubted whether a rendezvous over aerodromes would be reliable. Evill
favoured the maintenance of the current practice, although it would lead to
an increase of the frequency of calls from No 11 Group, 'who will be reluc-
tant to wait before calling for assistance'. [33]

Having read Evill's advice, Dowding gave judgement. Although he
appeared unwilling to intervene in what was patently a considerable difference of opinion between his two Group commanders, the C-in-C sided with
Leigh-Mallory. 'I will not press 12 Group to send single squadrons into battle,' he minuted, 'or to rendezvous in the battle area.' [34] At first sight this
appears to be a refutation of the criticism of the C-in-C, that he did not exercise powers of leadership during a sharp quarrel inside his Command, but
the enigma is that he did not side with Park, who was attempting under
severe handicaps to implement the Dowding system. Later accounts of the
battle, including Dowding's own recollections, neglect to acknowledge that
he did approve of Leigh-Mallory's interpretation of the tactics required. In
reality, burdened with a defensive system which required a single commander to be effective, the C-in-C was being indecisive.

Noting that there had been a small change in German tactics over the
previous few days, Park issued another Instruction to Controllers on 11
September. This shows that he had come to appreciate the use of squadrons
in pairs over his Group area. It is difficult to say whether the idea was
brought about by No 12 Group's policy of employing Wings, or whether he
realized from his own experience and his squadrons' that better results
might be achieved and fewer casualties suffered by using larger formations.
Controllers were told to despatch squadrons 'in pairs to engage first wave of
enemy'. Spitfires were to tackle the fighter screen, and Hurricanes the
bombers and close escorts. In the case of squadrons to meet a third wave of
attack, 'they should be sent in pairs as follows: Debden and North Weald
squadrons together; Hornchurch and Biggin Hill squadrons together; Kenley and Northolt squadrons together'. Controllers were then advised to
name the base over which the pairs of squadrons would rendezvous and to
select one of the squadrons to be the leader. It was important for the two
squadrons to maintain close contact. This policy was as far as Park would

go in linking squadrons; to the apostles of Big Wings it was no more than a half-hearted attempt. [35]

Undoubtedly Park's small but significant change of policy came at least partly from a meeting held at Uxbridge on 30 August. The Official Narrative points out the general feeling in No 11 Group that larger formations should be used and, if necessary, extra squadrons be drafted in. Suggestions for increasing the strength of Sector patrols were rejected, firstly because of the heavy demands already made on pilots, and secondly because of 'the Commander-in-Chief's policy of maintaining No 11 Group at a strength of three day fighter squadrons in each Sector and no more'. Wing Commander Beamish, OC at North Weald, offered the eminently sensible suggestion that two squadrons in one Sector should go into action together, but the idea was rejected 'though the Group Commander was clearly sympathetic to the idea of larger formations if there was time to assemble them'. Later, Park agreed that the time had come for larger formations to be employed, and plans were made for pairs of squadrons from adjacent Sectors to rendezvous before engaging the enemy. However, his critics would note the delay in implementing the policy because, although applied for the first time on 2 September, it did not become the rule until the second week of the month. [36]

It is noticeable here that Park was constrained by Dowding's insistence on limiting the number of squadrons in each Sector and on not organizing reinforcement from No 12 Group, which had the inestimable factor of time in arranging squadrons at height before they engaged the enemy. The minutes of this meeting add weight to Leigh-Mallory's and Bader's case for the employment of the Duxford Wing. [37]

Even before Dowding issued his minute of 10 September refusing to force No 12 Group to alter its methods of employing fighters, the Duxford Wing under Bader's command had flown patrols down into No 11 Group's area. On 7 and 9 September they employed three squadrons, Nos 19, 242 and 310, while another, on 11 September, consisted of four squadrons, before the battle over London reached a climax on the 15th, when the Wing was in action twice, using five squadrons each time. [38] Leigh-Mallory took a keen interest in these operations, travelling to Duxford on the 13th to hold a conference. [39]

The change of policy which had caused the Germans to alter the *Schwerpunkt* of attack to London quickly became counter-productive, and in this matter the Luftwaffe suffered from a grave misjudgement, again resulting from faulty Intelligence. Unknown to Dowding, the Air Ministry, Churchill or British Intelligence, Hitler decided to call off Operation Sealion on 17 September. [40] The air battle continued, but the contest which the RAF had set out to fight had been won, or, more exactly, had not been lost.

However, this brought no pause to the civil war then raging between two commanders inside Fighter Command. The reason for the switch of policy given in the War Diary of the German Naval Staff on 17 September was that the RAF 'was by no means defeated'. In Britain, however, although hints came of changes in the enemy's plans, there were still indications that the preparations for an invasion were either well advanced or even complete. Consequently there could be no relaxation of effort.

Although the Germans were not alone in submitting, and believing, greatly exaggerated claims of aircraft destroyed or damaged, such miscalculations harmed them more than the RAF. Their basic aim was to destroy or incapacitate Fighter Command before launching a seaborne invasion, while Dowding's intention, on the other hand, was not to overwhelm the Luftwaffe, or even, *pace* Big Wings, to cause an abandonment of attacks. Instead, by using defensive techniques, the Germans were to be held at bay until intemperate weather rendered invasion impossible.

During the period 26 August to 7 September, Luftwaffe claims were from three to four times greater than the RAF's true losses. For example, Luftwaffe claims for the five days 26 and 28 August, 1, 3 and 7 September totalled 309 machines, whereas the exact figure was 96. [41] It was small wonder that, when Kesselring launched the great raids of 15 September, some Luftwaffe aircrew had been told that the RAF were down to their last 50 fighters. The shock of reality was intense as squadron after squadron of Hurricanes and Spitfires met the incoming German bombers and not one bomber formation reached its target unmolested. [42]

On that day things went well for Fighter Command. There had been no massive raid since 7 September, airfields had suffered fewer assaults, and the new designation of squadrons had enabled many of No 11 Group's units to renew their strength. Morale was certainly higher than it had been a fortnight earlier. [43]

In terms of tactical application of resources, the Germans did little on the 15th to advance their own cause. The morning build-up over the Pas de Calais was slow and thoroughly detected by British RDF, which gave Park the benefit of time to prepare squadrons. Thereafter, Luftwaffe formations had to fight laboriously all the way to London and, as they reached the capital at midday, the Duxford Wing of five squadrons joined in a heavy onslaught, scattering the bombers into a chase which continued over many parts of Kent. As the next raid did not grow until about 2pm, Fighter Command squadrons were offered an unexpected respite for both men and machines. Then, an even larger formation of bombers, heavily protected by fighters, was again detected, tracked and met over London by the combined strength of six squadrons from No 11 Group, two from No 10 Group and, from No 12 Group, the Duxford Wing of five squadrons. Once again, the Luftwaffe formations were broken up and suffered heavy casualties as they turned for France. A comment on that day's activities, written in No 12 Group's Operations Record Book, showed Leigh-Mallory's belief that attacks on German aircraft should be made to a co-ordinated plan. It stated that Bader's Wing attacked the enemy 'according to plan – the Spitfire

Squadrons dealing with the enemy fighters and the Hurricanes the bombers'. [44]

The results of the day brought comfort to No 11 Group, whose squadrons had borne the brunt of the early incursions, and that gave satisfaction to Park. The intervention of the Duxford Wing provided a sense of achievement for the pilots of No 12 Group and, in Leigh-Mallory's view, justified his praise of the Big Wing. Nevertheless, Park was not to know the significance of that day's fighting in the context of the main air battle, nor could he predict what problems the Germans might pose next. Therefore, on 16 September another Group Instruction was issued, headed 'Engagement of Mass Attacks'. [46] In the first section he listed seven deficiencies noticed over the previous week, and in two of these he showed an awareness of the value of squadrons working together. One was that individual squadrons were being detailed to big raids, while the other was that some squadrons were not pairing up before tackling the enemy. Others again mentioned the fault of Group Controllers delaying in detailing a pair of squadrons on to individual raids.

Under the heading of 'Fresh Instructions' he issued new orders for dealing with very high flying enemy fighters, now operating at between 25,000ft and 30,000ft. His fifth heading, on diversions by enemy fighters, showed an awareness of the importance of using aircraft in greater than single squadron strength. '1. Detail not less than several pairs of Spitfires to fighter screen. 2. Get ample Hurricane squadrons rendezvoused in pairs in the region of sector aerodromes. 3. Get Northolt and Tangmere squadrons to readiness, to despatch as Wings of three squadrons to intercept the enemy's second or third wave which normally contains bombers.' This part of the document is revealing in refuting the often-stated view that Park did not believe in the value of squadrons working together in No 11 Group. The impression is gained, nonetheless, that the pressure from No 12 Group was beginning to tell, and that he was going out of his way to recommend pairs and Wings as a result. His opponents at the Air Ministry, not completely comprehending his difficulties, would have called this a late, and Damascene, conversion.

The very next day the debate on the value of Big Wings was given further impetus when Leigh-Mallory submitted to Stanmore a report on his Group's Wing patrols employed on four days during the first half of September. [46] He opened by reasoning that, as the Germans had used large formations of both fighters and bombers, adequate responses could not be made by single squadrons, therefore Wings had been employed with definite roles in which Spitfires tackled the fighters while Hurricanes dealt with the bombers. Concerning the first Wing patrol of 7 September, Leigh-Mallory voiced Bader's usual complaint of being called too late, which resulted in a lack of sufficient height when engaging the enemy. German fighters were able to attack them from the sun.

Bader's influence over his Group commander was also shown in the report on the second Wing patrol of 9 September, which finished by saying that 'the leader of the Wing' considered that more than twenty further bombers could have been destroyed if he had had additional fighters. German formations encountered on the third Wing patrol were described, and it was pointed out that Spitfires tackled the fighters, while No 74 Squadron attacked the bombers. [47]

The report continued by setting out tactical conclusions from the first three patrols. There had been two main difficulties, both of which were attributed to lack of fighter numbers. In the first place there were insufficient aircraft 'both to neutralise the enemy fighters and to attack the bombers successfully', while in the second, many enemy bombers could not be attacked because there were no fighters left 'with sufficient ammunition to carry on the engagement'. In listing his conclusions, Leigh-Mallory, once again using Bader's arguments, stressed the need for greater numbers. In his view at least two Spitfire squadrons were required to tackle the fighters and three others to break up the bomber formations.

However, accounts of the fourth and fifth Wing patrols, both on 15 September, made fanciful claims. Hurricanes had destroyed 'all the Dorniers they could see', and another squadron, encountering bombers, 'promptly destroyed the lot'. German fighters were unable to protect their bombers, which were eliminated by the three Hurricane squadrons 'at their leisure'. To his credit, throughout the report Leigh-Mallory never criticised No 11 Group in the manner that Park had reserved for complaints against No 12 Group. An equal fault, however, was committed in Appendix A, when setting out the number of enemy machines claimed. The long-term danger resulted from an acceptance of the accuracy of these totals, especially by the Air Staff, whose belief from pre-war days had been that the scale of attack would be reduced by heavy losses. For them, in their contest with Dowding, Bader's figures were manna from Heaven.

To place No 12 Group's case in perspective it is necessary to set their claims against the actual German casualties for those days. According to Leigh-Mallory, during the five Wing patrols 105 German aircraft were shot down, with 40 probables and 18 damaged, giving a total of 163 aeroplanes. Later figures, extrapolated from German records, show that on the four days in question the total Luftwaffe losses from all sources, including those aircraft not on combat missions and those judged at less than 100 per cent write-offs, totalled 234 machines. [48] Breaking the figures down further, on 7 September the three squadrons of the Duxford Wing claimed to have destroyed 20 German aircraft, and the whole of Fighter Command's claims for that day totalled 103 destroyed; the actual total was 41. It is revealing to set the Wing's claims for enemy fighters shot down on their five patrols against the figures now known. No 12 Group's figure for Bf 109s and Bf 110s destroyed was 48 machines, but the reality was that the combined total achieved by all squadrons of Fighter Command on those five occasions was 81. [49] The cardinal point is not so much that claims were exaggerated, as they certainly were by both sides, but that Bader's assertions, transmitted under the signature of his Group commander, were used as a potent weapon by those who wanted to remove Dowding and Park.

Leigh-Mallory sent two letters with his report. One, to Dowding, was reasonably non-committal, leaving the C-in-C to draw his own conclusions. He hoped that as pilots gained more experience results would improve, and claimed that matters were 'distinctly encouraging'. [50]

In the other letter, to Evill, Leigh-Mallory was far more forthcoming. 'I am convinced myself that it is the correct way to tackle these large German formations,' he wrote, adding that the Wing operations needed much more experience. He was sure that they would progress in time and, again, called them 'distinctly encouraging'. [51]

A small yet interesting enigma surrounds Leigh-Mallory's report, which was written on 17 September and forwarded to Headquarters, Fighter Command, where, six days later, Dowding announced that he was 'sending a copy to the Air Ministry for information'. However, someone at Stanmore had already done so, and the document was commented on by Crowe and Saundby in London on 22 September. How was Dowding by-passed by this copy? A possible explanation is that Evill, who showed sympathy towards No 12 Group's employment of Wings, and who would have seen the report before Dowding, rapidly forwarded a copy to the Air Ministry without telling his C-in-C. An alternative explanation is not easy to find. [52]

On 22 September Dowding sent the Air Ministry a copy of Park's report, dated 12 September, entitled 'German Air Attacks on England, 8th August - 10th September', which detailed the events of that month, especially the strain exerted on his Group. [53] Never a man to mince words, Park not only explained his perennial views on the tactics best suited to No 11 Group, but also laid about him with criticism of Headquarters, Fighter Command, and of the Air Ministry. He had been particularly disconcerted by requests for information even while he was completely absorbed in fighting the battle. The organization established at No 11 Group had worked well, but was inadequate to provide answers 'continually being demanded' by Stanmore for forwarding to the Air Ministry, with telephoned requests for information before squadrons had taken off, while they were flying, and then seeking casualties.

Park pointed out the burden on his Intelligence staff, who could not cope with such enquiries, received 'from Higher Authority from early morning to late at night', a remark hardly likely to endear him to the recipients of the report. Yet they had offended further by trying to obtain information for the Air Ministry by telephone requests directly to him or his Operations staff. Such 'importunate demands' had choked telephone lines and impeded staff in their duties, he added, with sharp strictures.

Thus senior officers at the Air Ministry, within a short period, had laid before them accounts of each Group commander's activities, policies and hopes. At this stage the divisions over the tactical employment of fighters grew deeper, still without decisive intervention from Dowding.

PART 3: AIR MINISTRY OPINION ON TACTICS

On 22 September at the Air Ministry, Group Captain Crowe, Deputy Director of Air Tactics, forwarded Leigh-Mallory's report to Air Vice-Marshal Saundby, Assistant Chief of the Air Staff, Technical Requirements. He included a minute which described it as 'most interesting' in its reference to Wing patrols, 'which have recently proved so successful'. He added, 'It is to be hoped that the wing tactics developed by No 12 Group will be followed by the other groups', thereby showing an ignorance of their differences of geographical position, if nothing else. [54] Saundby's subsequent minute went further, stating, 'It shows that the policy for escorting bombers by single seater fighters fails when there are sufficient fighters to contain the escort fighters and deal with the bombers', and added that the Air Fighting Committee had reached that conclusion 'years ago'. The report was then passed on in the general direction of Douglas. [55]

Dowding entered the lists on 23 September, at a time when he was being heavily pressed on the measures required to meet night bombing. [56] He wrote, in his own hand, a minute to Evill which contained one of his infrequently displayed shafts of humour in official documents. He was sure that Leigh-Mallory was thinking along the right lines, although the figures offered did not support his theory. 'More aircraft per Squadron were brought down by the combin. strength of 3 squadrons (though fewer bombers)'. A pun followed, concerning the Free Czech Squadron, No 310. 'Little Check is placed on the estimate of 310 Sqn. (joke) who generally are exuberant in their claims.' He added that some claims were 'mere thoughtful wishing', but he wanted Leigh-Mallory's report to be forwarded to the Air Ministry, adding that the figures in the Appendix were 'only approximate'. [57] On the same day he wrote to Leigh-Mallory, thanking him for the report which he had read with interest, but his tone was guarded and, instead of calling for an urgent review of tactics, the C-in-C appeared to do no more than engage in debate by correspondence. [58]

The next day a copy of the report was sent to the Air Ministry with a covering note, although, unknown to him, they had had one for three or four days. Dowding repeated his reservations over the claims made, but concluded with an unequivocal approval of Leigh-Mallory's tactics, a fact ignored by those who have blamed the AOC No 12 Group for being uncooperative. 'The losses incurred by the Wing were reduced,' Dowding noted, 'and I am, in any case, of the opinion that the AOC No 12 Group is working on the right lines in organising his operations in strength'. [59] Consequently Dowding was both aware of and involved in the controversy. It is understandable that some of those who knew the principals at the time, as well as historians later, have reflected on why he failed at that stage to bring together the chief antagonists and resolve their differences, because he, as C-in-C, had not only to make policy but also to ensure that it was enforced. In this respect it is also noticeable that Newall, CAS and therefore Dowding's senior officer in the Service, did not intervene, although he must have known the extent of the controversy. Possibly this added weight to the case of those who wanted him replaced.

On 24 September Douglas wrote a strongly worded minute in reply to Saundby's observation, and thus gave a firm momentum to the wheels of change already turning in the Air Ministry. He claimed to have received recent criticisms about Fighter Command's tactics, especially those in No 11 Group, in the way they tackled large enemy formations. 'It is alleged,' he wrote, 'that squadrons go up with no very clear idea as to how many other squadrons are in the air and no instructions as to how they are to work in co-operation with them.' For example, he went on, even in 1918 in France some aircraft had been sent to hold off the fighter screen while others attacked the bombers. He feared that the points made in Fighter Command's tactical memorandum on dealing with escorted bombers were not being followed in practice. There was need for a co-ordinated plan of action, and it was undesirable for squadrons to attack piecemeal, 'without any idea of what other squadrons are in the air, and what they are doing'. He believed that problems could be solved; three or four squadrons could have the same radio wavelength. The DDAT was then asked to consult the staff of Fighter Command 'and see what can be done. I would like to know the result.' [60] On reading this note, Saundby minuted the DDAT, asking for a report. He showed his preference when adding, 'the fighter wing tactics now being tried by 12 Group have a bearing on this'. [61]

Douglas maintained his criticisms of Park in a note written on 28 September for the benefit of the Chief of the Air Staff and the Vice-Chief of the Air Staff, a copy also going to the Director of Home Operations. He made no mention of Park's attack on 'Higher Authority' or of his opinions on fighter tactics, but selected a different target for censure. 'You will notice that Air Vice-Marshal Park's report deals almost entirely with day fighting,' he wrote. 'Night fighting is barely mentioned, save for a brief reference in the final paragraph.' Douglas felt that the question of night raids, at that time a particular burden for Fighter Command, might have been dealt with more fully. [62]

Douglas had a growing concern with night defence, in which he was deeply involved. Yet his failure to examine the details of Park's opinions on day fighting can lead to one of two conclusions. Either he disagreed so strongly that he was not prepared to spend time discussing them in writing, or the ideas had been discussed verbally at the Air Ministry and a general opinion formed which there was no need to write down. Either way, Park appeared to be on a losing wicket.

By this time Park was ready to express firm views to his Controllers on what he considered to be the weaknesses of Wings. An instruction of 28 September remarked that bomber raids were being made without close escort and without high fighter screen, so it had been hoped to link three squadrons in a Wing, but they took too long to form up and could lose contact. It appeared to him that three squadrons took twice as long as two squadrons to reach a given point, and precious time could not be spared while they were organizing. Controllers therefore should put up pairs of squadrons, although three might occasionally be needed 'in the winter and frequently in the coming Spring', when it was hoped to take the offensive. That final sentence showed an optimism and aggressive spirit denied to Park ever since he had taken command of No 11 Group in April. The litany of defence and disaster had restrained him and darkened his steps, but there were some shafts of light by late September as pressure had eased a little, morale had risen and the supply of new pilots and machines had grown encouragingly. Now he was thinking in terms of engagement which would have drawn approval from the Air Staff – had their commendation not already been awarded to Leigh-Mallory. [63]

The next day Park went further, firing a heavy broadside against No 12 Group in a letter to Stanmore entitled 'Major Tactics in Home Defence'. [64] Frustration concerning the criticisms made of him, both overt and covert, showed through. He started by commenting at some length and with considerable praise on the role played by No 10 Group. They were called on only when a heavy threat developed. Conversely, they could call on reinforcement from No 11 Group, and it is noticeable that Park stressed the speed of response in saying 'these are always provided immediately if No 11 Group is not heavily engaged'. The arrangement had worked for the previous two months, and followed the principles he believed to be incumbent on all Groups of Fighter Command. 'The Group requiring reinforcement shall state the number of Squadrons required, when and where, also the height they are required.' That was the basis of his belief, and he assumed that his C-in-C agreed. Both Groups had to keep in close touch to avoid confusion.

Park went on to force home his opinion. Matters had worked very well with No 10 Group because he and their AOC agreed that it was essential to get a small number of squadrons to the point required, instead of calling for a slow-forming Wing which would arrive after the enemy had bombed and turned for home. In another sharp swing at No 12 Group he said that they might 'bag' more enemy aircraft, but would fail to prevent the bombing of vital targets.

Warming to the attack, he turned with bitterness to Leigh-Mallory's approach. Arrangements here, he remarked, had led to confusion with the

Observer Corps, his squadrons and Sector Controllers. Giving detail, he listed two occasions in August when No 12 Group had been requested to cover Debden and North Weald. However, both had been bombed because, believing that the task would be covered, he had despatched his own squadrons to fight further south. He had therefore asked that requests for assistance from No 12 Group should be made to the Command Controller, but even that had failed. Recently, upon enquiring whether their squadrons were patrolling the North Weald-Hornchurch area, he had learned that they were 'somewhere down near the Coast'.

Heaping Pelion upon Ossa, a member of his staff had been told by 'a formation leader of No 19 Squadron' that the Duxford Wing never patrolled the North Weald-Hornchurch area, 'but went off down into the Dover area when ordered to reinforce'. Therefore, on the previous day he had declined the Command Controller's suggestion of seeking help from Leigh-Mallory only to learn shortly afterwards that he had 'a Wing of five squadrons in the Hornchurch area'. Park's descriptive complaint gives an impression of the Duxford Wing acting as a type of independent robber band plundering its way across his Group territory, a description to which Squadron Leader Bader might not have taken exception. In the letter he explained what confusion could result. The fact that some formations had recently 'roamed into Kent' uninvited and unknown to his Controllers might have accounted for Observer Corps reports of large raids in East Kent. However, when he sent his own squadrons to investigate, they found only 'friendly fighters'. His note carried an air of exasperation.

He set out five points to which he believed No 12 Group should adhere when asked to reinforce. First, they should send squadrons 'where and at the height requested'. Second, no fighters should be sent unless asked for. Next, his Controllers should be informed of the whereabouts of these squadrons. Fourth, no squadrons should alter their patrol lines without informing his Group Controller. Last, No 12 Group, when asked for two or three squadrons, should not waste time trying to form a Wing of five squadrons. These five points underscore the benefit that employing one overall commander would have brought to Fighter Command.

The Duxford Wing's claim of victories irked Park, and he wrote that their eagerness 'to obtain a good "bag" is understandable', but offered his own belief that the primary task of fighter squadrons was to protect aircraft factories, Sector aerodromes and London Docks; gaining high scores was only a means to that end. The letter maintained its attack to the end. The final paragraph praised the offensive spirit of No 12 Group and suggested that the best way of channelling it would be for them to be exchanged with his own squadrons. Many of these were tired, lacking sleep and relaxation because of constant raids and night bombing. He was sure that some of his squadrons would be glad of an exchange for a month 'to have a spell of undisturbed nights'. Reinforcing squadrons, he concluded, had advantages because they entered the battle after the enemy had been tackled by No 11 Group aircraft, 'whose one endeavour is to meet the enemy bombers, plus escort, *before* they reach their objectives'.

Park was battling alone against a rising tide of criticism and his C-in-C was offering scant support for his contentions regarding tactics in a day battle which, though being fought on a reduced scale by the end of September, was still occupying the full skills and attention of Fighter Command. Without doubt an important reason for this was the amount of time and thought Dowding was having to allocate to the expanding problem of night defence, so no clear statement concerning day tactics came from Stanmore, whereas others were closely examining recent events and possible changes.

On 1 October Park sent another paper, entitled 'Wing Formations', this time to the Commanding Officers of his seven Sector Headquarters and to each fighter squadron under his command. [65] The document clearly set out Park's views on the use of Wings, yet opened on a defensive note, evidence of his awareness of the criticisms being levelled at his handling of the battle. 'There is a feeling among pilots in some Squadrons,' he began, 'that the only way to defeat the enemy raiders against this country is to employ our fighter Squadrons in Wings of three Squadrons.' The object of his note was to explain why such formations had been used 'off and on during the past five months' yet were not the usual method of employing fighters in home defence.

He referred to the use of fighters during the French campaign, when he had employed the squadrons first in pairs, then in Wings of three. Conditions then were quite different, because there was time to gather formations before sending them across the Channel. The difference now was that the enemy 'can and has made four heavy attacks in one day', with minimal warning given. The best results over France, he added, were not obtained by Wings of three squadrons, but by pairs working together.

Each of the next three paragraphs contained the phrase 'experience has shown', reinforcing the fact that he was not dealing with theoretical tactics but with what he had learned in the harsh reality of battle. Wings were, in his view, uneconomic in home defence and had frequently been attacked while climbing. It was better to have one squadron of fighters over the enemy than three squadrons climbing from below, and London Sectors rarely had time to bring a Wing to height before the bombs fell. Here, however, if the premise is accepted that Bader's main aim was to enter the battle at height, and not to suggest that No 11 Group should form Wings, then Park is again missing the potential of integrating the Duxford aircraft into the defensive system. No steps were taken to combine forces and thereby add to the defence.

He then set out one of the greatest difficulties of employing squadrons from various Groups in a co-ordinated defence. Without VHF radio in all aircraft, three squadrons in a Wing could not work on a common R/T frequency. The Dowding System, built meticulously round the ability of RDF stations and the Observer Corps to locate the enemy, and the judgement of Controllers in guiding squadrons, could accommodate pairs of squadrons working on a common frequency, but not a Wing of three. The only person who could decide on the number of squadrons to employ was, in Park's opinion, the Group Controller, who had 'the complete picture of the enemy's movement on a wide front, from Lowestoft to Bournemouth'. Nevertheless, he concluded, Wings would probably become more common in the following Spring. [66]

Bader disagreed with this policy, wanting more power of decision to be taken by commanders of flying formations actually in touch with the enemy. This opinion was shared by others, such as Group Captain H. Darley, then OC No 609 Squadron in No 10 Group, who believed that Controllers did not understand the importance of the weather. He could tell a 'Junkers 88 day', a 'fighter-bomber day', or a 'big bomber day', and could use his discretion accordingly. [67]

On the same day that Park published this detailed report, a quite different view was displayed at the Air Ministry. Obeying Saundby's instructions of 27 September, Group Captain Crowe replied at some length in the form of a minute, noting that two days earlier he had discussed matters at Uxbridge. 'From various conversations recently' he had learned that fighter squadrons had gone into action with little plan for co-operative endeavour. To overcome the difficulty of making rendezvous for squadrons coming from different aerodromes, he suggested that Wings should operate from the same, or adjacent airfields. They could fly from as far back as Hatfield or Northolt and thus meet the enemy at operational height after a straight climb, instead of following the customary practice of flying away from the coast to gain altitude, which meant that they 'do not actually intercept any quicker than units further back'. If squadrons of a Wing were stationed together, units would 'get to know each other', discussing tactics and combat, and pilots would learn to co-operate as a team. He noted that both Park and Leigh-Mallory had detached fighters to engage the high-flying escorts while others met the bombers and, referring to the Duxford Wing's operations on 15 September with five squadrons, considered that even with the benefits of VHF a Wing leader should not be required to control more aircraft than that.

The first suggestion that a conference should be held appeared in his eighth paragraph, when referring to Park's methods of dealing with large raids. The development of such plans, Crowe suggested, should be discussed 'in conference with the Fighter Group commanders and the C-in-C, Fighter Command'. His minute concluded by mentioning the advantages that VHF sets would bring to Wings, and that they were being delivered at the rate of 680 a month for fighters and one-and-a-half sets a week for Sector Stations. [68]

Saundby read the minute, added a brief note and passed it on to Douglas who, by now, was taking definite steps within the Air Ministry to alter policies. Not only was he a firm supporter of Big Wings, but he was also playing an increasing role in night air defence. In both fields he was opposed to Dowding's general policy. Douglas wrote, 'This is all right as a beginning. But I am still far from happy.' In his view a Wing was better than a Squadron, and a Group needed a tactical plan which allowed Wings to fight as their commander saw fit. He asked for Stevenson, the Director of Home Operations, to see the papers and, after discussion, to hear his views. [69]

In the meantime, Leigh-Mallory was keeping in close touch with those airmen through whom he was able to intervene in the battle. On 3 October, a day of poor weather when few demands were made on his squadrons, he visited Duxford again for discussions. [70]

At the same time, investigations were being made at Stanmore into the strong and detailed criticisms made by Park on 29 September. Group Captain Lawson, G/C, Ops 1, passed a minute to Evill. If No 12 Group squadrons had been 'wandering over Kent', he could imagine the confusion. In his view, Park's arrangements, if followed, should work well. [71] In the midst of an increasingly acrimonious argument Evill took a balanced view and, with his customary succinct appreciation, wrote a summary for the C-in-C. He mentioned Park's request for a speedy despatch of small numbers, and Leigh-Mallory's preference for sending a Wing, but added, 'I do not think it would be correct to imply that 12 Group are not prepared to send smaller formations when these are urgently needed. In fact I have knowledge of their recently having sent one and two Squadrons to 11 Group's assistance.'

He explained that there was 'a fundamental difference of attitude between the two Groups'; this related to pressure of time. Evill believed it wrong for No 12 Group's Wings 'to rove without control over 11 Group's Sectors', and presumed that Dowding wanted that stopped. While granting that Park's requests were reasonable, he believed that some of No 11 Group's squadrons had been adversely affected by fighting constantly against larger numbers. A Wing could be of great help to them because it was bad for the Germans if a large formation was employed sometimes. He felt that Park should recognize this fact and should arrange to 'use the strength of the Duxford Wing against a mass raid'. At the end he expressed his belief that an increase in the use of VHF radio would make the control of a Wing practicable. So, too, would 'good co-operation between Groups'. [72]

Dowding was left in no doubt of the extent of the problem and its background. Evill's minute had explained the 'fundamental differences' without taking sides and had made suggestions for using the strengths of both Groups, but he acknowledged that the C-in-C alone had authority to act decisively in the matter. Some later accounts portray Dowding as a victim of the Big Wing controversy and wrongly accuse Evill of not notifying him of

115

the quarrel. However, he did know. The puzzle is that he took no immediate, firm step to resolve the problem when a meeting between him and the Group commanders was patently called for. Possibly the cares of meeting the German daylight assault had temporarily drained his energies, and certainly the increasing demands placed on Fighter Command's attitudes towards night fighting were exercising both his mind and patience. In Bader's later opinion, he was reaping the unwelcome fruits of not having a single commander to control the whole battle. For whatever reason, Dowding was comparatively slow to react. [73]

PART 4: INDECISION AT FIGHTER COMMAND

On 8 October Dowding wrote to Leigh-Mallory with an air of indecision, enclosing Park's letter which complained so bitterly about No 12 Group's alleged irregularities. 'You have spoken to me about your desire to meet the enemy always in maximum strength,' he said, adding approvingly, 'and this is, of course, a sound principle of war.' He next asked for comments on Park's contention that small reinforcements arriving on time were preferable to a stronger force appearing after the attack. Then he posed Park's criticism of Wings failing to patrol where asked after entering his area uninvited. [74]

It is noteworthy that Dowding neither passed judgement nor set down his own policy. At that stage he was well aware that the abrasive quarrel was offering no help and succour to the running of the Command, and the response throws doubt on the acceptance of a later claim, when, writing of Park, he said, 'I wish he had kept me more personally informed about his difficulties with Leigh-Mallory. I now know that he tried to fight it out for himself . . . but I might have been able to help him more. When the time came for me to intervene it was too late . . . too late for both of us.' From the evidence of documents, the C-in-C's memory here was less than infallible and, unfairly, implies blame on Park for not speaking out soon enough. [75]

Leigh-Mallory, obviously stung by Park's criticisms, replied at once and hoped Dowding did not consider that his men were 'merely trying to get a "bag"'. In his opinion there were two main objects of Wing formations. The first was to meet the Germans on equal terms, thereby incurring fewer casualties, and the second was to raise the morale of squadrons whose spirits had been depressed by constantly having to tackle 'overwhelmingly superior numbers of *GERMAN* aircraft'. The Wing, in part, had achieved both objectives. In his main letter Leigh-Mallory set out briskly to refute Park's allegations, and blamed the bombing of aerodromes on the late call for his squadrons. On the thorny issue of timely assistance being preferred to greater help arriving later, he made the telling comparison that 'the distance from DUXFORD to HORNCHURCH is approximately the same as the distance from HORNCHURCH to ASHFORD in Kent', and said that if he were allowed to put up the Wing when the Germans were over the French coast there would be ample time for them to reach Hornchurch. On his own initiative he had got squadrons airborne over Duxford because he knew that they would be called late, not until the enemy were between Maidstone and London, but he wanted squadrons to be called at the same time as those of No 11 Group.

As for Park's recommendations for action by No 12 Group, Leigh-Mallory agreed with some but not with others, because they ignored the advantages to be gained if those squadrons were called off in good time. He then dealt with the accusations of his squadrons 'roaming over Kent', and agreed, but claimed that they had been ordered there by Headquarters, Fighter Command. On other occasions events followed naturally from his pilots patrolling over Hornchurch and seeing enemy formations close by, 'immediately to the south', which were, naturally, engaged. Having dealt with Park's complaints, Leigh-Mallory went on to the offensive. He noted that the Germans had caused heavy damage in London recently. If his aircraft had been scrambled when the enemy were at the French coast they would have been at 20,000ft before the enemy arrived, and 'many raids which did penetrate over London would have been engaged before reaching there'. The letter closed strongly and patriotically, claiming that he wished to co-operate with No 11 Group with the main object of preventing the enemy from reaching London, and Duxford was well situated for that. In view of the importance of the capital, Leigh-Mallory hoped that he might be allowed 'to render assistance which I believe would be most effective'. The evidence of this letter certainly suggests that Leigh-Mallory was not recommending the employment of Big Wings by No 11 Group, in spite of later accusations that both he and Bader did so. [76]

Next day Park wrote to Dowding with suggestions for incorporating No 12 Group's Wing into his defensive system, recommending they be placed under the control of one of his Sectors and, to achieve their best, should live and work there for a time. Possibly some squadrons could be exchanged with his own, or perhaps a Wing of three squadrons could be sent each day to operate under the Kenley or Biggin Hill Controllers. His letter misses the point of employing the Duxford Wing to its best advantage. The drawback of placing No 12 Group squadrons 'to live and work' in Park's territory was the loss of time and height to be gained by their flying from airfields further north. It reinforces the impression of two Groups fighting separate battles with disjointed aerial forces. Here was a fine opportunity for Headquarters, Fighter Command, to blend them into one. They missed it. [77]

By then the nature of German attacks had changed and, although large raids were made in the south after 15 September, they did not again reach the intensity and scale of the earlier offensive. Wings were called into action and employed on later dates but, as the Germans set aside their plans for a seaborne invasion, the Luftwaffe, having suffered so heavily, adopted a new role. [78] On 16 September Goering held a conference with commanders at his forward headquarters and new tactics were selected. Big raids were to be attempted only in the best weather, and then by bombers flying under heavy escort. Attacks were to be maintained so that the British were unaware of 'Sealion' being postponed, and Goering still hoped, anyway, that his enemy could be defeated through destruction of the economy and the shattering of civilian morale. [79]

Yet, as ever, he lacked the sustained interest required for successful leadership. On the 21st he returned to Rominten for some hunting, and one of his pilots, Adolf Galland, who visited him there five days later, wrote that no mention was made either of the war in general, or of the Battle of Britain in particular. [80] Although the daylight battle is regarded by some writers as only one part of the continuing German offensive against Britain, Goering knew that in this phase his Luftwaffe had failed, for the first time, to gather the fruits of a decisive victory. If the German Air Force was not defeated, its considerable efforts were, at the very least, greatly frustrated.

According to Telford Taylor, by 16 September 'the main emphasis of the bomber offensive was shifting toward night operations'. Day bombing was 'dwindling rapidly' and, apart from a few belated though accurate raids against aircraft factories, the last massed bomber attack was launched on 30 September. [81] Sure proof of the Luftwaffe's inability to force an issue was shown by the increasing use of Bf 109s and Bf 110s as fighter-bombers in annoying raids of pinprick proportions. The raids on aircraft factories were worrying, bringing heavy criticism of the Air Ministry where, ironically, Beaverbrook's loud, constant and sometimes intemperate pleas for their protection put further pressure on his friend, Dowding. The impression was given that Fighter Command and AA guns were incapable of rendering an adequate defence, and on 6 October Beaverbrook complained of this in a memorandum to Churchill. 'The balloon barrage is too thin,' he wrote. His next words reflected the widespread apprehension being felt over the night Blitz, when he added censoriously, 'Just as important as night bombing is the defence of aircraft factories and their aerodromes'. He finished in best staccato style, 'Two Hurricanes lost at Northolt yesterday. Can we have action now?' [82]

The exasperation he could rouse in others is sensed in a reply from his old adversary, Sinclair, on 10 October. 'As I have repeatedly told you over the telephone and in letters,' he stated, 'I do not yield an inch in my anxiety to give all possible production [sic] to the factories you mention.' Nor is it difficult to assess Sinclair's feelings for Dowding from the tone of the next sentence in which, one suspects, with some relief he laid the responsibility for all air defence at the door of the C-in-C. 'It is not, as you suggest, a job for the Air Staff, but for your devoted friend, the C-in-C, Fighter Command. I am sending him your letters at once and asking him to do all he can to meet your requirements as I know he himself will be anxious to do.' [83]

A minute written by Evill to Dowding on 13 October showed that the SASO was feeling concern over several matters which went to the root of the strategy and tactics employed by Fighter Command. 'You recently instructed me to keep an eye open on the progress of day operations,' he began, then went on to list the faults he had noticed. One of these was that reports submitted after action by Groups, especially No 11 Group, gave 'no general statement of the action taken'. He complained that, 'we do not know whether their Squadrons are sent up singly or in twos or threes,' and went on to say that little was disclosed 'about the way in which they conduct operations'.

Evill appeared diffident over suggesting remedies. 'I fully understand that you delegate the tactical conduct of operations to the Groups,' and they should be shown no 'lack of confidence', yet the staff at Headquarters, Fighter Command, 'is in no position to appreciate reliably what the Groups are doing'. He felt sure that Groups had 'some system whereby they instruct Controllers as to tactical methods and dispositions', but these were not known at Stanmore. [84]

The SASO, unintentionally or otherwise, was underlining the feeling that tactical leadership was lacking at the time, and in this Evill shared the opinion held in the Air Ministry, particularly by Douglas. Insufficient information was being provided for the Command's headquarters, although as Dowding was not controlling the battle immediately it is difficult to know what changes to strategy and tactics such information would have brought. As Park had complained earlier, there was often a surfeit of demands – from 'Higher Authority' – which meant that both Stanmore and the Air Ministry wanted to know what was going on. The solution would have been for a single commander to control the battle. He would have received reports and acted immediately by amending tactics as necessary and, not having a double jury sitting at his shoulder, would have been able to synchronize the actions of various Groups as he saw fit.

An interesting deduction emerges from Evill's minute. When Douglas minuted Saundby on 24 September he offered no source for his claim that it had been 'alleged' that squadrons were being sent up with no instructions of how to work with others. The source could have well been Evill. It is unclear whether he voiced his criticisms before or after Douglas gave them prominence, but it could have been the former. [85]

Dowding's reply to Evill is also of interest. Instead of appreciating that the minute touched on a severe weakness in the method of command, he merely asked that the report form should be changed 'so that they would have to get the information and give it to us, or else confess their failure by leaving the compartments empty', a rather opaque instruction to solve a problem requiring the light of leadership. Evill's reply to that again asked for Groups to submit studies, reviews and recommendations after their operations, but no solution to this problem came until after the Group commanders' conference of 30 October, towards the end of Dowding's time as leader of Fighter Command. [86]

While Headquarters, Fighter Command, were examining the claims and counter-charges exchanged by Park and Leigh-Mallory, an apparently innocuous note arrived for Dowding from the Air Ministry. Sent by Stevenson, the DHO, it announced 'a small conference' called by Newall, the CAS, to be held in his room on 17 October for the purpose of discussing 'major tactics by fighter formations' and receiving a report on the progress of night interception. He enclosed an Air Staff note which was a commentary on fighter tactics produced by Stevenson himself. His points were no neutral attempt to discuss Wings, but a commendation to promote them, going virtually hand-in-hand with Leigh-Mallory's beliefs, as taken up by Douglas at the Air Ministry. [87]

In the Introduction he referred to Park's report and soon opened his criticism in line with the current Air Staff opinion. 'But he does not report whether squadrons were vectored into the air battle singly, in pairs or in larger formations. Nor does he report upon the allocation of role to the squadrons employed in a general action.'His second paragraph was a reminder that the Air Staff had foreseen the launching of mass raids and that Dowding had 'welcomed this form of attack as the one he was best able to meet'. However, it was realized that much remained to be learned about the best method of deploying a large fighter force against such an attack.

Stevenson then referred to Leigh-Mallory's report, a copy of which, significantly, was attached to the agenda, and noted that 'no less than 105 enemy aircraft were destroyed at a cost of 14 of our fighters'. By using a force of between three and five squadrons 'the enemy's mass formation was broken up and severe casualties inflicted at slight cost'. He explained that the object of the 'Balbo' was threefold: to neutralize German fighters, break up the bomber formations and then shoot down the bombers afterwards. Looking ahead, he predicted heavier attacks in the future, and said that the lessons learned should be applied 'to enable the fighter force to operate at maximum efficiency'. He believed that the German Air Force had been defeated in their attempt to gain 'day air superiority' over Britain, but added, 'we must be prepared in all respects to defeat enemy mass formations effectively'.

He referred to the attached note from the Air Staff as 'a basis for discussion', but no more than a cursory glance revealed that most of the discussion had already been held in the Air Ministry, and the results were a foregone conclusion. It had become apparent, the document stated, that sometimes 'our fighters have been meeting the enemy on unequal terms both as regards numbers and height'. To overcome the disadvantage, fighters should be flown in units 'large enough to deal with enemy formations', and should be well controlled. Several disadvantages suffered by RAF squadrons were then listed. There had been numerical inferiority with lack of co-ordination between squadrons and Groups, and formation leaders had planned few operations together. Fighters had often been put up with a height disadvantage, and a number of squadrons could not be operated together because of the limitations of high-frequency radio.

There followed a clear statement of what the Air Ministry wanted. The minimum fighter unit to meet large enemy formations should consist of three squadrons, and in certain circumstances two Wings, called a 'Balbo' might be formed. One of the squadron commanders should be present with the Sector Controller to regulate the Wing, and Stevenson did not foresee insuperable difficulties if Wings were not in radio contact with their Sectors. In those conditions, he reasoned, the large enemy formations would be clearly visible from a distance, 'and vectoring therefore will be unnecessary'. The influence of Bader is felt here, with the assumption that a Controller's task was no more than to place the fighters close to the enemy and leave the rest to the Wing commander's judgement. It is known that the Air Ministry held some Controllers in low esteem, and Sinclair had written to Beaverbrook a fortnight earlier, stating that 'the lack of good Sector Controllers has been a weak point in Fighter Command for a long time'. [88] Stevenson did not suggest a way in which the tactics of the two Groups might be readily and amicably blended into an effective whole, but his reasoning certainly assumed that the Dowding system, so intricately designed, was to be bypassed.

The accompanying agenda was a reinforcement of what Dowding and Park regarded as prejudice, but what the Air Ministry saw as a dynamic new approach. For example, Item 2 asked three questions, and the second and third of these presumed an affirmative answer to the first. 'Is it agreed that a larger fighter formation than a wing should operate as a tactical unit? If so, is it agreed that this unit should consist of two wings? By what name should such a unit (referred to in these Agenda as a "BALBO") be known?' Obviously these questions demanded positive and agreeable answers, allowing no scope for nonconformity. The only apparent neutral item was the last, which stated briskly that Dowding would give a short report on the current position of night interception. [89]

Park replied at once to Stevenson. He explained what, in his carefully reasoned opinion, were the vices of using Wing tactics in his area and the virtues of his own Group's formations. His annoyance is sensed as he once again repeated his principles. His Group had employed Wings of three squadrons 'in May, June, July, August, September and are still using them when conditions of time, space and weather make them effective'. He complained that Stevenson's note appeared to be based on the experience of No 12 Group's Wings on five occasions only. As the Duxford Wing's claimed results had been included in the papers for the conference, Park asked that those of Nos 10 and 11 Groups should also be circulated. He then returned with tenacity to his basic belief. 'I may be wrong,' he wrote, 'in imagining that our primary task is to protect London, Aircraft factories, Sector Aero-dromes, against enemy bombers, and not merely to secure the maximum bag of enemy aircraft after they have done their fiendish damage.' That appeal fell on deaf ears. Park's final paragraph was another swing at No 12 Group squadrons which, he asserted, mainly engaged outgoing, not incoming raids after they had been attacked 'by pairs of Spitfire also Hurricane Squadrons located around London' and they and their close escorts had been 'pretty badly shaken' by AA gunfire. [90]

By this time the opponents of Dowding and Park were clear on the course to follow, and took pains to prepare a case. For example, it was probably not unrelated that Wing Commander Woodhall, Controller of the Duxford Wing, was called to Headquarters, No 12 Group, for a conference on 16 October. Matters were not to be left to chance. [91]

While that smaller conference was in progress, an effort was being made at Stanmore to investigate Leigh-Mallory's claim that his squadrons had been 'roaming over Kent' because they had been ordered there by Head-quarters, Fighter Command. The results were inconclusive because the Con-troller's records were insufficiently detailed, but Evill minuted Dowding and threw doubt on Leigh-Mallory's assertion. On such occasions, he noted, the conditions of strength, area and form of action were laid down by No 11 Group. He then sagely expressed reservation over whether No 12 Group always conformed, and added that such matters were difficult to check. [92]

There follows an interesting and revealing addition to the minute sheet. Dowding obviously studied Evill's note, and jotted down a few words in pencil. First, he boxed in 'Information to 11 Group as to position of 12 Group's Squadrons'. Under that, also boxed, was 'Barnett?', probably a ref-erence to Squadron Leader R. Barnett, formerly OC of No 234 Squadron, who had been removed from his command on 13 August. At one side he wrote '8th October. Raids not plotted.' It is, however, the final note that dis-closes his realization of what was needed, in spite of later protestations of ignorance of the problem. The C-in-C pencilled in 'Compose differences between Groups'. Although for a variety of reasons he failed to do it, his own future, as well as those of his Group commanders, might well have been different had he succeeded. [93]

This minute proves the extent of Dowding's fallibility of memory on the matter of the controversy. As late as 1961 he told Robert Wright that he knew nothing of the difference between Park and Leigh-Mallory 'until it had reached a fairly advanced stage'. Then, 'to his great surprise', Sinclair men-tioned Leigh-Mallory's views, 'based on the idea put forward by Bader'. However, Dowding's assertion is contradicted here. [94]

The extent of the 'battle within a battle' taking place at Fighter Com-mand from 7 September to 16 October is not widely recognized, because much attention is naturally given to the RAF's success in preventing the Luftwaffe from gaining aerial supremacy, without acknowledging the grave disquiet emanating from the Air Ministry over tactics. In reality, but unknown to the principal antagonists, the controversy had lost most of its point by the end of September as German tactics changed. Their disagreements were concerned with what might have been, not with what was, or would be.

At that stage, Fighter Command looked to Dowding for decision in leadership that he was either unwilling or unable to offer. As his hesitancy allowed the controversy to simmer, it is understandable that officers at the Air Ministry, under the prompting of Douglas, pressed for definite action and requested a conference. The question must be asked why Newall, as CAS, took no lead in the matter. The fact that they backed the claims and cause of Leigh-Mallory showed their readiness to support anyone who believed that Dowding was failing to make the best use of resources. In doing so they gave an omnibus blessing to the employment of Big Wings as a *sine qua non* ingredient for all Groups, thereby missing the point of Leigh-Mallory's and Bader's argument, which referred only to the possibilities open to the Duxford Wing, used over Park's area, where there was no time to gather local squadrons into Wings.

By 16 October mistrust of Dowding's powers of command in the day battle resulted in a forceful campaign to have him replaced being well under way. That much is generally acknowledged. What is less frequently appreciated is that there were, at the same time, fears over his attitude to meeting the growing menace of the night bomber.

6

NIGHT AIR DEFENCE

PART 1: THE BACKGROUND TO NIGHT AIR DEFENCE

The publication in 1981 of Group Captain Haslam's article, 'How Lord Dowding Came to Leave Fighter Command', restored some balance to assessments of the leadership of the RAF 40 years earlier. [1] The piece was prompted by two contributions by Len Deighton which praised, excessively in Haslam's opinion, Dowding's leadership during the Battle of Britain. [2] Haslam criticised that very quality in the C-in-C, claiming 'it was precisely for his apparent lack of control of leadership' that he was replaced, but then opened a further and largely unexplored field of controversy between Dowding and the Air Staff. The documentary evidence, he suggested, showed that Dowding was removed not so much for his handling of daylight raids as for his response to night attacks.

Since the Battle of Britain so much attention has been paid by historians and writers to the ebb and flow of the daylight battle, especially as this was conspicuous to millions of people, that the threat at the time from night bombing has received scant attention. As the Luftwaffe failed to overwhelm Fighter Command by a daylight campaign, paving the way for a seaborne invasion, Dowding has been accorded general acclaim for his part in keeping Britain in the war. This judgement, however, has overlooked the importance to the air campaign during the early autumn of 1940 of the alternative German strategy, and of Dowding's efforts to counteract it. If Haslam's claim is examined, strong evidence emerges that, especially from 7 September when the first heavy night attack was launched against London, a number of influential Service leaders and politicians were gravely worried at Dowding's reaction to the new crisis. There were three reasons for this.

In the first place, by the nature of his appointment the C-in-C, Fighter Command, was responsible for the aerial defence of the United Kingdom by both day and night, a fact freely admitted by Dowding himself. [3] If the nation's aerial defence was found wanting, the responsibility and attendant blame were reckoned to be largely his. Secondly, when pressure grew for rapid and urgent changes to be made to the night air defence system to counter the major new threat, Dowding appeared unwilling to comply rapidly, showing what the Air Staff considered to be his customary stubbornness and lack of co-operation. Thirdly, and underlying these two reasons, Dowding's opponents in the Air Ministry, already critical of his handling of the day battle, were not displeased to find another cudgel with which to beat his declining reputation. They made the most of it.

Consequently a point often unrecognized is that, by the time Dowding was called to the Air Ministry conference of 17 October, largely to discuss the supposed infirmities of his day fighting tactics, there was a strong current of opinion highly critical of his conduct of night air defence. These feelings were not limited to his long-standing adversaries inside the Air Council. Mistrust of his policies, emanating from the Ministry of Aircraft Production, was being laid forcefully before the Prime Minister, and the essential political support which the C-in-C had received from Beaverbrook and Churchill was waning. A close examination of minutes and papers relating to night air defence, essential to give a balanced view of the leadership, strategy and tactics of Fighter Command at the time, certainly strengthens Haslam's claim.

Nonetheless, what his article fails to underline, as Dowding's critics of 1940 also conveniently failed to observe, was that the weaknesses of night air defences, in terms of suitable fighters and ground equipment, were not the fault of the C-in-C, Fighter Command. The general neglect of the RAF until the late spurt from 1938 had to be laid at the doors of the government of the day, or of the Air Ministry. It was permissible to disagree with his employment of available resources, but unfair of politicians to have provided so little, because the feeling existed in pre-war days that night defence should not take too great a fraction of the whole national effort. [4]

Many people who had lived in Britain during the First World War were well aware of the potential dangers of night bombing. Much of the German aerial campaign launched then, less than a quarter of a century earlier, consisted of attacks made at dusk or during the hours of darkness. The effect, especially on civilian morale, exceeded the cost in terms of airships or bombers lost. German ambitions from 1915 to 1918 were similar to those of the Luftwaffe in 1940, because they were attempting 'to unnerve the British public, to make life unbearable by destroying their homes' and to cripple the means of supply. In this way they intended that heavy casualties would force the British people to demand peace, 'and sacrifice their national honour rather than suffer a continuance of air attacks'. [5] German aircraft had dropped almost 9,000 bombs, weighing 280 tons, at night, killing 1,413 people and injuring almost 3,500. About half of the casualties were incurred in London, where 62½ tons were dropped, affecting the output of munitions. [6] The effect of these raids was clearly remembered in 1940 by those aged over 35 and, as bombers had developed in power and numbers, the prospect of new attacks brought great trepidation.

In 1934 a writer recollected the effect of one single raid made by Gotha bombers only seventeen years earlier. [7] For several weeks afterwards, London's Underground stations were packed nightly 'to suffocation' by an estimated 300,000 people, while half a million others went into cellars. He wrote, 'the mere rumour of a raid was sufficient to stampede thousands to these refuges'. Industrial production was affected as, for example, a false report of one Zeppelin approaching Scarborough led to lights being extinguished in munitions factories situated as far apart as Nottingham, Bath, Gloucester and Worcester. [8]

The British defence system in 1940, therefore, was faced with no new problem when the Germans intensified night raids, because thousands of civilians had undergone the ordeal before. The new factor for them was that technological advances enabled greater numbers of enemy bombers to carry larger loads, probably including gas, at higher speeds than in the previous war. [9] Their hope was that similar progress would enable the defensive system to meet the threat successfully, which had happened in 1917-18 when countermeasures led to the scaling down of German raids. [10] It was, perhaps, fortunate for public morale that civilians had little idea of the extent to which, in night bombing, the attacker enjoyed immunity. In the later words of General Pile, C-in-C, AA Command, 'at that time night fighter defence was deplorably inefficient'. [11] And, as the Ministry of Information's official survey pointed out in 1943, with a frankness not always displayed in Government publications, 'London at the time was not adequately defended. All over England there was still a shortage of anti-aircraft guns.' [12]

Although night air defence was causing increasing concern by the outbreak of the Second World War, it was not in the forefront of RAF planning. When government and, subsequently, RAF policy changed from the end of 1937, and more particularly after the international crises of 1938, greater attention and resources were allocated to Fighter Command, but the expectation was that the main German raids would be made in daylight. [13] Most of Dowding's countermeasures were aimed at parrying those and, as Fighter Command's resources were hardly extensive, few were available for night defence. The first reason for this was that accurate navigation in darkness involved considerable problems, so that by the outbreak of war the RAF could not guarantee that British bombers would easily reach and identify targets in Germany, and the Luftwaffe was thought to share the problems. [14] Secondly, both air forces were geared to daylight campaigns and, as one pilot wrote later, no air force would launch night attacks if they 'could manage to do the job by day'. [15]

The Luftwaffe, a mainly tactical air force developed to co-operate closely with ground units, saw little need for night bombing, yet had aircrew who were at least comparatively well prepared for flying in darkness. According to Galland, bomber crews received adequate experience in night and blind navigation operations as part of their normal peacetime training. [16]

British countermeasures against night bombing took two forms before 1939, and it was anticipated that, together, they would prevent the Germans from achieving the disruptive effect on peoples' lives which had been experienced in the First World War.

The first was the theory of the value of the counter-offensive, generally accepted within the RAF during the 1930s. This 'Trenchard Doctrine' led to a slow start in the creation of an adequate fighter defence against day attacks, let alone against those made at night. It was a fragile strategy that relied on the threat of retaliation from a Bomber Command which was at the time incapable of causing irreparable damage to enemy targets. Yet the theory held that the only really effective air defence in the long term was to sustain a more powerful offensive than the enemy's. [17]

Nonetheless, in assessing Dowding's attitude it should be remembered that before 1939 the C-in-C himself subscribed to this policy. Writing as Chairman of the Home Defence Committee in February 1937, he stated categorically that local defences 'however numerous and efficient cannot alone provide an adequate measure of security', adding that 'offensive action will be ultimately more efficacious in reducing the scale of attack on Great Britain than a vast increase in the number of local defence fighters'. [18] While lecturing at the Staff College three months later he displayed similar sentiments. Home defence could never be ensured by fighters and guns, he believed, unless 'the bombers are systematically destroying the enemy's machines, reserves, factories and fuel supplies'. No disciple of the Trenchard Doctrine could have put the case for bombers more succinctly or enthusiastically. [19]

The second form of counter-measure was more obvious to the British people and guaranteed to bring greater reassurance to those suffering the enemy's onslaught. Ground defences consisting of anti-aircraft guns, searchlights, sound detectors and balloons were positioned mainly around large cities, industrial centres and a number of aerodromes, following the precepts and methods employed during the First World War. The system was based on the assumption that sound locators would detect aircraft, searchlights illuminate them and guns destroy them, with additional help from night fighters.

An assumed weakness in the defence system was a shortage of anti-aircraft guns. This was, to some extent, overcome in daylight when enemy machines, often flying in close formation, could be seen and engaged, but difficulties were magnified in darkness, when bombers flew individually or in small sections. General Pile pointed out that, after Dunkirk, an estimate was made that 3,744 heavy anti-aircraft guns were needed for Britain's defence, yet on 11 July only 1,163 were available,[20] a figure that had grown to no more than 1,271 by 21 August.[21] Similar shortages were found in all types of anti-aircraft equipment, from light guns to searchlights, and from balloons to gun-laying RDF sets, of which there were only eleven in the London area by 9 September.[22] Consequently the two main planks on which Britain's night air defence was based were far from sound in 1940, yet, as German night attacks intensified, many people looked naturally to Fighter Command, which had done so well in daylight operations, to bring relief.

The ability of RAF fighters to intercept German bombers was linked closely to the development of RDF. As far as daylight raids were concerned, the system evolved was of inestimable value, but when, in the later 1930s, what was considered to be the lesser problem of night defence was explored, three extensive difficulties were encountered. [23]

Firstly, RDF was designed to locate and track enemy aircraft as far as the coast, where, in daylight hours, the Observer Corps would take over and airborne fighters make visual contact. Churchill had predicted a drawback to this scheme in June 1939, when he commented that reliance on the Observer Corps was 'a transition from the middle of the twentieth century to the early stone age', a criticism later proved to be less than fair. However, during the hours of darkness, once bombers had passed the RDF stations they were 'lost', as no method of inland tracking existed. [24]

Secondly, a method had to be evolved during night raids of bringing the defending fighter close enough to the bomber to make an attack. Little imagination is needed to appreciate the gulf between achieving this in daylight and in darkness. Much patience and ingenuity were required from ground stations to reach this goal, even when inland tracking was developed, because the airborne interception apparatus carried by fighters was necessarily small and incapable of working at distances over three miles.[25]

Thirdly – and this a problem which had dogged the RAF from pre-war days and still had not been satisfactorily resolved by August 1940 – a suitable night fighter was required for the specialist role. Existing Hurricanes and Spitfires, well developed for daylight interception, suffered disadvantages in night combat, particularly in the glare from exhausts, which impaired pilots' vision. Blenheims were better suited, but lacked the speed to track and catch the faster German bombers.

The critics of Dowding's efforts at night defence overlook his interest in experiments made before the war, which were slow to produce results owing to factors beyond his control. After visiting the Bawdsey experimental station near Felixstowe in July 1939,[26] the C-in-C wisely recommended the ideal night-fighter should carry a two-man crew, one to fly and the other to concentrate on navigation. The aircraft, he suggested, should be twin-engined, with unobstructed forward vision and good weight-carrying abilities.[27] The Bristol Beaufighter met these requirements, and the Mk II, which flew in 1941, had four 20mm cannon and six machine-guns. The Air Ministry ordered 300 even before the prototype flew on 17 July 1939 but, because of teething troubles, machines did not leave the factory until August 1940, allowing no time for squadrons to be adequately trained before the Luftwaffe's night offensive began. In fact, they were not operated in efficient numbers until early 1941, when the Blitz had been under way for four months.[28]

Experiments relating to RDF and its incorporation in a defensive system had been in progress since the setting up of the Committee for the Scientific Survey of Air Defence (CSSAD) under the chairmanship of Sir Henry

Right: No 19 Squadron, the first in Fighter Command to operate Spitfires, flew the type during the battle. Here one of its pilots, Sgt George Unwin, climbs out of his aircraft after a sortie at Fowlmere, a reactivated First World War aerodrome. Note the 'Popeye' marking just forward of the cockpit.

Below: After the climax of the daylight air fighting, No 610 Squadron was transferred from the south-east of England to Acklington, where this pilot group photo was taken. The timing of the movement of squadrons into or out of the main battle zone was one of Dowding's greatest problems.

Above: The success or failure of the Dowding System depended on the rapid assessment of enemy movements from radar, and corresponding Fighter Command movements. WAAF plotters are here seen at the map table from which RAF Controllers will direct the squadrons. The work of these 'unsung heroines' was crucial.

Above right: Air Vice-Marshal Trafford Leigh-Mallory, Air Officer Commanding, No 12 Group. During the battle he wanted greater use to be made of his 'Big Wing' flying from Duxford under the command of Douglas Bader.

Below: The Heinkel He 111 was the largest twin-engined bomber used by the Luftwaffe throughout the battle. A typical bombload was up to 4,000lb, and bombs were stored vertically, tumbling as seen here when dropped.

Right: Oberstleutnant Werner Molders, one of the Luftwaffe's most successful fighter aces, is here talking with Reichsmarschall Hermann Goering, whose leadership in the battle was often at fault.

Below: This Dornier Do 17 has been brought down relatively intact. The oldest and slowest bomber design operated by the Luftwaffe, it was increasingly unable to defend itself over the skies of southern England, but could withstand a surprising amount of punishment.

Above: Squadron Leader Douglas Bader examines the RAF view of Hitler on one of No 242 Squadron's aircraft. Bader was a passionate proponent of the value of the Duxford Wing used in conjunction with No 11 Group's squadrons, and found an ally in Leigh-Mallory.

Left: With the arrival of the night blitz, when a concentration of the Luftwaffe bombers found the target, the effects were devastating. This is a street in Coventry after the infamous raid of 14 November 1940.

Above: The Air Officer Commanding No 11 Group, Air Vice-Marshal Keith Park. After the battle he was removed to Training Command and his post went to the man with whom he had disagreed so bitterly, Air Vice-Marshal Trafford Leigh-Mallory, AOC No 12 Group.

Below: Air Vice-Marshal W. Sholto Douglas, Deputy Chief of the Air Staff, took over from Dowding on 25 November 1940. Their beliefs in air tactics had differed from pre-war days.

Left: Junkers Ju 87 Stuka dive-bombers in formation. An intergral part of *Blitzkrieg* tactics, the pinpoint accuracy achieved by their near-vertical dives was crucial in overcoming points of resistance, or destroying vital ground targets. However, the Stuka was an easy target over Britain, as Fighter Command pilots discovered. After severe losses it was withdrawn from further action in the Battle of Britain.

Left: Lord Beaverbrook, Minister of Aircraft Production, seen in a later photo with an American counterpart. Beaverbrook's reorganization of aircraft manufacture and supply gave Dowding the fighters he needed during the battle, building on much of the work already achieved by Air Marshal Sir Wilfrid Freeman.

Left: The Chief of the Air Staff, Air Chief Marshal Sir Cyril Newall, is shown centre. A number of politicians and senior airmen believed that he lacked driving force in leadership, yet his achievements in the RAF have been underestimated.

Right: Marshal of the Royal Air Force Lord Trenchard, pictured during a tour of stations and headquarters in the Middle East. Trenchard, 'The Father of the RAF', worked closely with MRAF Sir John Salmond to remove both Newall and Dowding.

Below: Possibly the finest aircraft in the Luftwaffe inventory in 1940, the Junkers Ju 88 was a fast medium bomber and, with *Blitzkrieg* much in mind, had a dive-bomber capacity. Heavily armed by the standards of its contemporaries, this view shows the 'gondola' forward under the nose section that housed a useful 20mm cannon.

Left: Sir Archibald Sinclair, the Secretary of State for Air, was leader of the Liberal Party and a close colleague of Winston Churchill in the War Cabinet. Sinclair and Dowding held each other in low mutual esteem.

Right: Bristol Beaufighters were just entering the night battle as Fighter Command struggled with AI radar to deter the bombers by night. Their heavy armament and improved interception methods brought growing success during the early months of 1941, after Dowding had left Fighter Command.

Left: The opening stage of the Battle of Britain saw daily attacks on Channel convoys by the Luftwaffe, partly to deny much-needed coastal trade and partly to test RAF defences. Scenes like this were frequent in June and July 1940. The escorting destroyer at the extreme right appears to have anticipated the fall of bombs and avoided danger by rapid acceleration–note the sharp bow wave.

Left: Despite No 11 Group's sterling efforts, some Luftwaffe bombers reached their targets. London was the scene mainly of the last stage of the battle as the night Blitz attempted to destroy the morale of a nation. Fire, dust and smoke shroud the sky-line, but the dome of St Paul's Cathedral stands out intact.

Right: Heavy AA defences were initially little more than a morale booster for the British public, but the ground defences gradually evolved better tactics, including fighter-free gun zones. Their increasingly accurate fire had a detrimental effect on the Luftwaffe bomber crews, forced to fly higher and bomb less accurately.

Above: The man whose sympathy for Dowding was ultimately subordinated to the needs of the war, yet who believed that he should be honoured and not forgotten, Winston Churchill. Here he is seen on a bomber airfield later in the war.

Below: Laying plans; Hitler in conference. The Führer's basic lack of understanding of air warfare and his delay in opening attacks on Britain were of great help to the RAF, especially Fighter Command.

Tizard in 1935. [29] From then until the early days of the war there was a constant and sometimes tortuous struggle to translate the benefits of RDF for Fighter Command. By February 1939 Tizard wrote to Dowding that, although difficulties over daytime fighting were being solved, he was 'mainly occupied with the night problem now', which was different, more serious and needed further experiments. [30] In July 1939 attempts were being made to equip night fighters for air-to-air combat 'in view of the present relative weakness of our night air defence'. [31] At the same time experiments continued with RDF, so that by the outbreak of war a ground station could place a fighter within five miles of its target and the aeroplane's airborne interception (AI) apparatus could guide it from three miles down to 200 yards, by which distance it was hoped that the pilot could see the enemy machine. [32]

Limited Luftwaffe night activity in the early months of the war was a blessing for the RAF, but basic problems remained. [33] In March 1940 Air Vice-Marshal R. Peck, an Assistant Chief of the Air Staff in the Air Ministry,[34] asked the CAS to form a committee to co-ordinate measures for defence at night and link up research and development by making practical experiments. There could, he wrote, be no doubt 'of the magnitude and urgency of the position of night interception',[35] a point proved by the fact that, by the following month, there were only six squadrons of Blenheims in Fighter Command, and these alone specialized in night fighting.[36] Peck's request was met by the formation of the Night Interception Committee on 14 March. At the committee's first meeting its chairman, Air Marshal Peirse, was prophetic, predicting that even if the Germans began daylight raiding with large numbers of aircraft, 'our good defences would force him to adopt night bombing'. Their meetings continued the progress being made, but with no speedy or radical breakthrough, so that by May the Chiefs of Staff Committee reported, 'our defence against night attack is still far from effective'. They doubted whether night attack alone would bring German victory, yet showed the long-held fear that morale was more vulnerable during the hours of darkness. [37]

Consequently, as the German offensive opened in the west on 10 May, Fighter Command, sorely pressed to hold the Luftwaffe's day onslaught, was even less prepared to counter night bombing. Nonetheless, in June night air defences had some success, largely because at that stage bombers flew low enough to be detected by searchlights, a fault soon remedied by the Luftwaffe. On the night of 19/20 June *KG 4* lost five He 111s.

Worse was to follow, however. At that stage information about German scientific and technological advances in air warfare was laid before Britain's political and Service leaders, who were thereby confronted with problems of night defence far greater than they had anticipated. [38]

On 21 June Dr R. V. Jones, a young scientist attached to the Air Ministry, attended a Cabinet meeting at which he unfolded to a sombre audience his knowledge and predictions of German advances in work on radio beams. Research over several months had shown that the laborious advances in defensive science and technology made by Britain had been overtaken by those of the attacking enemy. While the introduction of RDF into night fighters was making slow progress in the RAF, it became known that the Luftwaffe had at its disposal apparatus for laying radio beams across targets hundreds of miles distant. For example, the *Knickebein* beam was about 400 yards wide, could reach 300 miles and bombers could be guided along it with remarkable accuracy. Although Jones was at first confronted by the sceptical doubts of some other scientists, it soon became evident that the Luftwaffe's work was well advanced. [39]

The Germans had solved the problem of marrying science to technology with comparative ease. Theirs was the simpler task. It is far more straightforward to locate a large and static object such as a city, with a beam using a powerful ground transmitter, than it is to follow an aircraft, a small, moving target, using an airborne device. The information provided by *Knickebein* was transmitted to bombers through the Lorenz blind-approach receiver which all aircraft carried to assist landings, so crews required no special apparatus or training. The more accurate *X-Gerät* apparatus was fitted to aircraft of *Kampfgruppe 100*, which then acted as pathfinders, attacking targets with incendiaries to light them for the following main bomber force. In this way Luftwaffe bombers, guided by beams emitted from carefully located beacons, could be led to targets over mainland Britain. [40]

The extent of the threat had been unveiled to the Air Staff five days earlier. Those specially involved were Air Marshal Sir Philip Joubert, ACAS (R), Air Commodore Nutting, Air Commodore Lywood, of the Directorate of Signals, and, naturally, Sinclair, Newall and Dowding. When Joubert, the chairman, asked Dowding what response he believed should be made to the threat, the C-in-C answered in one word – 'Jam!'. Countermeasures were immediately set in hand under No 80 Wing to locate and jam or distort the beams. Masking beacons, known as 'Meacons', were set up and had reasonable success, but the extent to which the attackers held an advantage over the defenders soon became obvious. [41]

The Prime Minister himself was aware of the problems involved, largely through the closeness of Professor Lindemann, his scientific adviser. Lindemann, despite harbouring some early doubts of German ability to lay beams, soon recognized the threat and reacted with the enthusiasm of the converted. [42] Churchill, while appreciating Fighter Command's magnificent defence against daylight raids, now had to face new dangers from a campaign of night bombing which was far more difficult to counter. Consequently Dowding's reactions to German moves and, more especially, his response to advice offered, were of critical importance and under sharp scrutiny. In fairness to him it should be noted that on 16 July he did warn the Prime Minister of the potential dangers to civilian morale of night bombing, saying that there was no adequate night fighter for interception.

The widely accepted view that the overall failure of German daylight mass raids was the prime, or only, cause of the change to night bombing masks an important point. This is that, during the summer of 1940, although the Luftwaffe's main objective was to defeat Fighter Command, there was an intention to erode British economic power by bombing factories, docks, roads and rail centres by night. These targets, selected even before the war started, were raided with increasing regularity after the defeat of France in June enabled German Air Force units to be moved closer to Britain. Nonetheless, the relief brought to bomber crews, who could now fly in darkness without fear of attack from Hurricanes and Spitfires, should not be underestimated, and the night bombing campaign certainly restored their morale. [43]

These raids served a number of purposes. They provided good experience for crews in using beams to reach targets in darkness. They were also a constant disturbance to industry, transport and civilians, whose morale was tested. The raids were carried out with far lighter losses than had been incurred in daylight,[44] and were at least partly a riposte to night attacks made on German targets from July 1940. That month marked the opening of the RAF's strategic bombing offensive, which was not concluded until the end of the war. [45] The night bomber offensive should therefore be weighed in conjunction with, not separate from, the main Luftwaffe daylight campaign. [46] If this fact is accepted, an accurate assessment can be made of the reasons for Dowding's removal in November. The unified strategy is demonstrated particularly by examining some of the areas raided by night while the day battle was still in progress. For example, on the night of 10 July attacks were made on western Scotland, the Home Counties and the east coast. A Heinkel He 111 was shot down just after midnight on 26 July while laying mines in the Bristol Channel, while on the same night a Do 17 failed to return after bombing Rochford aerodrome. On 30 July raids were made in south Wales and the Midlands and, during the night of 15 August, after extensive day attacks had been launched, 70 bombers struck at places as diverse as Birmingham, Crewe, Southampton and Bristol. [47]

At Goering's Karinhall conference on 19 August, the decision was taken to increase the combination of day and night attacks on Britain, the latter being allocated to *Luftflotte III*, many of whose fighters were moved forward to the Pas de Calais to take part in the new offensive being launched against Fighter Command airfields. The way was prepared for night bombing on a greatly increased scale, particularly as Goering ordered raids against the British aircraft industry. He suggested that units should be allocated 'particular areas which they will come to know better during each successive raid'. Consequently the first really heavy night raid occurred on 28 August, while the daylight onslaught on Fighter Command was reaching a peak. That night, 160 bombers of *Luftflotte III* attacked Liverpool, an important industrial and transport centre within German plans. Raids on the city followed on each of the three succeeding nights, showing the Luftwaffe's determination to strike at a large target. [48]

Noticeable in these attacks was the inability of Fighter Command to intercept enemy aircraft. For example, on the night of 27 August, while German bombers crossed England to raid targets in the north, the Midlands and East Anglia, and while mines were sown in at least six points round the coast, Fighter Command put up 47 sorties. Only one intercepted a bomber – unsuccessfully. Three defending fighters, a Spitfire, a Hurricane and a Gladiator, crashed. [49] At that stage the Germans certainly held the initiative at night and were confronting Dowding with problems of daunting proportions. This was galling for him because in day raids his Controllers, although heavily pressed, could follow the enemy and direct fighters towards them. In darkness Fighter Command appeared unable to prevent the Germans striking at will.

Air Ministry Intelligence appreciated the growing scale of night bombing. A report on 3 September estimated that, between 8 August and 2 September, the Luftwaffe had employed an average of 160 bombers in day attacks and 120 at night. In the last week of the period the figures had been considerably higher, at 230 and 220 respectively. In the first week of September an aviation journalist noted that 'night raiding was widespread and hardly any of the larger industrial centres and ports of England and Scotland escaped'. However, a vital and redeeming feature, resulting from the Luftwaffe's lack of a truly heavy bomber, was that each aircraft carried only about one ton of bombs. [50]

PART 2: THE NIGHT BOMBER OFFENSIVE OVER LONDON

The turning point for the RAF came on Saturday 7 September. Not only did the change of target for day attacks from airfields to London take Fighter Command by surprise, but the subsequent night raid on the capital added to existing fires, some of which burned for days afterwards. Among these, in the words of a later official publication, were 'nine conflagrations (huge spreading areas of flame), nineteen fires that would normally have called for thirty pumps or more, forty ten-pump fires, and nearly a thousand lesser blazes'. A blaze at the Anglo-American Company's oil works at Purfleet had not been extinguished by 13 September. At one turn, the Luftwaffe had struck a grievous blow at the capital city. [51]

Churchill visited London's East End later in the day and saw for himself not only the suffering of ordinary people, but also the results of the RAF's inability to hold off the enemy. A few days earlier he had learned that, in the whole of the United Kingdom during August, 1,075 civilians had been killed by air attack and, as Gilbert points out, 'As the German raids intensified, Churchill was concerned by their effect on the population'. [52] The bleak reality was that during the night assault on London the capital's defences had

offered scant protection, only six night fighters taking off. As a German invasion was believed to be imminent and the invasion codeword 'Cromwell' was
issued at 8.07pm, it was essential that public morale was sustained and every
effort made to increase the effectiveness of AA guns and night fighters. [53]
London's ordeal, with its attendant worries for politicians and Service leaders, continued for several nights. Extra numbers of guns were sent to the capital in an effort to bolster morale, but it was not until 10 September that the
defences were able to put up a heartening, though inaccurate, barrage. [54] On
the night of 8 September 412 civilians were killed and 747 seriously injured,
and on the following night more than 1,700 casualties were suffered. [55]

An official account of the raids later claimed the Germans believed that
by concentrating on the east of the city, 'where there was a large and
crowded population', such panic would be caused that the Government's
position would be endangered and they would be forced to make peace. The
old fears over public morale were never far from the surface. 'Chips' Channon, after driving back through the East End on 16 September, wrote in his
diary 'the damage is immense, yet the people, mostly Jewish seemed courageous'. [56] The Germans, with no conspicuous success in the day battle,
made the most of the damage caused to their enemy's heartland. Broadcast-
ing directly from a bomber over London on the night of 11 September on
the German Home Service, an official of the Propaganda Ministry reported
that he could see 'the blazing metropolis of England, the centre of plutocrats
and slave holders, the capital of the world enemy number one'. After the fall
of bombs, he continued, 'but we still circle over the city a few times, so that
those below should hear that we are here'. [57]

The sudden intensification of night attacks, causing such great damage
for so small an expenditure, naturally led to the raising of urgent questions
over defence. As Gilbert points out, 'public concern was focused on the
Blitz'. How had it happened, and who was responsible for the Germans getting through? The Official Narrative notes that, while bombs were falling in
London, 'two Hurricanes were patrolling their Sector station at Tangmere
though they had received no instructions to intercept the enemy'. Guns in
the Inner Artillery Zone did not open fire until 9pm, 25 minutes after bombs
had landed in Battersea. [58]

The difficulties of firing a barrage at night were immense. It was estimated that, to give a one in fifty chance of bringing down a machine flying
at 250mph and 'crossing a vertical rectangle ten miles wide and four miles
high' (i.e., from the barrage balloons up to 25,000ft), about 3,000 3.7in
shells would have to be fired every second. Not surprisingly, it was recognized that only aimed fire would be effective. [59]

The root of the matter was that, while anti-aircraft guns were seen and
heard to be attempting something, however ineffective, Fighter Command
was doing little. The RAF's lack of both suitable apparatus and adequate aircraft to prevent night bombing was of small interest to civilians, who under-

stood nothing of airborne interception or ground controlled interception (GCI) but wondered why the fighters which were defending them so staunchly by day could not offer similar protection during darkness. A writer of the time asked if a special night interceptor was being planned. Pilots who had experienced night flying 'must have found by now whether or not the effective night fighter's characteristics are quite different from those of the day fighter'. [60]

In assessing the role of Dowding and Park in this new emergency, it should be remembered that the great raids on London started on the very day of the C-in-C's conference to discuss Fighter Command 'going down-hill'. There, his policy was criticised by Douglas, whose expanding influence within the Air Ministry is deduced from the preparations made for the later conference of 17 October. As Dowding's leadership in day fighting was coming under searching examination, the new failure of night air defence added to his troubles. The criticism also embraced Park, a close disciple of the C-in-C, whose squadrons guarded the capital's southern approaches. [61] Radical methods were needed swiftly to meet the new threat, with necessary improvisations, but Dowding's careful and methodical mind was not tuned to variations. He knew that the Beaufighter was the real solution to the problem, and that sending Blenheims, Defiants, Hurricanes and Spitfires into the night sky would lead to the destruction of few bombers. His policy was that there was little relief for targets which Germans were locating so accurately and attacking almost at will.

Dowding's report in October said that the enemy's navigational aids were so effective that he would 'be able to bomb this country with sufficient accuracy for his purposes without even emerging from clouds'. He went on to say that the Germans could bomb in the poorest weather, a 'most depressing fact'. [62]

The differences in outlook between the C-in-C and Douglas were shown in the latter's memoirs, when he wrote that Dowding had come to believe so strongly in radar equipped fighters 'that he had become a little blinded, I felt, to the more simple hit or miss, trial and error, use of single-engined fighters'. He and other influential RAF senior staff felt that, in spite of the disadvantages, an effort had to be made. [63] Dowding's attempts to meet the threat were demonstrated on 9 September, when about ten gun-laying radar sets were borrowed from AA Command and mounted at searchlight posts in the Kenley Sector, which lay on the path into London. The positions were linked to No 11 Group's Kenley Sector station, which then tried to guide night fighters towards the incoming bombers. In theory the sets, which were capable of plotting aircraft within 40,000ft, should have been a welcome addition to the defences. Dowding pinned faith in them, but in practice the AI sets in aircraft failed and the weather was poor. The so-called 'Kenley Experiment' continued, but without either the success or subsequent relief hoped for. [64]

On 11 September a meeting of the Night Interception Committee was held at the Air Ministry under the chairmanship of Sinclair to examine problems urgently. There was much discussion, during which Dowding explained seven methods of operating night fighters, but talk appeared to solve no problems. That point was undoubtedly noticed by Douglas, Joubert, Slessor, Saundby and Stevenson, all critics of the C-in-C's attitudes towards day defence, and all of whom were present. [65]

The slow development of RDF and fighters in night defence led to suggestions for unorthodox remedies, one of which had appealed to both Churchill and Lindemann for some time. This involved the dropping of small aerial mines, either from aircraft or attached to balloons drifting along the bomber stream. Lindemann minuted Churchill on 11 September, recommending their use as a stop-gap measure until the arrival of AI, claiming that even 100 mines might bring down 'a noticeable proportion of machines'. The Prime Minister, ever attracted to an adventurous enterprise, forwarded the minute to Newall and Dowding, enthusiastically encouraging them to examine the idea because of the urgency of the threat. [66] Such plans were regarded without favour by most senior RAF staff, who thought them rather bizarre. In his memoirs Douglas said the plan was ridiculous, 'a complete waste of time and effort', which gave Fighter Command 'a particularly acute headache'. His anger was also displayed in a letter written in 1961, in which he stated that the project, codenamed 'Mutton', wasted 'millions of pounds and tens of millions of man hours'. Nonetheless, such fulminations removed neither the threat nor the pressing need for a remedy. [67]

PART 3: THE SALMOND COMMITTEE

The new and radical approach needed in night air defence emerged on 14 September, not, as might have been expected, from the Air Ministry, but from the Ministry of Aircraft Production. Beaverbrook wrote to Sinclair, informing him that Marshal of the Royal Air Force Sir John Salmond, from his staff, was to undertake an enquiry in his Ministry related to the preparation of night fighters, and asked that the Air Ministry should provide all the information required. [68] Beaverbrook's letter received an instant and surprisingly agreeable response from a Ministry which appeared suddenly grateful that someone else had taken an initiative. On the same day Newall wrote a reply, welcoming the move,[69] and the Air Ministry sent a letter to Dowding, informing him that Salmond was to undertake 'a thorough enquiry into the equipment and preparation of night fighters', but then going further. The Air Council wanted the enquiry to be extended to cover 'all matters in connection with air fighting at night which are of common interest to the two Ministries'. They suggested that Air Vice-Marshal Quintin Brand, AOC, No 10 Group, should be a representative at the forthcoming enquiry. [70]

The choice of Salmond was widely approved. He was highly respected, formerly CAS, senior in age, rank and service even to Dowding and had been appointed Director of Armament Production in the MAP. The move was a shrewd success for Beaverbrook, whose worries over the effect of night bombing on his factories were given further fuel on 11 September, when he read a report, sent from Churchill, on the German *Knickebein* and *X-Gerät* navigation beams. At the same time, he was meeting the problem with an initiative sadly lacking in his old adversaries at the Air Ministry. [71]

Salmond was far from unwilling to serve, and it could well have been that the investigation of night defence began at his instigation. Evidence for this is strong. He had had a close working relationship with Lord Trenchard for some time, and they were the nation's two most senior airmen. Their attitudes, as shown from correspondence in the early days of the war, included dislikes of a separate Army Air Service, of dropping leaflets instead of bombs on Germany, of lack of governmental aggression – and of Newall. Also, neither man held Dowding in special repute. Trenchard's biographer wrote of a slight rivalry, or jealousy, holding them apart, in spite of a bond of mutual esteem. In their dealings over Dowding esteem outweighed rivalry or jealousy. [72]

On 12 September Salmond wrote to Trenchard, enclosing a copy of a paper on night fighting which he had given to Beaverbrook on the previous day. 'He said that he would show it to "someone" last night,' Salmond reported. 'Who this may be I do not know.' Salmond stressed the extreme importance of the matter and hoped that Trenchard would join him in what was obviously to be a crusade against the tardiness of developments in night defence, and thereby against Dowding. He claimed to have the names of those who had 'intimate experience in night fighting and its organization during the last war', so there would be no shortage of experience to work from. [73]

Salmond moved with the briskness and despatch for which he was renowned, and the first meeting of his committee was held at 10am on 16 September. As the enterprise had started at the MAP, this and the committee's two subsequent meetings were held at Thames House South, the headquarters of Beaverbrook's Ministry, and not at the Air Ministry, a point of some importance. The meeting's minutes[74] show that the discussion was held mainly among Beaverbrook's officers, with Salmond, Freeman, Tedder and Sowrey present, while Stevenson was the sole officer from the Air Ministry who was present all day. Douglas and Joubert, in the morning and afternoon respectively, sat in on the committee, and evidence was taken from two officers experienced in night fighting in Blenheims, and from a scientific officer attached to Fighter Command.

The meeting provided Douglas with a platform for criticising Fighter Command's practice over filtering, suggesting that the RDF information might be given straight to Groups; in this he received Tedder's support. The

Air Ministry representatives reported that Dowding 'did not care to risk air-craft, and particularly crews, in operations over enemy occupied territory', underlining his policy of offering careful defence rather than showing an aggressive spirit. Joubert then criticised the current use of night fighters, say-ing that he would be content with eighteen squadrons and claiming that AI equipped Blenheims were 'just wandering round in the hope of making a contact', but Stevenson strongly opposed Tedder's suggestion, which would have horrified Dowding, that separate day and night Fighter Commands might be considered.

The second meeting was held next day, when the committee comprised five of Beaverbrook's officers and two from the Air Ministry. [75] Those called to give evidence included an officer of the Fighter Interception Unit and Air Vice-Marshal Quintin Brand, who was dismayed that young pilots relied so greatly on radio telephone instruments and believed that they 'should be taught real air pilotage'. Details of the working of AI were given and its weaknesses pointed out, with the note that some operators 'were not suit-able for the work'. The presence of Squadron Leader Max Aitken can have been no random choice; not only had he been OC No 601 Squadron, with a fine record in action, but also he happened to be Beaverbrook's son. Judging by the committee's later conclusions, his contribution made an impact. His opinion, certainly not shared by all other pilots, was that the Hurricane was a good night fighter 'in the hands of a pilot who was well experienced in night fighting'. He also believed that experienced pilots aged at least 26 were better for night work, which could be done by those 'who had had enough' of day combat, and that AI was 'a valuable adjunct' in night interception, for which separate squadrons were essential.

It is noticeable at this stage, while many urgent changes were being sug-gested and evidence taken from various quarters, that no voice had been heard from either Headquarters, Fighter Command, or from No 11 Group, which were most closely involved. The most charitable explanation is that the committee's members, realizing Dowding's and Park's responsibilities at the time for day defence, thought it unreasonable to make extra demands. There exist, nonetheless, two pieces of evidence against that interpretation. One is that Dowding was called on to attend the third and final meeting of the committee on 18 September, and the other is that the committee's rec-ommendations, in the form of a report, were produced, dated and signed by Salmond on the previous day, after the second meeting and before Dowding had been heard.

The third meeting lasted only for the morning,[76] with questioning of Dowding and Major General Newton of AA Command. Dowding agreed that a night fighter unit should be formed, and 'would not oppose' a night fighting section being added to Fighter Command. He was, however, against too great a decentralization of control, believing that too much was left to Sector Commanders. After explaining various methods of employing night fighters, he objected to the delegation of filtering from his headquarters to Groups. During the afternoon Salmond, Tedder and Sowrey of the MAP, together with Joubert of the Air Ministry, drafted some conclusions, yet the bulk of the committee's work and the production of their findings had been finished after the first two days. The report, consisting of eighteen points, was then sent speedily to all relevant parties. The production of such a clear and concise series of recommendations within so short a time, to meet an urgent problem, had been a remarkable achievement.

At that stage, in spite of Fighter Command's inability to halt the night bomber, Churchill certainly still held Dowding in high regard. On the evening of 21 September, together with Lord Gort, the C-in-C dined at Chequers with the Prime Minister. German night bombing was discussed, especially their use of parachute mines, and there was talk of retaliation. In relating the visit, Colville wrote that Dowding produced a paper about night interception, which Churchill described as 'masterly' to Beaverbrook. It concerned future prospects, with the skilful use of AI in Beaufighters and gun-laying radar. Dowding was suggesting what would be done and could offer no sovereign remedy for the present, a point noted by others at Chequers who were less impressed than Churchill. Colville's diary for the following day referred to Lindemann, 'who says, *sotto voce*, that Dowding's "masterly" paper is his first admission of a number of facts which have been impressed on him for ages'. Considering Lindemann's influence over the Prime Minister, it was a bad omen for Dowding that this opinion was held of him. This factor was to recur in October, when Lindemann complained that Fighter Command could do more to counter radio beams. [77]

Having received the Salmond Report, the Air Ministry acted quickly to discuss and implement its proposals. On 22 September Sinclair met Beaverbrook at Thames House South to examine the document,[78] and the Air Council was convened two days later to review recommendations. Salmond, Douglas and Joubert were present to elucidate various points, and all appeared to be most enthusiastic. [79] Subsequently, three days later, a copy of the Salmond Report was sent to Dowding, together with a letter from the Air Council which examined each paragraph and then set out proposals which the C-in-C was required to implement. In general the Air Council accepted Salmond's suggestions, with wide agreement and undoubted relief over the general aims, a number of which were contrary to Dowding's belief and practice. [80]

PART 4: DOWDING *V* THE AIR STAFF

While the C-in-C that day was mulling over the report and the Air Council's letter and finding fault with many of the proposals, Salmond and Trenchard were exchanging letters whose contents display a mutual determination to relieve Newall and Dowding of their commands. When the question of Dowding's removal from office is explored, the correspondence proves that the question of his attitude towards night defence was crucial in resolving his fate, and also that Salmond's and Trenchard's part in ensuring it has previously received insufficient acknowledgement. In his letter Trenchard stated, 'Yesterday I told you that I was going to call up and see if I could go round and see Beaverbrook and talk about one or two things. You said that if I did there was something you very much wanted me to say.' He added that he would see Beaverbrook within two or three days, but would not fix the time until he had heard from Salmond. [81]

Salmond's immediate reply is a remarkable letter, because there appears to be no document in any public collection which is more openly critical of Dowding and, being private correspondence, it lacks the restrictions of a formal minute or note. [82] At the time many voices obviously criticised the C-in-C, but from those in high office who wrote opinions, this letter is the most powerful example, giving the historian insight both of the writer and his subject. Salmond opened by speaking of the failure to cope with night bombing, adding that on his report to Beaverbrook he had included a note recommending that 'Dowding should go'. Because of his close work with the C-in-C, Beaverbrook expressed reservations, however, and 'is now a bit shaken on it'. When Sinclair was told the same thing, 'I could see that he was frightened of putting it forward', although Salmond believed that the CAS and, almost without exception, the Air Staff, agreed with him.

The attack then turned to include Newall. Before the previous day's meeting of the Air Staff, Salmond told Newall that he would raise the matter of Dowding, but he 'seemed a bit rattled at the prospect' and asked Salmond not to do so. Yet previously he had claimed that he was extremely keen for the C-in-C to go, referring to 'what enormous difficulties he and the Air Staff had had in getting him to accept new ideas on fighting at night'. In Salmond's view, Dowding had no qualification as a 'Commander in the Field', lacked humanity and imagination, and was living on the reputation gained by his pilots in daylight combat. Next, the fates of Dowding and Newall were linked, showing the growing feeling that general changes were needed in the leadership of the RAF. [83] Beaverbrook had suggested that, if Dowding had to go, so should Newall, who also carried responsibility. Salmond raised no objection, listing what he saw as the CAS's frailties during the Norwegian and French campaigns. 'If you see Beaverbrook I would very much like you to bring up the matter of Dowding, and also of Newall', he concluded, 'because I believe that with these two in the saddle, we are not getting the best we should expect.'

This letter clearly shows the depth of feeling held by some other senior officers inside the Air Ministry against retaining Dowding at Fighter Command, and also demonstrates how both Service and political leaders were being made aware of the controversy. What has not emerged from most previous writings on Dowding's removal is the intensity of Salmond's opposition to him, which is clear from a note in Salmond's own hand at the top of the letter. It reads, 'My views which I eventually explained to the Prime Minister who practically blew me out of the room – after three weeks I met him again in the "Other Club". Winston said I was right. Dowding had gone, "but it nearly broke his heart"'. He then adds, chillingly, 'Had the Prime Minister not agreed I had decided to appeal to His Majesty'. Salmond's relentless energy for change was indeed a scythe.

As Dowding left Fighter Command on 25 November, Salmond's meeting with Churchill could not have been held before about 4 November, although he had written to the Prime Minister on 5 October. In determining Churchill's attitude towards removing Dowding, which has received some unjustified criticism, it is noteworthy that, in the period from late October to early November, as will be shown, he heard direct criticism of the C-in-C from Flight Lieutenant P. Macdonald, MP, probably between 18 and 24 October; from Salmond around 4 November; and from Sir Reginald Clarry, Vice-Chairman of the 1922 Committee, on 6 November. This rather destroys the ill-conceived notion that Leigh-Mallory engineered a political plot to remove Dowding.

Dowding's attitude to the proposed changes over night fighting is summarized on his copy of the Salmond Report. As was his custom, he read the document and made blue crayon marks to emphasize his opinion of the proposals. Agreement with a point was denoted by a tick, some reservation or doubt was given a question mark, and disapproval was registered with a cross. Of the letter's eighteen points, fourteen were marked. Beside these are three ticks, five question marks and no fewer than nine crosses. [84]

The C-in-C's long-standing reputation for lack of co-operation was, in the minds of the Air Ministry, strongly reinforced by his reply, written on 27 September, in which he examined the suggestions individually but was unimpressed by many. He dismissed the proposals for removing filtering from Headquarters, Fighter Command, to Groups, which had been rejected by him in January 'and was finally disposed of'; he asked to be 'spared the necessity of discussing the question afresh'. Other suggestions were rejected as impractical, premature, unwise or beyond his understanding. [85] Dowding, however, was not alone in marking documents. An unknown hand at the Air Ministry added comments beside points in his letter. These included, 'The need is already urgent and long overdue', 'Pert', 'The same reason which has prevented any change months ago', and 'Obstruction. Why?'. [86]

Differences between Dowding and the Air Ministry are clear from their receptions of the Salmond Report. A note from Sinclair to Beaverbrook spoke of 'useful discussions' from 'Sir John Salmond's very useful Committee', and referred to changes 'which I know you are as anxious as I am to press on with'. Sinclair gave as particular needs AI sets and Mk IV AI equipment, adding that anything that could be done to accelerate Beaufighter production would be most welcome. [87] The urgency can also be deduced from a minute sent by Saundby to Douglas on 30 September, giving details of tests made on Blenheims without turrets and recommending that all rear armament should be removed from these machines. [88]

The next day, while moves were being made at the Air Ministry to promote the employment of Big Wings in day fighting, thereby altering Dowding's policy, the C-in-C was called to a meeting on night air defence. Of those present, including Sinclair, Salmond, Joubert and Douglas, not one could be called an ally of Dowding, an impression reinforced by the minutes. When the C-in-C asked for it to be placed on record that, in his view, transferring filtering directly to Groups would not improve the efficiency of night interception, Joubert, not to be upstaged, asked for his opinion to be recorded that such delegation *would* improve interception both by night and day. Dowding's letter to the Air Ministry was discussed 'paragraph by paragraph', the subsequent draft note stated. [89]

At Headquarters, Fighter Command, on 3 October, Evill examined the copy of Salmond's report and minuted the C-in-C, asking what action should be taken on its various suggestions. Referring, for example, to paragraph 2, dealing with filtering at Groups, he asked on what lines action should be started. Dowding's reply was curt and categorical; 'NONE, except what Air Ministry specifically orders. D.' [90]

By the turn of the month the defences had enjoyed scant success against a growing night bomber offensive. Fighter Command's Order of Battle for 3 October shows 52 day squadrons and 11 night squadrons, with a further 4½ squadrons forming. [91] Yet, during the previous month, while the Luftwaffe had flown an estimated 6,135 sorties at night, only four German bombers had been destroyed by fighters. Such a small credit had to be set against the debit of 1,500 civilians killed in the week ending 26 September, 1,300 of them in London. A further 1,700 were killed in the city during the following seven days, apart from heavy damage suffered. [92]

Such attrition concentrated the minds of politicians on the question of air defence, and none more than the Prime Minister. Events over the following few weeks gave him the opportunity of viewing Dowding in a different light, because previously he had dealt with a C-in-C at Fighter Command who was by himself, in active and apparently successful control of the battle against day raiders. Now Churchill was judging him against a novel background where Dowding sat among a group of other senior RAF officers who disagreed strongly with his policies on night defence, with the arguments and tensions becoming apparent. This raised questions over his leadership. Were all of the C-in-C's many opponents misguided and spiteful, or was there more than a grain of truth in their assertions?

On 3 October Eric Seal, the Prime Minister's Private Secretary, drew his attention to the disquiet felt. Seal had talked with Lindemann, and wrote of their shared belief that more could be done to prevent night bombing, with the suggestion that Churchill should 'send for the responsible officers' of Fighter and AA Commands 'and probe deeply into the details of what they are doing and ask for day to day reports of progress'. He added ominously that Dowding had the reputation of being conservative 'and of not being receptive to new ideas'. [93]

The barrage from Trenchard and Salmond continued next day. The former wrote that recently he had done all he could 'of rubbing in about Dowding, and I am going to rub in again today', adding that he knew of some of his views reaching 'the right quarter'. He believed that it would be difficult for Portal, the CAS designate, to dismiss Dowding unless further pressure was exerted. His next sentence could imply either a degree of deviousness for which he was not noted, or an attempt to distance himself from responsibility for the impending execution. 'I feel your pressure has done as much good as anything I know from what I have heard from other sources,' he wrote, 'but I never mention that you and I are working in agreement on the matter as I feel it is more use our apparently being independent but working for the same cause. '[94]

Bolstered by such support, Salmond had no hesitation in writing to Churchill with a directness which aimed straight at the target. 'I am most anxious to put to you the case for a change in the holder of the important position of Commander-in-Chief Fighter Command,' he began. 'Recently on Lord Beaverbrook's instructions, I have carried out an enquiry into Night Air Defence, the result of which, together with what has since occurred, make a change, in my opinion, imperative.' He finished by showing that his was no lone voice. 'This opinion is also very strongly held by most, if not all, Service members of the Air Council.' That night in London more than 200 people were killed or injured, adding weight to the Prime Minister's responsibility to have the best leader in charge of night air defence. [95]

The pressure on Fighter Command and its leaders was maintained inadvertently by Beaverbrook, who still lost no opportunity of crossing swords with the Air Ministry over the protection of his factories. On 30 September Beaverbrook telephoned Sinclair, suggesting that fighters should be stationed next to factories where possible, but Sinclair, in a courteous and rational reply, explained the impractical nature of the scheme. Two days later Sinclair extended an olive branch by sending Beaverbrook a copy of an American newspaper report, written by the journalist Helen Kirkpatrick, which commented on the rift between their two Ministries and was highly critical of Beaverbrook. Sinclair called it 'Mischievous and contemptible tripe,' written by a correspondent of 'eccentric opinions'. [96]

None the less, this did not prevent the Minister of Aircraft Production sending a memo to Churchill on 6 October, complaining of damage to the Hawker factory at Langley and saying that the balloon barrage was too thin. 'Can we have action now?,' he finished. A minute of the same date claimed that the Secretary of State for Air and the Secretary of State for War should protect factories still in production. Naturally, any extra demands on Fighter Command compounded Dowding's task at a difficult time. [97]

In his memoirs, General Pile noted that when a problem of high importance arose, Churchill immediately took over the chairmanship of meetings on the subject. As he became increasingly aware of the intricacies of aerial defence he ordered a Night Air Defence Committee to be formed under his leadership. [98] Dowding was required to attend the first meeting, on 7 October. Around Churchill sat seventeen officers and officials burdened with the daunting task of blunting the night Blitz, but of these only Beaverbrook and Pile could be listed as Dowding's possible allies. Those who regarded the C-in-C in a less favourable light included Sinclair, Newall, Salmond, Douglas, Joubert and Lindemann, a formidable opposition. Overall, business was conducted at pace with discussion, *inter alia*, of Beaufighters and AI, G/L radar sets and AA personnel. [99] Later, Newall chaired a smaller meeting whose report was endorsed by the Prime Minister, and the committee were tackling a desperate problem with energy and combined purpose. [100]

However, Churchill was now witnessing at first hand the divisions which had grown between Dowding and other senior staff. A particular point of controversy was the decentralization of filtering, and the C-in-C wrote to the Secretary of the War Cabinet detailing disagreements with his colleagues. Regarding the Salmond Report, he claimed to have agreed with all the proposals, 'but in some cases unwillingly and under pressure'. Churchill had asked him for a report of points of disagreement, and in this Dowding said that the greatest issue was decentralization of filtering, with which he disagreed very strongly, and detailed twelve points to support his view. The episode underlined what Dowding saw as adherence to his basic principles, but his opponents viewed as proof of stubbornness and unwillingness to co-operate. [101] Churchill was left to draw his own conclusions, but before doing so he minuted the Air Ministry, seeking their opinion on filtering, and thereby presented them with an opportunity of showing how far apart the two sides were. [102]

Dowding dined at Chequers on 13 October, and reported that German night attacks lacked purpose because they failed to concentrate on one target, or to make the best use of incendiary and high-explosive bombs, news that was greeted with relief.[103] Nevertheless, Churchill's worries were far from removed the following night. While he was dining with Sinclair and other ministers a particularly heavy raid was launched with 365 aircraft, during which bombs landed near Downing Street and much heavy damage was caused. [104]

On 16 October, while Dowding was still wrestling with the controversy over employing Big Wings in the daylight campaign and preparing himself for the following day's conference on fighter tactics, Churchill ordered his name to be added to the list of officers entitled to see Enigma decrypts. This proves the error of those who later claimed that the C-in-C had been privy to these reports throughout the daylight battle.[105] At the same time, Churchill learned that in the previous week nearly 1,400 people had been killed in London alone. [106] The magnitude of the threat from night bombing had not lessened, and he had experienced at first hand the subsequent controversies inside the RAF. Rightly or wrongly, Dowding had given the impression of believing himself to be the only man in step.

Consequently, Haslam's assertion that it was the C-in-C's handling of night raids that eventually led to the call for his replacement has much evidence to support it. Nevertheless, this cause must be set beside potent criticism of his control of day fighting tactics, through Park and Leigh-Mallory. His opponents at the Air Ministry found fault in him for both. The burden of the dual obligation can best be realized by exploring Dowding's problems on certain days in a period of just under six weeks. For example, on 15 September, while the C-in-C was following each step of an intense daytime battle, his mind was also exercised by the previous day's notification of the creation of the Salmond enquiry. [107] On 27 September, when heavy daylight raids were aimed at London and Bristol, with some fighter-bombers penetrating to the capital,[108] Dowding was sending his uncomplimentary observations on the Salmond report to the Air Ministry. [109] And on 8 October Dowding wrote not only to Leigh-Mallory concerning Park's complaints against the Duxford Wing,[110] but also to the War Cabinet with highly critical views on filtering. [111] As the relief of the load carried especially by No 11 Group arrived in late September, the troubles of the night campaign expanded.

As Dowding prepared for the conference of 17 October he was well aware of the weight of opposition gathered against him, and appreciated that his adversaries were trying to impale him on a Morton's Fork of criticism, concerning his conduct of day and night fighting. They were intent on disparaging him for either one, or both. It could not have escaped his attention that a guiding hand behind the ground swell of opposition was that of Air Vice-Marshal Sholto Douglas, Deputy Chief of the Air Staff.

7

CHANGES AT FIGHTER COMMAND

PART 1: A CRITICAL MEETING

There has been deep disagreement and controversy over the circumstances of Dowding's and Park's last days at Fighter Command. Both attended the Air Ministry conference on 17 October at which Douglas, Leigh-Mallory and Bader were among those also present. This meeting, it has been suggested, was part of a plot behind which lurked No 242 Squadron's Adjutant, Flight Lieutenant Peter Macdonald, MP, who had brought the controversy over Wings to the Prime Minister's attention, probably after prompting from Leigh-Mallory. Therein, according to a number of writers, was the prime, or only, reason why Dowding and Park were replaced as soon as conveniently possible after a political conspiracy at the top level. [1] Both men went virtually unrewarded, carrying with them seeds of rancour which grew throughout the remainder of their lives. In 1968 Park still felt compelled to comment that, 'to my dying day I shall feel bitter at the base intrigue which was used to remove Dowding and myself as soon as we had won the battle',[2] while Dowding's similar feelings were channelled through Robert Wright's book, published in the following year. [3] Was there a 'base intrigue'? A careful examination shows that, between the conference and the replacement of both leaders, a number of previously little-recognized factors emerged, appearing as pressures from both political and Service sources.

The meeting of 17 October has assumed a position of such importance for those who see it as a carefully staged plot to undermine Dowding and Park that a detailed review of the occasion is revealing. The first point to appreciate is that this was a meeting which Dowding himself should have called, because the lack of liaison between his two subordinates had led to an antipathy between them which affected the most efficient deployment of Fighter Command's resources. In Douglas's later view, anyone seeing Park and Leigh-Mallory facing each other would realize the strength of the clash 'between these two forceful personalities'. The fact that Douglas took the initiative and convened the meeting can be seen as a step taken in a plan for his own advancement, but Dowding's indecision had left a vacuum which someone in authority had to fill. Headquarters, Fighter Command, had failed in this, so the responsibility was taken at the Air Ministry, where Newall was at the end of his time and the lead was taken by his deputy, Douglas.

When Dowding and Park arrived at the meeting they found their opponents waiting in metaphorical Big Wing strength, with Quintin Brand their only possible sympathizer or ally. Looking round, they could count six senior officers who were, or had been, opponents of their policy. These were Douglas, Joubert, Leigh-Mallory, Slessor, Stevenson and Crowe. A seventh, Portal, the CAS designate, though not a party to the previous stages of controversy, favoured the majority view. What came as a complete surprise to Dowding and Park was the presence of Bader, taken along by Leigh-Mallory, in the words of a later writer, as 'one of the men actually doing the daily job'. [4] However, neither then, nor in later official correspondence, did Dowding or Park object to Bader's presence. [5] In the absence of Newall, who was indisposed, Douglas took the Chair. Although there was some later disagreement over the minutes, those published give a reasonably full impression of what was covered. [6]

The agenda is usually examined in terms of daylight tactics because, of the 27 items noted in the minutes, 22 dealt with that subject and they provide the apparent reason for the calling of the meeting and its main content. Yet the shorter part dealing with night air defence, although covered by only five items in the minutes, was important in underlining Dowding's differences with the Air Staff. It reinforces the contention that the controversy over employing Wings in daylight battles was far from the sole reason for the subsequent changes made in Fighter Command's leadership.

Douglas opened the meeting by setting out three propositions to be considered. The first was to outnumber the enemy; the second was to have a co-ordinated plan, with some squadrons engaging fighters while others tackled bombers; and the third was for the top layer of fighters to be higher than the enemy's. These ideals, he admitted, could not always be obtained, but he invited comments. In response, Park opposed the use of Wings in his area for reasons of time, distance and cloud, and claimed that, for him, pairs of squadrons had achieved better results. [7]

When Dowding entered the discussion he made no reference to the controversy which had soured his Command, and anyone who believed that he would restate his basic doctrine of controlled defence, or even praise No 12 Group's policy or offer the balm of compromise was disappointed. Instead, he began by discussing the early identification of the size and intentions of groups of raiders and of improving Control systems. It is noticeable that he did not speak up forcefully on Park's behalf. [8]

Leigh-Mallory, in his turn, said that he was anxious to help No 11 Group, declaring that his Wing of five squadrons would be airborne in six minutes and 'over Hornchurch at 20,000 feet in twenty-five minutes'. If the formation intercepted only once in ten sorties, all would have been worthwhile. Then Joubert continued his criticism of the existing system by mentioning the shortness of warning given to Groups, a point of long-standing dissension between him and the C-in-C. Dowding replied that his orders were for an arrow to be placed on the Operations Table as the first 'counter' was received, although very-high flying raids presented problems.

As discussion developed, with Park defending his position, it was generally agreed that extra fighter support would lead to more of the outnumbered enemy being destroyed. Dowding then said that, with his Group commanders, he 'could resolve any difficulties of control involved in sending such support', a rather surprising claim in view of his signal failure to achieve this earlier. All believed that the time factor was a great difficulty.

Bader's presence has been seen variously in terms ranging from a Machiavellian plot to an honest attempt to inject a practising pilot's realism into the Air Staff. From the minutes he appeared to say little, with a contribution reported by only 41 words, and he apparently reminded his listeners that time was the essence of the problem, with a large number of fighters likely to obtain the most effective results. However, the fact that he was produced on the day like a trump card by Dowding's opponents, to show that Wings worked in battle, had greater significance than his few words.

After the weeks of controversy, with accusations and counter-claims, the meeting proceeded surprisingly quietly. Portal sought, and received, an assurance that No 12 Group's other responsibilities would not be affected by the despatch elsewhere of a Wing; the importance of early warning from RDF was stressed; then Douglas summed up. He emphasized the value of Wing formations, noting that they would operate over No 11 Group's area and that Dowding would 'resolve any complications of control'. Sometimes two Wings, provisionally known as a 'Balbo', 'for want of a better name', would fly together and all squadrons would operate from the same Sector, being controlled by the Sector Commander. However, the fighter leader of a mass formation would dispense with Sector Control and lead his aircraft into action. When VHF radio was used, in theory a maximum of seven Balbos could be operated. Wings would fly from aerodromes where they would not have to turn to gain height advantage, and would consist, if possible, of the same squadrons.

The meeting then turned to night interception and, from the minutes, Dowding's disagreement with Air Ministry policy, a battle that had grown since 7 September, became clear. He was unwilling to meet the proposal that two Hurricane and two Defiant squadrons should form a night fighting Wing 'on a 1914-1918 basis', believing that employing Hurricanes at night was dangerous and unsound. He had agreed reluctantly to accept the Air Staff decision to do that, showing what his opponents viewed as an uncooperative attitude.

By the end of the meeting all of Park's pleadings over previous weeks had come to nothing, and he left realizing that methods would change. The C-in-C had uttered no public word to support his case and had been outmanoeuvred. Park later claimed that Douglas 'was the public prosecutor' and that he and Dowding 'were condemned – that is the only word'. [9] On the other side, the result was a triumph for No 12 Group, and Leigh-Mallory was to be allowed to participate in the remaining battle on his own terms. Bader's belief in independent control for a commander leading a large Wing of fighters had received an official accolade, and this conference marked an important advance in his career.

But the day also marked the emergence of Douglas, who thus far had been involved in the controversy only by way of minute sheets, through staff in the Air Ministry and by pressure applied behind the scenes. Through attending meetings of the Salmond Committee just a month earlier, then the first meeting of the Night Air Defence Committee on 7 October, he was well aware of the disagreements over night defence. Therefore, when opportunities of leadership were offered he was not slow to take them, and after the meeting of 17 October his hopes were closer to realization.

On 20 October the draft minutes of the conference were issued and copies despatched with requests for any amendment. [10] As might have been expected, the reactions fell into two categories. Those favouring Big Wings, that is 'The Air Ministry Group', were prepared to accept them with only minor alterations. Dowding and Park, whose practices had been questioned critically and, to a lesser extent, Quintin Brand, were dissatisfied and requested changes.

Not surprisingly, the first counter-attack came from Park, whose reply enclosed a sheet of amendments which he asked urgently to be included 'because I cannot agree to the important statement which I made being omitted'. The Air Staff note, he complained, 'contained some misinformed criticism' of his policy. At the meeting he had spoken from previously typed notes which he now wanted to be added to the minutes as a 'statement by AOC 11 Group'. This codicil, however, was guaranteed not to find favour with his adversaries, claiming, for example, that Douglas, Dowding and Portal had all agreed with Park's current policy, which should be continued against future mass bomber attacks. Nor, possibly, were they to be impressed by his criticism of the morale of No 12 Group's squadrons, which had been taught that in the south-east area safety could come only by employing Wings of four or five squadrons. Nor again would they approve of the complaint that the Duxford Wing caused confusion to fighter and ground defences south of the Thames and to the air raid warning system. Park, a doughty fighter, was determined to speak out in his own defence against what he saw as injustice. [11]

Dowding's reply was remarkable, making no defence of the policy which he had instituted and Park had put into practice. Instead, his main attention was fixed on smaller quibbles. He disliked the word 'Balbo', although he was prepared to accept 'Wing', 'Swarm', 'Mass' or 'any term that anyone can think of in preference to "Balbo"'. He showed more awareness over the references in the minutes to night defence where he was resolutely opposing change, asking that it should not be said that he agreed 'reluctantly or otherwise' to Hurricanes being used at night, because 'I am carrying out orders which I believe to be dangerous and unsound with our present strength of fighter squadrons'. For Dowding's opponents this comment encapsulated his intransigence. Although related to night defence, it summarized for them the need for a general change in the leadership of Fighter Command. [12]

Leigh-Mallory, not unnaturally, was pleased to accept the main part of the minutes. His only queries concerned the radio control of Balbos by High Frequency, but he contended that, with the existing Group and Command frequencies, seven Balbos could be operated simultaneously through VHF radio. [13]

Park's request for the inclusion of his statement was a matter for discussion within the Air Ministry, and a minute was sent to Douglas asking whether alterations should be made to meet it. [14] Stevenson replied on his behalf on 31 October with a refusal, and the comment that Park's criticisms were not 'appropriate to the minutes of a meeting of this kind'. [15] The reply, sent to Park the same day, informed him that the Air Staff would not agree to the inclusion of his statement, partly because of its length and also because it was held to be out of keeping with the minutes, which were 'intended more as an aide-memoire than as a detailed report of the discussions'. [16]

When Quintin Brand queried several points in the minutes he also was told that no alterations could be made. The Deputy Chief of the Air Staff 'was anxious to keep the minutes as short as possible', but his letter would be placed on the relevant Air Ministry file. [17]

By this stage the momentum gathered at the meeting, especially under Douglas's leadership and guidance, was maintained and the accuracy or fullness of minutes was not to impede it. Those officers in the Air Ministry searching for changes in the leadership and tactics of Fighter Command were in no mood to allow 'The Old Guard' any room to manoeuvre. Dowding had raised little complaint, but Park's defence had to be by-passed. Subsequently the final minutes emerged on 1 November and were distributed both to those who applauded them as an innovative triumph and to the minority who felt their bias. [18] Dowding's criticism of the word 'Balbo' cut no ice at the Air Ministry and the name continued to appear, but his complaint over changes in night defence received a better hearing and the minutes reported his opinion of 'a dangerous and unsound policy'. They added that he agreed 'with reluctance to implement the Air Staff decision', a phrase that underlined his differences with his colleagues.

PART 2: A CONTINUING CONTROVERSY

Any thought that the conference would bring a rapid declaration of peace and goodwill was premature. The controversy continued, not only over the content of the minutes, but also through the subsequent degree of co-operation between the two sides. This was primarily because neither Leigh-Mallory nor Park had changed opinion about who was to exercise command of squadrons flying over No 11 Group's area. Park believed that the Duxford Wing should operate where and when he chose, but Leigh-Mallory wanted them to be under the control of his Controllers at Duxford, flying together as a composite force.

However, the nature of the day battle had changed. The *raison d'être* of employing Wings to break up mass attacks no longer held, because during late October many sorties were made by Bf 109s and Bf 110s converted into fighter-bombers, making fast hit-and-run raids. Balbos were of limited use in countering these tactics, so although the conference had looked forward to a new style of defence, a different approach to problems was required at the end of September, when German plans altered course. The last big raid by a mass German formation in daylight was made on 30 September, with four major attacks across Kent and two others over Portland. [19]

In one sense this was an acknowledgement by the Luftwaffe that their basic aim of overwhelming Fighter Command before launching a seaborne invasion, and of breaking public morale, had failed. Later German views – those of Kesselring, for example – sometimes refer to the campaign against Britain as part of the general Western air war, lasting from May 1940 until June 1941, an indivisible offensive. Yet it was at least the magnitude of their losses and the accompanying pressure on aircrew which caused them to change course from the day battle in the form they had wanted. Between 30 June and 30 September, 621 of their bombers were destroyed. This in itself was a victory and solace for Fighter Command. [20]

The new tactics, using fighters in a way never intended by either their designers or pilots, were certainly troublesome. Nonetheless, small formations of fighter-bombers, each equipped with one 250kg bomb, flying at great heights and racing in to drop tiny loads on London or on airfields, were more of a nuisance than a threat of defeat to the RAF and civilians below. To meet the threat, steps were taken by Dowding and Park. These were necessary for several reasons. First, the Bf 109 with a two-stage supercharger had a better performance above 15,000ft than either the Hurricane or Spitfire. Additionally, both RDF operators and the Observer Corps had difficulty in detecting and tracking German fighters flying so high and fast, especially during cloudy weather. When the change of Luftwaffe tactics was recognized in late September, two Spotting Flights were formed whose dangerous task was to fly very high and send reports back to Headquarters, No 11 Group, on the height, size and direction of incoming raids. [21]

Leigh-Mallory wrote to Park the day after the conference, offering the services of the Duxford Wing,[22] but while Park appreciated the gesture, he could not forget past criticisms. [23] He would be pleased to have the Duxford squadrons, he wrote, 'if possible once a day'. He added that it was essential for his Group and Sector Controllers to know the Wing's position so that ground defences could be warned and 'confusion to the fighter defences and the issue of unnecessary air raid warnings' avoided. Park laid down six points under which he would be prepared to accept the Wing entering his area via the Hornchurch Sector. These, he claimed, not allowing tact to override previous controversy, would prevent his own squadrons 'wasting their time investigating friendly aircraft'. After listing those elements in his area that had earlier been confused by the operation of the Wing, he finished with the hope that 'it will get some good fighting'.

When Park sent Evill a copy of the letter, he stressed that the new German tactics would give the Duxford Wing little time to reach the action before the enemy 'would be on their way home'. [24] Therefore he had offered No 12 Group the choice of flying a standing patrol, which they had declined, preferring to receive sufficient warning to reach the battle 'before the enemy has slipped out of Kent'. Never losing an opportunity of expressing what he believed to be the frailties of the Duxford Wing when operating over his territory, Park wrote again to Evill on 26 October, regarding misunderstandings between the two Groups during the previous day's actions. [25] Leigh-Mallory had sent four squadrons south, but reports of their position had been received from No 12 Group only while they were north of the Thames, and after that they had to be tracked by the Observer Corps. Near Gravesend, the Wing 'broke up and apparently returned home by single squadrons'.

Park had felt uneasy about the activities of the Wing, and had ordered his own squadrons to intercept a raid which they had erroneously been reported as engaging. 'Two good Spitfire squadrons' caught the enemy 'in spite of the absence of the Duxford Wing' before any vital point was bombed, he wrote, hammering home his lessons. As a result of the failure, Leigh-Mallory had now agreed to try 'the simple procedure suggested to him in my letter of October 20th', and Park, who had always doubted No 12 Group's ability to fix the point of its Wing south of the Thames, wanted this information passed on to Dowding. Yet when the report was laid before the C-in-C on 27 October, he still appeared indecisive, minuting that No 12 Group should go south only by invitation and that they might be needed 'in their own territory'. [26]

A remarkable step was then taken; one which, had it occurred two months earlier, could have altered the whole nature of Fighter Command's activities. Belatedly – and far too late to change the pattern of events – Dowding produced an order for Park and Leigh-Mallory, entitled 'Reinforcement of No 11 Group by No 12 Group' and announced with an air of decision previously lacking that 'the following principles are laid down'. [27] The first was that No 12 Group should be given good notice when help was needed. Then came the imputation that, in the past, No 11 Group had requested assistance too soon, and that in future it would probably be limited to times when raids were building over the Dover Strait. The fifth point was that Leigh-Mallory should not send less reinforcement than required, 'but he may send more at his discretion', a palliative to his views and also proof that Dowding, in spite of later claims to the contrary, was not disapproving of Leigh-Mallory's policy. As if to redress the balance, he next said that it was 'imperatively necessary' for No 12 Group to inform Park of the position of their formations, which should stay within range of R/T control. He ordered that arrangements should be made directly between the Groups, and that No 12 Group should inform the Command Controller of action taken.

To maintain the momentum, Evill minuted the C-in-C next day, seeking permission to publish a memo to Controllers to explain their new role, but Dowding asked him to wait in case the Groups suggested alterations.[28] However, it was too late to amend the entrenched attitudes of both sides, and over subsequent days Headquarters, Fighter Command, showed great interest in the activities of the Duxford Wing over No 11 Group's area.

On the following day Park issued Instruction No 35 to his Controllers. [29] This informed them of the later arrangements made for operation of the Duxford Wing and did not, for once, enumerate the faults of the past, but offered a statement of future procedures. By 0900 hours each day it was hoped that the No 12 Group Controller would inform his counterpart at Uxbridge when the Wing would be at 'Readiness'. Then, as soon as Park's headquarters learned from RDF that enemy aircraft were gathering over the French coast, Leigh-Mallory's Controller would despatch his squadrons of the Duxford Wing to a position near Hornchurch, waiting for them. The Hornchurch Controller would follow the Wing's progress, notifying its location 'at frequent intervals'.

Park also wrote to Evill and examined claims made by No 12 Group squadrons, especially the 'Dux Balbo', when they had operated during September over what he termed 'No 11 Group territory'. [30] He pointed out that their claims of the proportion of the enemy destroyed, compared with their own losses, were far higher than those made by other squadrons during six months of intensive fighting under his control. That included 'just about every squadron in the Command!'. Park was highly critical of No 302 (Polish) Squadron, 'said to be one of the best performers and prime movers in the Duxford Balbo'. Although working with two of his 'excellent squadrons', its results had been poor when flying in a Wing of three squadrons, or as one of a pair, when 'it had done worse'. The squadron had failed to maintain contact with other squadrons, and had suffered losses when its pilots could not find their way home. He claimed that these points were listed to underline a major criticism of Wings, namely that their squadrons failed to develop essential fighting tactics and could not 'fend for themselves'. Looking ahead to the forthcoming winter's vagaries of weather, when squadrons would have to work alone, he added bitterly 'the No 12 Group mania for Balbos had done a grave disservice'.

In examining three recent occasions when the Duxford squadrons had come south, Park said that they had not found, let alone engaged, the enemy, whereas pairs of No 11 Group's squadrons, guided towards the enemy, had achieved immediate results with those raids. The Wing had failed, in his opinion, because the Balbo's squadrons were 'pre-occupied in maintaining their mass formation'. He was for ever telling his squadron leaders to be flexible in tactics, yet Leigh-Mallory's men were imbued with the idea that it was unsafe to fly in formations of less than five-squadron strength. He personally had visited Nos 74 and 302 Squadrons to explain to them the different conditions obtaining in his area, where they were close to the Luftwaffe. Relentless to the last in his scorn, he compared No 12 Group's results unfavourably with those of Nos 10 and 13 Groups, and he obviously had little faith in Leigh-Mallory's support. In No 12 Group, 'the Balbo idea had weakened the offensive spirit of individual squadrons'.

Reports of action submitted by No 11 Group were examined at Headquarters, Fighter Command, on 29 October, when the raids were mainly attacks on London by Bf 109s, hardly easy targets for a Balbo. This was a day of importance in estimating the strengths and weaknesses of Big Wings. The first report dealt with morning intruders, showing that RDF gave about 35 minutes warning.[31] According to the times shown by Park, No 12 Group's contribution was less than promising because the Wing was requested at 1030, did not get off the ground for 17 minutes and left Duxford at 1107. An accompanying criticism claimed that with an earlier start they could have intercepted a raid made on the Charing Cross area. Park could not forbear to add that No 602 Squadron, operating alone, tackled 50 Bf 109s without loss to themselves, emphasizing his opinion that 'a resolute Squadron well led is more than a match for the enemy fighters'.

His more severe censure of the Duxford Wing was included in the report on the afternoon battle, during which some 200 enemy aircraft attacked in three waves, bombing several aerodromes. [32] The No 12 Group Wing, he claimed, took off at 1608 with three tasks. The first was to patrol the Maidstone-Sheerness line, then to intercept two raids that were crossing the Thames Estuary into Essex, and finally to make a sweep across north Kent. Under the heading 'Action by Fighter Squadrons' he showed the worrying aspect of Fighter Command's policy at the time, in that two Groups with differing backgrounds and leaders enmeshed in rivalry were required to co-operate over one area without the benefit of a single commander.

At 1630 the Duxford Wing was asked to intercept the raids that were approaching Essex, but could not be contacted because of R/T traffic between them and their home base. The opportunity of engaging the enemy disappeared, and North Weald was bombed before a pair of No 11 Group squadrons could fly there. Nor, according to Park, did the Wing carry out the next allotted task, which was to intercept raids heading for Biggin Hill. Instead, they were recalled by Leigh-Mallory, who had received reports of bad weather and 'was afraid of the difficulty of landing so many squadrons on one aerodrome'. Fortunately, he added, the Germans took no advantage of the gap left in the defences, probably because they saw extra No 11 Group squadrons climbing in the Biggin Hill area.

Such reports, regularly issued by Park, show a sense of frustration and error that would, in less straitened circumstances, have bordered on farce. Nevertheless, bitterness restricted his vision and promoted inflexibility over incorporating the Duxford Wing into a composite defence system. He was attempting the superhuman task of implementing a barely workable policy in which he lacked faith, in collaboration with a fellow commander for whom he felt scant respect. Above them, the C-in-C who had planned for a battle against unescorted bombers was strangely hesitant in ensuring clarity over tactics to be followed in different circumstances.

Nonetheless, Evill as SASO continued to carry out his duties conscientiously and gathered details of the Duxford Wing's activities, resulting from Park's accusations. A report written by Group Captain Lawson, G/C Ops. at Dowding's headquarters, dated 2 November, noted that the Balbo, which had been ordered off in good time, need not have assembled over Duxford but could have gained height while flying south to the patrol area.[33] Then came criticism of Park's policy, with the question of why the Wing was called for so quickly when there were additional squadrons in No 11 Group which could have been used. This was less than fair to Park, who had been pressed repeatedly to call on No 12 Group for help after giving them early warning. Lawson then showed an appreciation of the demanding role laid on Park when he said that it was 'almost impossible for No 11 Group, or No 12 Group for that matter, to control effectively the Wing when it passes into No 11 Group's area'. This was the nub of the problem, and should have been foreseen and addressed long before.

He next mentioned an attempted solution in which some No 11 Group fighters would fly with the Wing over the southern area and, using an R/T frequency, enable all aircraft to be plotted by Park's Controllers, but Lawson added with no small reservation that it remained to be seen how the plan would work out in practice. He finished on a note of doubt, suggesting that the Wing's operations in the south had brought few benefits and the events appeared to support Park's views. The Wing seemed to be too unwieldy for rapid operation. Also, No 12 Group should watch for possible assaults on their own area when the Wing had gone south, and at least one squadron should be retained in the Duxford Sector.

Evill passed the report to Dowding with several conclusions and recommendations.[34] In the first, he too failed to comprehend Park's invidious position concerning requests for assistance from Leigh-Mallory. He wondered why the Duxford Wing had been called within five minutes of the plot of the day's first raid, which was made by only nine aircraft. That judgement passed by the roots of the controversy. In Evill's view, no call for assistance should have been made before the second or third attacks, but he also acknowledged, with regard to the afternoon raids, the basic problem of controlling the Balbo over No 11 Group's area. He concluded that, in view of German raids on East Anglian aerodromes, No 12 Group should be careful not to neglect 'its own responsibilities'.

Dowding's minute in reply displayed insensitivity towards the antagonism that had festered for months. [35] On the one hand, Leigh-Mallory had been desperate to get his Wing into action in the south. On the other, Park had been blamed for calling them too late, yet the C-in-C's response announced that No 12 Group should not be called in unless Park's squadrons were in trouble. 'It is absurd to call on No 12 Group,' he finished, 'when only two of 11 Group's Squadrons have been dispatched,' a reply hardly likely to satisfy either of his Group commanders.

The simmering controversy was not yet resolved, but had lost much of its point through the changes in German strategy and tactics. These presented the RAF with the awesome task of countering night bombing, a burden that came increasingly to occupy Dowding's attention. Nonetheless, there was still time for him to issue another and, as it transpired, final Operational Instruction on 13 November, regarding the reinforcement of No 11 Group by its neighbours, a document divided into 'Principles' and 'Procedure'. [36]

Under the former heading, attempts were made at compromise which, however, failed to address the fatal weakness that, when in action outside its own area, the Duxford Balbo was being asked to serve two masters simultaneously. The Wing's employment would be limited to 'special circumstances' and No 11 Group should meet most responsibilities with its own squadrons. The actual methods for the Balbo were to be decided by No 12 Group, 'subject to the allotted task being adequately performed', and Leigh-Mallory was reminded of his duty to protect his own area. Nevertheless, the enemy might be surprised by 'an occasional large formation by pre-arrangement', which sounded more like arranging a social calendar than meeting an unexpected German mass raid.

An innovation suggested under 'Procedure' brought some relief to No 11 Group's Controllers by ordering that the Big Wing should not fly south of the Thames, or of the south bank of the Estuary. Generally, No 12 Group would have two squadrons at 15 minutes 'Readiness', and requests for more would come from the Command Controller. In action, Duxford would have control of its own squadrons while No 12 Group would be given, simultaneously with No 11 Group, 'all available RDF information down to the latitude of Dungeness-Gris Nez', which Leigh-Mallory had begged for during the previous months. Such arrangements, nevertheless, however carefully they were planned, depended for fulfilment on a large degree of goodwill and co-operation. Whatever quantities of those virtues had existed in early August had evaporated by mid-November when Instruction No 43 was produced in a belated attempt to mend fences.

In fact, Park and Leigh-Mallory were still at loggerheads through the weapons of written reports right up to 17 November, by which time the C-in-C had learned of his posting on a mission to the USA. Here was proof indeed that Dowding had failed to solve their disputes. The last argument resulted from Park's report of No 11 Group's activities in September and October in which, once again, he lost no opportunity of belittling the Dux-ford Wing. [37] 'In ten sorties it effected one interception and destroyed one enemy aircraft', he claimed, showing at every turn a dislike of the Wing and offering no single word of thanks for their efforts, or for incorporating their strength into the defensive system. Leigh-Mallory's reply to these points was equally direct, again blaming the lateness and paucity of information from No 11 Group as the prime cause for the lack of success of his Balbo. [38] In his view, the Duxford Wing had proved that a formation of up to 60 fighters could be controlled satisfactorily and suffered fewer casualties.

Dowding's vacillation over these differences, in which he was able to sympathize with both points of view simultaneously, lasted until the end. In a letter to the Air Ministry on the day after the Prime Minister had confirmed Sinclair's decision to remove him from Fighter Command, he wrote that he supported 'the 11 Group rather than the 12 Group point of view', yet added that this opinion 'must be qualified by the remark that the use of small forma-tions must not involve attempts to climb in the presence of the enemy who has already achieved height superiority'. Once again he was failing to offer a clear policy to be followed harmoniously by both Group commanders. [39]

PART 3: INVOLVEMENT OF POLITICIANS

Writers who have examined Dowding's controversies with the Air Staff have made much of the conference of 17 October, but have overlooked the signif-icance of another problem facing the C-in-C that day. A letter marked 'Per-sonal and Private' arrived from Churchill, enclosing a paper on night air defence written by Admiral Phillips, Vice-Chief of the Naval Staff. [40] The paper had been produced at the Prime Minister's request, and was 'purely private and for my information. I send it to you on the same footing.' Dowd-ing was asked to comment. It appears that Churchill, while realizing how far Dowding's views and approach diverged from those of his colleagues, appreciated the weight of responsibility laid on his shoulders and was offer-ing help. The gist of the paper, however, was similar to the thoughts of the Air Ministry and therefore unlikely to find favour.

Phillips wrote that, to his knowledge, many RAF officers 'both on the higher and lower levels' held the strong opinion that the problem should be tackled in different ways. Airborne Interception promised well for the future, but did not 'deliver the goods today', so simpler methods should be introduced, employing eight-gun fighter squadrons. There were, claimed

Phillips, 65 squadrons in Fighter Command, and three should be employed on night interception to counter the great menace of the Blitz.

Like a number of Dowding's critics, he looked back to what had happened during the First World War, when two fighter squadrons had stopped raids on London 'in about six weeks', then compared the situation with Fighter Command's inability at the start of the current war to protect North Sea convoys by using 'more scientific methods'. It had succeeded, he asserted, after the Admiralty's suggestion of returning to 'simpler bow and arrow methods' of patrolling the sea lanes. The Admiral also believed that fighters should patrol over London on 'Fighter Nights', when the guns would be silent. He was sure that the population would be satisfied if enemy aircraft 'were brought tumbling down on the housetops'.

Dowding's reply gave the Admiral's opinions no quarter.[41] The note was returned with marks beside twelve points on which he commented, often laconically, parrying almost every suggestion made. The C-in-C referred to the plan for employing fighters as a 'Micawber-like method of ordering them to fly and wait for something to turn up', but in his view the only salvation lay in having AI for fighters and radio aids for searchlights. He added in his own hand that he would try a Fighter Night, but thought it unlikely to succeed. 'Will wish to try when fighter is better than gun.' One mark of a great tactical commander in war is his readiness and ability to improvise, but in this Dowding was singularly lacking in the face of what was feared to be a considerable threat. Undoubtedly his search for an ideal night air defence was laudable, but it failed to meet the problem. Churchill, who would not have forwarded the Admiral's suggestions had he not favoured them, was unlikely to be impressed with the reply.

Soon after this, the Prime Minister gained further evidence of the gulf between Dowding and the Air Staff when he received a reply from Sinclair to his minute enquiring about the details of filtering. [42] In essence, Sinclair believed that Dowding's principle of passing all filtering through his headquarters brought earlier air-raid warnings for civilians, but led to squadrons being called to action less quickly. The Air Ministry preferred filtering to go straight to Group headquarters, firstly because this had already been done since the formation of Nos 9, 10 and 14 Groups and secondly, in the case of night interception, because Salmond's 'authoritative committee' had recommended it. Thirdly, when all aircraft were shortly equipped with Identification Friend or Foe (IFF), filtering would be decentralized, and lastly, when larger numbers of aircraft were encountered in 1941 the Fighter Command filter room would be overwhelmed by congestion. Once again, the Prime Minister was forced to question Dowding's principles. In this case the Air Ministry gave the impression that, whereas the C-in-C's scheme had worked in the past, they had longer vision and were planning for the future.

The rising star of Douglas's ambition was seen on the same day, when he chaired a meeting on Lorenz beams,[43] and over the following week he was present at several investigations into the urgent changes needed in night air defence. Also, on 21 October he attended the second meeting of the Night Air Defence Committee,[44] again with Churchill as chairman, and was able to see the Air Ministry overriding Dowding on a crucial matter; they ordered that three eight-gun fighter squadrons should be earmarked for night fighting. [45]

The taking of three Hurricane squadrons was an important step in Dowding's decline, epitomising the superseding of his logical approach to night defence by the pragmatism of the needs of the moment. There was no time to develop an ideal solution and, with so many squadrons available, emergency measures had to be taken. Although many pilots recognized the Hurricane's general unsuitability as a night fighter, the feeling that something should be done rested in the minds of many and was summarized by one of No 85 Squadron, posted south on 23 October. Two days earlier was Trafalgar Day, 'and "England expects"'. He added that fighter pilots had a duty to defend Britain by night as well as by day and, as London was being bombarded, 'where were we, its appointed guardians, yet incapable of defending its seven million citizens?'. It was high time to come to their rescue, and the challenge 'could not be refused'. [46]

The Prime Minister's perception of the widening gulf was sharpened by a letter he received from Dowding on 24 October, complaining not only of the cost of changing the filtering procedure, but also of 'the expenditure of my time in arguing with the Air Staff every intimate detail of my organisation'. He added a point of which Churchill was now acutely aware, and one which could no longer be overlooked. The C-in-C wrote, 'I have to fight the Air Staff on so many important issues'. [47]

During October British scientists drew deductions from the bombing pattern adopted by the German pathfinder *Geschwader*, *KG 100*, and their predictions were an accurate assessment of the techniques which would be employed at various stages later in the Blitz and which were subsequently used by the RAF. A note from Lindemann to Churchill on 24 October suggested that, as the *Geschwader* were dropping many incendiary bombs which could not be aimed accurately, the aircraft were probably fitted 'with special devices to assist in blind bombing on these expeditions', so that they could start fires on the target which following aircraft could see. [48] Such predictions from scientists were worrying for the Government, and brought the question of defence against night bombing to wider notice. There was also concern over the growing rate of civilian casualties, which were so much heavier in night raids than during daylight attacks. Quoting official figures, a contemporary aeronautical magazine gave the casualties for September as 6,954 killed and 10,605 seriously injured, an average of 250 killed and 350 injured every day, so although civilians had proved to be remarkably resilient under attack, there was constant pressure on morale. [49]

From the end of October until mid-November Dowding's control over night defence was often bypassed. He still had hopes of profit accruing from the Night Interception Trials he held in the Kenley and Tangmere Sectors, but the results were disappointing as a rapid solution to problems. [50] The C-in-C spent much time on them. 'I am just off on a nocturnal expedition,' he wrote to Beaverbrook on 29 October, 'and will ring you when I get back and try and fix a convenient time for a short talk.' [51] It is now obvious that his aim for the ideal requirement was admirable, seeking fighters equipped with AI and controlled by ground radar. For him, the 'nocturnal expeditions' had confirmed his belief that haphazard methods would bring only 'an occasional fortunate encounter', but the Germans were still bombing at will. [52]

Far greater impetus came from the Air Ministry, where a note on 26 October from Sir Arthur Street, the Permanent Under-Secretary, to various officers, demanded action on the Salmond Report and showed how it should be registered. [53] Group commanders later held a conference to discuss night defence,[54] and the next day Churchill, at a meeting of the War Cabinet Defence Committee, summarized their problem. National survival, he stated, depended upon 'the maintenance of life in this island', and that postulated an excellent air defence and 'successful countering of night bombing'.[55] The extent of the problem facing the nation and, his enemies would have claimed, Dowding's failure to meet it, is displayed through examining the figures of successes achieved by night fighters. During September and October the Luftwaffe flew an estimated 11,180 sorties at night, causing widespread damage and taking a heavy toll of civilians, especially in London. In that period the RAF shot down seven machines.[56] One senior officer recollected that, in an effort to counter criticism, Dowding insisted, on a night of bad weather, that the Defiants of No 264 Squadron should be put up to demonstrate that Fighter Command was trying to do something. Crews were instructed to bale out if they were unable to land.[57]

An example of political intervention in the affairs of the RAF was shown earlier, when Irene Ward's contribution was noted.[58] Those who believe that there was a political plot to overthrow Dowding are mistaken, but certainly several politicians exercised what they recognized as their duty and right to offer opinions on matters of air defence, and a number of these related directly to Dowding's strategy and tactics in battle.

The Adjutant of Douglas Bader's No 242 Squadron was Flight Lieutenant Peter Macdonald, then aged 45, who held a dual role. Not only did he have duties with the squadron, but he also carried the considerable responsibility of being Member of Parliament for the Isle of Wight, a position he had held since 1924. Macdonald was perfectly placed to hear the complaints made daily by his squadron commander at Duxford, that there was little opportunity of becoming involved in the main battle. At some stage of the controversy Macdonald visited Parliament and met Harold Balfour, the Under-Secretary of State for Air. According to Balfour's autobiography, he refused to discuss the disagreement with Macdonald, who 'then asked if I could arrange for him to see Churchill'. Balfour replied that he could not, but that as an MP he had the right to seek an interview with the Prime Minister. Macdonald followed up this advice, and through the agency of one of Churchill's secretaries, probably E. A. Seal in view of his feelings towards Dowding, a meeting was arranged. After that, according to Balfour, 'down the pipe-line came the Churchill enquiries'.[59]

None of the books that relate the incident offers a date for the meeting, and the only remaining source of information, the Chartwell Papers, will not be open for some years. Even there, according to Martin Gilbert, the Prime Minister's engagement diaries, 'though full are not complete'.[60] Balfour is unreliable. He speaks of his own visit to Duxford on 2 November before referring to Macdonald's intervention, which was, in his story, followed by the Air Ministry conference of 17 October. He also mentions visits made to Duxford by the Prime Minister and also the Secretary of State for Air 'just a week before he asked me to pay my visit'. On examination, the Duxford Operations Record Book shows that Sinclair was there on 26 October in company with Sir Louis Greig and Sir Hugh Seeley, but there is no mention of a visit from Churchill, an event hardly likely to escape mention in the aerodrome's record.[61] Probably Macdonald's meeting with the Prime Minister occurred in the week following the Air Ministry conference of 17 October. Then, when Churchill asked for further investigations to be made, Sinclair visited Duxford on the 26th, an event also mentioned in Sir Hugh Dundas's diary for that day, and Balfour about seven days later.[62]

Macdonald's intervention was most likely made on his own initiative and not, as some have suggested, as part of a conspiracy instigated by Leigh-Mallory or Bader. Sir Denis Crowley-Milling, who flew in No 242 Squadron at the time, has stated categorically that 'Douglas Bader, L-M and all of us were totally unaware of this approach', and Bader learned of it only after the war.[63] Others have impugned ignoble motives to this action, yet no one has produced any evidence to support the accusation. Macdonald's purpose is uncertain. The kindest explanation offered is that he was fulfilling a Member's duty of informing the Prime Minister, in the national interest. Another reason offered is that he saw the opportunity of becoming involved in affairs of State in which he believed No 12 Group to be in the right. The least charitable critics accuse him of 'sneaking' behind the back of a C-in-C to whom he should have demonstrated loyalty.[64]

What has seldom been recognized by those who link Dowding's fate solely to the controversy over daytime tactics is that the Prime Minister, by the time of Macdonald's intervention, had possessed for over two weeks Salmond's forthright letter asking for Dowding to be replaced. At the same time Churchill himself, through his chairmanship of the Night Air Defence Committee, had been able to make a close judgement of the Commander-in-Chief, Fighter Command, and his relationship with his colleagues.

As soon as Balfour had visited Duxford he wrote a report, generally known as the Balfour Memorandum, in which his judgement firmly supported Bader and Wing Commander Woodhall, the Duxford Sector Controller, who had lost no opportunity of laying before him their ideas and grievances. [65] Balfour stated that his visit had confirmed fears gained by Sinclair in the previous week that there was a conflict of operational views between the two Groups. The differences had 'become a personal issue with the pilots', with No 12 Group feeling resentful against Park and his Group, and also against the Air Ministry.

A catalogue of dissatisfaction followed. Balfour wrote that no improvement had come after the conference of 17 October and the Duxford Wing had not engaged the Germans since the end of September, a comment which displayed a lack of awareness of the change in enemy tactics. Duxford squadrons were always called too late to fly into action as a Wing. They were facing resistance from No 11 Group, who appeared to 'object to their poaching on that Group's territory and are jealous of the Wing Formation being likely to shoot down 11 Group Germans'. Nonetheless, they claimed to have friends in No 11 Group who were entirely sympathetic to them, agreeing that the Wing was being ignored or wasted. These No 11 Group pilots were 'fine material', but as a result of constantly facing enemy forces in superior numbers were becoming 'unnecessarily shaken in their morale' and, Balfour added, were not holding off the enemy, which could be achieved by employing larger formations. Bader had told him that the Wing looked forward to a renewal of mass daylight raids, when, given time to gain height and position, they were certain of causing heavy casualties. Yet there had been a complaint that the Fighter Command Controller was not permitted to transmit RDF information from south of the Thames. Woodhall had obtained some from the Observer Corps, but this initiative was now stopped.

Copies of this memorandum were sent immediately to Sinclair and Portal, and to Douglas, who wrote to Dowding, enclosing a copy of the findings, with a covering letter that left no doubt where his sympathies lay. [66] Douglas referred to the differences between Park and Leigh-Mallory which 'were so patent at the conference', and asked the C-in-C to act decisively. The quarrel was leading to bitterness not only between the two Group commanders, but also between the squadrons in the two Groups. This situation had been apparent for some time, and could not be allowed to continue. He asked Dowding to remedy matters by 'an authoritative statement of your views', a not unreasonable request for a decision which would be better than an intervention by the Air Ministry trying to act as referee.

Douglas again unfolded his colours by approving of Leigh-Mallory's viewpoint. It would be good sense, he suggested, for the Wing to be encouraged, even by attacking the enemy on the way home, which was a restatement of his belief held from pre-war days. He claimed to have a feeling 'which may not be justified', that Park had 'a subconscious aversion to

161

another Group coming down and fighting in his area', but hoped that more information would be passed to No 12 Group to assist their quick response. Finally, he asked that the matter should be left in Dowding's hands, adding the postscript, 'The Under-Secretary of State asks me to say that he hopes Bader will not get into trouble for having been so outspoken'.

The memorandum was passed by Dowding to Evill for investigation, and the SASO concisely dissected it into four points. The first, regarding insufficient RDF information being passed to No 12 Group, had already been dealt with by him through an Order. Their complaint about being refused Observer Corps reports had arisen because, according to the Southern Area Commandant of the Corps, these requests interfered with essential work. Thirdly, answering the grievance of the Wing being called too late, Evill believed that, on the contrary, they had been called far too early recently by No 11 Group. The last point, relating to lost opportunities of destroying enemy aircraft, was now out of date because the Germans had changed their style of attack. [67]

Using Evill's Minute, Dowding instantly replied to Douglas, rebutting each point made yet admitting the extent of the controversy. [68] He agreed that there was so much mutual ill-will and friction that he had decided to withdraw the control of combined operations between the Groups from Park and Leigh-Mallory and 'issue orders through my own Operations Room'. At last there was to be a single commander in battle. Dowding went on to point out that such continuous operations of the Wing of five squadrons could not be justified presently, and that No 12 Group should guard their own area. Leigh-Mallory had commitments of his own and 'should "keep his eye in the boat"'. Finally, obviously riled, the C-in-C replied to the postscript, wondering why an Under-Secretary of State had listened to accusations from a junior officer against the AOC of another Group, then written them down 'with the pious hope that the officer will not get into trouble'. He scathingly suggested that Balfour, who had been in the Service during the Great War, should have known better.

He then turned to Bader, the rising star for some senior RAF officers. Dowding believed that Bader had been responsible for a good deal of the ill-feeling caused and, whatever his other merits, he suffered 'from an over-development of the critical faculties'. It might be better to move 'young Bader to another station where he would be kept in better control'. The pilot's 'amazing gallantry' would probably protect him from disciplinary action. By this time, however, unknown to him, Dowding was approaching his final days at Fighter Command. Ironically it was he, not Bader, who was about to be moved 'to another station'. For Dowding's opponents, Bader's aggressive attitude epitomized a new chapter in the war, so ranks were closed to protect the chief practitioner of flying Wings in action.

On 17 November, after Dowding had learned of his own future, Portal, the new CAS, wrote to him, referring to the correspondence which had followed the Balfour Memorandum. [69] The order was severe, informing him that Sinclair had directed that no reproof should be offered to either of the two Duxford officers for what they had said. The sharp edge of criticism found in so many of Dowding's previous responses to the Air Ministry had left him when a reply was made. He wrote simply that 'no reproof has been or will be offered by me to either Woodhall or Bader'. [70]

As Under-Secretary of State for Air, Balfour had a duty to be concerned with events at Fighter Command. He possessed a dual qualification for this, through his experience as a former fighter pilot and also in his role as a politician, answerable to Parliament. There is no doubt where his beliefs lay in the controversy. The extent of Balfour's involvement will probably never be fully known, although as he was an astute politician with 'an excellent political nose',[71] it must be suspected that his influence was strong. For example, on 5 November, during discussion with Stanley Bruce, he spoke of differences between the Air Ministry and Beaverbrook, who 'could only think of the war in terms of a fortnight ahead' and had influenced Churchill. Both agreed that the appointment of Portal and Freeman had made 'a great improvement in their higher direction of the Air Force'. The talk then turned to the feeling that the time had come when 'Dowding should be removed from the Command of Fighter Command', which Bruce put down to the C-in-C's 'incapacity to co-operate with anyone'. Balfour's main argument was that the tide was running strongly against Dowding, who would be replaced within three months. In that case, would it not avoid friction if he were to go immediately? As a replacement, Balfour had suggested Joubert but, according to Bruce, 'he was only one of several that they have in mind'. [72]

Another recorded political intervention came on 6 November, when Sir Reginald Clarry, one of the vice-chairmen of the 1922 Committee, wrote to Churchill. He had chaired a meeting and had been asked to write and tell the Prime Minister of the lack of confidence felt for Dowding by 'certain quarters of the personnel of the force', and this gave grave concern to his Executive. Churchill's reply recommended that the 1922 Committee should not become 'a kind of collecting house for complaints', but he obviously took notice of their opinion. [73] Where did Clarry gain his information, and who persuaded him to write?

The members of the Executive Committee at that time, under the chairmanship of Mr W. Spens, appeared to have little interest in, or knowledge of, Air Force matters. The closest, probably, was Admiral Sir Murray Sueter, who had had connections ever since his Royal Naval Air Service days. Others, such as Colonel Charles Ponsonby or Mr W. Emrys Evans, were hardly close to the wrestling match within the Air Ministry. The minutes of the meeting held on 6 November, at which 78 members were present, show no evidence of the origin of Clarry's complaint. After formal business, the Committee was addressed by Mr A. V. Alexander, First Lord of the Admiralty.

The nearest association with the controversy could have been through Macdonald or Balfour. Worries over night defence were raised at the meeting of 16 October, when it was suggested that a debate be held 'in Secret Session on Air-Raid Defence generally, and especially of London'. Concern over Dowding's leadership on night defence was prevalent then and, as the conference on day fighting tactics followed the very next day, there could have been a connection. If so, the link might have been Balfour, who later addressed the Committee on 4 December on methods being adopted to counter the night Blitz. [74] Others taking an interest in the air war at this time included Sir Louis Greig and Sir Hugh Seeley, both of whom had accompanied Sinclair during his visit to Duxford on 26 October.

Certainly a number of politicians were well aware of Dowding's difficulties with the Air Ministry. For example, Hugh Dalton, Labour MP and Minister of Economic Warfare, met Sinclair on 15 November and discussed Portal, the new CAS. 'I praise Portal,' he noted in his diary, 'and he says that there was strong pressure for Dowding which he is sure he was right to resist. Dowding has now got stereotyped, keeps things to himself, and has been losing the confidence both of his subordinates and his equals.' These remarks summarized the Air Ministry's opinion of the C-in-C. 'Within a few days,' Dalton continued, 'it will be announced that he is being shifted to a job in America where he can do very good work.' [75]

PART 4: REPLACING DOWDING AND PARK

Some of the greatest confusions regarding changes in leadership at Fighter Command after the Battle of Britain relate to the sequence of events leading to Dowding's removal from office on 25 November. These came to light – and underwent considerable scrutiny – after the publication of Wright's book in 1969. There, he quoted Dowding as saying that he was dismissed immediately by a telephone call from Sinclair 'in the second week in November'. Upon questioning the 'perfectly absurd' decision, Dowding was told that it was final, 'with no explanation for such a precipitate step taken'. For Wright this typified the long story of discourtesy shown to Dowding 'by officialdom', and he added the C-in-C's comment that 'they just got rid of me'. His confused diatribe continued over the following pages, where both he and Dowding gave the controversy over Wing tactics as the root cause of the dismissal, with no mention of differences over night fighting, or any other reason. [76]

Later, Wright blamed the part played by Churchill in Dowding's fortunes, suggesting that Service leaders who earned the Prime Minister's disfavour were replaced, and offering the example of Wavell. He added that, at about the time of Sinclair's alleged phone call, Beaverbrook suggested that Dowding should visit the USA and, 'at the Prime Minister's request', the C-in-C went to see Churchill. According to Wright, Dowding claimed that Churchill was unhappy about his being replaced at Fighter Command and expressed surprise that it had been done 'in the moment of victory'. [77] Wright believed that Churchill knew well what was going on. He wrote of 'the political intervention of the adjutant of Douglas Bader's squadron', adding that since Dowding's 'lone stand against Churchill at the Cabinet meeting of 15 May', until the controversy over Wing tactics, the C-in-C 'was a marked man'. [78]

Such unsupported accusation breeds dangerous myth, and elements of this emerged in January 1970 through correspondence in *The Times*. Marshal of the Royal Air Force Sir John Slessor questioned whether Sinclair would have treated Dowding in such a manner,[79] a point later supported by Professor R. V. Jones, who referred to the Secretary of State as 'a Minister of exquisite courtesy'. [80] Both correspondents spoke highly of Dowding, although Slessor suggested that possibly the C-in-C's memory was faulty.

Two broadsides were fired in reply. The first came from Dowding, who wrote, 'in a matter as grave as this, the record of what I remembered could not fail me', and asserted that Wright had recorded his experiences 'correctly and exactly'. [81] The next day Wright wrote of his intense search over a long period to find what had happened, but then trimmed by acknowledging that there might have been an interview, a point that throws some doubt on his research. [82] The waves of turmoil were quietened as, for the first time in the controversy, documentary proof replaced fallible memory and accusation, when A. J. P. Taylor's letter included Sinclair's notes on his meeting with Dowding, which had come from the Beaverbrook Papers. [83] An accurate assessment of the sequence of events in mid-November leaves little doubt that the removal of Dowding, which had been likely for some time, was carried out in a proper manner, although the spirit is open to question.

At the root of the matter lay two forces. First was the Air Staff's strong wish for new leadership at Fighter Command, and by early November, after he had seen and heard so many objections to Dowding, Churchill was prepared for this. The second force, however, is seldom recognized. It was that both the Prime Minister and Beaverbrook still held Dowding in high esteem and did not want a man of such great achievements and undoubted, although sometimes individual, abilities, to be dropped. There was a problem over his future employment because few opportunities were available. Portal had been appointed CAS on 25 October, thereby blocking that avenue. Although there was the possibility of creating a general post of inspectorate within the RAF, as had been previously arranged for Ludlow-Hewitt, this was unlikely as Dowding was *persona non grata* with so many senior staff.

The way out was discovered through Beaverbrook's Ministry, which was engaged at that crucial stage of the war in the essential, difficult and sensitive issue of obtaining aircraft and supplies from the USA via a Mission in North America. With American appreciation by November 1940 that Britain had survived the main blast of the German aerial storm, and with the welcome news on 2 November of Roosevelt's re-election, the time was propitious for the work to be pushed forward. No one appreciated its importance more than Churchill, who knew that Britain's only salvation lay through American aid and subsequent military intervention. [84] The question of sending a senior RAF officer to the United States as joint representative of the two Ministries for this work had been raised in mid-October. The names of Air Vice-Marshal Freeman and Air Commodore Slessor were mentioned, but Beaverbrook was not prepared to release the former officer. Sinclair wrote to him regretting this decision, adding 'I have no option but to send Slessor alone'. [85] Slessor, after some difficulties, reached New York on 8 November and later wrote modestly that there was a strong case for sending a senior Air Staff officer who was 'thoroughly in the picture of the latest expansion policy', and could discuss problems of requirements from American industry. [86]

This description certainly did not fit Dowding, but with the pressure to find him a post, together with his accumulated prestige from the daylight battle, Beaverbrook and Churchill decided to send him. The opening step was taken on 13 November, with an interview between Sinclair and Dowding. The C-in-C's memory of being dismissed over the telephone, and Wright's subsequent invective were wide of the mark, as is proved by an examination of the notes Sinclair carefully made and passed on to Beaverbrook next day. [87] He opened by explaining to Dowding the importance of the American Mission, which required 'the driving force of a strong personality', whose influence on American leaders would carry weight and go far to shape the United States air force of the future. The Americans had asked for Portal, but Sinclair was unable to release him. Beaverbrook had suggested Dowding, and the Secretary of State had agreed after carefully weighing 'all the factors in the problems involved'.

Dowding was not immediately impressed and gave no answer straight away. He wondered whether the Mission was temporary and asked if he would then return to Fighter Command. On being told that Douglas would be taking over there, he said that he would think the matter over and asked to see the Prime Minister, 'and so we parted'. Sinclair would have felt far less comfortable about the C-in-C going to Churchill on what was intrinsically a matter for the Air Ministry's decision had he not been assured that the Prime Minister was thinking along similar lines. He obviously wished to avoid receiving another written battering from Churchill over Dowding's treatment, as he had in August.

Therefore, when Dowding met Churchill on the morning of the 14th, Sinclair's decision was reinforced and a note of the meeting sent to the Secretary of State later that day. [88] According to this, Dowding at first expressed doubts about his ability to fulfil the mission, but Churchill told him that it was in the public interest 'of which I was the judge', and he accepted. The weight of those six words is not without importance, because they showed the manner in which Parliament was the final arbiter in Service matters. 'I have a very great regard for this officer,' concluded Churchill, 'and admiration for his qualities and achievements.' What Sinclair and the Air Staff saw as the removal of a burden from their necks was considered by Beaverbrook and Churchill as an opportunity to fill an important role.

The saga of removal was unfinished, however. History made by telephone calls often goes unrecorded, and although Terraine suggests that Luftwaffe success in bombing Coventry on the night of the 14th prompted the Air Ministry to phone Dowding on the 16th in an effort to bring forward the replacement, there appears to be no corroborated evidence of this. [89] The next day, nevertheless, in what was a tactless letter, insensitive in its treatment of the leader who had done so much for his Command, Portal, who must shoulder some blame for the C-in-C's poor treatment, wrote to Dowding. [90] He was asked to postpone his departure until the 25th because Douglas was unable to take over until then, and Dowding, who received the letter at 1.20am the following morning, having just returned from night operations, agreed to the request 'if that will be convenient to you'. [91] The replacement did take place on the 25th, when Douglas arrived at Stanmore.

Park left Headquarters, No 11 Group, at Uxbridge on 18 December, when Leigh-Mallory took over. The extent of their antipathy was later expressed by Park, who commented that his successor 'did not even bother to attend the usual formality', so he handed over to his SASO. [92] Supporters of Park sometimes show surprise that he was replaced, because he was younger than Dowding and had proved himself a leader of great competence in the furnace of battle. His policy of limited response, they claim, albeit forced on him by the geographical position of his Command, held off German attacks. Having occupied his post for only six months, he still had much to offer. On the other side, he was extremely tired and careworn by the end of the year and, in that view, replacing him was a wise move. He had a great contribution to make to Training Command, where he was posted, and future aircrew would benefit from his experience. [93]

In reality he was the victim of his closeness to the C-in-C. Within the Air Ministry, opponents of the current policy linked the two men, viewing Park as the executor of Dowding's planning. For them, changes in the top echelons of the RAF needed to be comprehensive. Portal had taken over from Newall and, to succeed Douglas, Freeman had been brought in as Vice-Chief of the Air Staff to follow his policies, on 25 October. There was to be a fresh start overall. [94]

The rancour felt by the supporters of Dowding and Park is heightened because their replacements appeared to be their greatest critics. In their view, Douglas and Leigh-Mallory were at the heart of an intrigue which first caused the Air Ministry to make a *volte-face* on the leadership of Fighter Command, and then brought the plotters themselves to power. Why was Douglas chosen to succeed Dowding? There were several reasons for this.

First, he had the qualifications and ability to do so, having been a successful fighter pilot in the First World War, and then having gained experience between 1918 and 1939 in a wide spectrum of posts. Age was on his side. He was 48 years old and, in a Service where younger men were being promoted, Douglas stood to benefit as a leader of ability and strong personality. He was, in the words of one historian, 'a very clever fellow', and if 'one had been interviewing Dowding and Douglas for a big job – one would have put one's money on Douglas'. [95]

Another reason in his favour was that he fitted far better than Dowding into the Air Ministry's plans for the next stage of the war. His spirit of aggression in aerial fighting matched more clearly their ideas of the employment of Fighter Command as an offensive, as well as defensive, force. His views on the value of Wings contrasted with those of Dowding, who was experienced in using his Command for defence but had less feeling for carrying the battle to the enemy. Thirdly, and this a reason of the utmost importance, Douglas at the Air Ministry was well placed to influence the influential. First among these was Sinclair, a man not noted for forceful leadership and who was, in Beaverbrook's opinion, governed by 'the bloody air marshals'. A revealing insight into Sinclair's relationship with Douglas was given in a letter written by the former after the war. 'You were my first friend at the Air Ministry,' Sinclair recollected. 'You helped me enormously in those early days . . . I felt as though I had won a battle when I got Fighter Command in your hands – and looking back, how right I was!'[96]

The importance of political support to senior Service officers is reinforced by exploring the relationship between Douglas and Harold Balfour. In the matter of the Wings controversy, Balfour's judgement lay clearly with Dowding's opponents, whose efforts were centred round Douglas, so the politician and the airman shared a common purpose. Douglas's advancement was also helped by the low esteem in which his immediate superior, Newall, was held by Beaverbrook and Salmond, Bruce and Dowding himself. In spite of Slessor's verdict that at the worst times he would emerge from Newall's office feeling as if he had just had 'a stiff whisky and soda',[97] others believed that the CAS was overwhelmed by the job. Douglas's own notes are instructive here, calling him 'a thorn in my flesh' during the first year of the war, 'especially during the time of the Battle of Norway and the Battle of Britain and the fighting in France'. He suggested that Newall worked too hard and was too conscientious, never leaving the Air Ministry, and 'consequently became an absolute bag of nerves' and 'worked himself to death'. [98]

The growing importance of Douglas emerged again as the Wings controversy developed, and it was he, not Newall, who called the conference of 17 October and directed its pattern. Whether the CAS refused to become involved because he was about to be replaced by Portal, or whether Newall felt unable to confront Dowding, is open to question. The result was that Douglas was seen to be involved decisively, an effect that counted to his credit. Then, as the argument over night air defence developed, Douglas found further powerful allies. Through his position within the Air Ministry he was able to lead the anti-Dowding faction, a stance obviously noted by Salmond, and then by Churchill, at committee meetings.

Douglas himself, an ambitious man, wanted a change of role. In his memoirs he claimed that Newall told him just before he left that he would shortly be offered a change, as he had been at the Air Ministry almost five years. 'I was quite pleased with this idea', he added. At that stage, Douglas said that he would have liked to command a Group in Fighter Command, as he knew more about fighters than about bombers. Shortly afterwards, however, Balfour, his old and close friend, announced that he was to replace Dowding, 'who was to retire'. [99]

The fact that Douglas and Leigh-Mallory succeeded Dowding and Park was not the end result of their scheming, and events of the time lack the elements of evil imputed by some writers. Both Dowding and Park had been under immense and unrelenting pressure of battlefield responsibility since the opening of the French campaign in early May. The strain clearly told after six months of fighting. When the decision to replace the C-in-C had been taken, it was not unreasonable that his successor should want, as AOC No 11 Group, closest to the enemy, a man in tune with his own outlook. This was no more than Dowding had done in selecting Park, first as his SASO, then to command that Group. The choice of Leigh-Mallory fitted in with the Air Staff's planning for Fighter Command's new role, so Park, a Dowding man, had to go.

Consequently, Dowding's decline after the conference of 17 October was both steady and certain. It had been the Air Ministry's intention since July that he should go by the end of October, so in their eyes the continuing clashes over policy made replacement inevitable. The decline can be best appreciated by exploring the cumulative effects of the differences concerning both night and day defence. The controversy between the two Group commanders was exacerbated after the conference with, again, a lack of decisiveness from the C-in-C. In night defence there were clear dissensions between Dowding and the Air Staff over filtering and the employment of Hurricane squadrons. Yet the fundamental addition to the armoury of Dowding's opponents was the power of political intervention. Through pressure from Sinclair, Balfour, Macdonald and Clarry, combined with the influential opinions of Trenchard and Salmond, both Beaverbrook and Churchill came to recognize the need for change. This they accepted reluctantly, but the measure became part of the RAF's new policies, which also involved the replacement of Newall by Portal. [100]

Dowding's treatment, therefore, was not the 'base intrigue' of a vendetta, or a plot engineered by conspirators. It was rather the result of a plan designed by politicians and Service leaders for the RAF, and inevitable as a different role was sought for Fighter Command in the war.

EPILOGUE

PART 1: AFTER THE BATTLE

Greater perspective of changes in the leadership of Fighter Command comes from a brief examination of certain events which happened over the two months following Dowding's dismissal. They show that on the one hand the controversy over the C-in-C smouldered and followed him to his new appointment in North America. On the other, Douglas tried immediately both to address the formidable task of meeting the night Blitz and employ Fighter Command in a more aggressive day role.

Correspondence written before Dowding's departure on the American Mission reveals that Beaverbrook and Churchill, while recognizing the need for Dowding to be replaced, were nonetheless concerned for his future. It also proves that the anti-Dowding caucus in the Air Ministry were determined not only to prevent him from returning to positions of power, but also were worried over the effect of his appearance in the USA.

Before the visit Dowding received information and advice, including notes on American scientific organization from Tizard and a memo from the Ministry of Aircraft Production. This listed requirements needed urgently, such as aero engines and gun turrets, and was sent to him on 28 November. [1]

The Air Ministry's worries over what they saw as Dowding's awkwardness in co-operation led to correspondence with Beaverbrook. Slessor, already in the United States, was less than pleased when he learned that Dowding was to join him. On 2 December he sent an urgent message to London, displaying fears over the forthcoming relationship between Dowding and the American Press.[2] He suggested that Dowding would be 'besieged by reporters', and although interviews 'will be distasteful to him' they had to be borne 'with as good grace as possible'. After offering much advice on the need for tact, he finished by suggesting that the Embassy could, if required, provide a member of the British Press Service 'to look after him'. Possibly Slessor was raising the spectre of Dowding's personality unnecessarily before the former C-in-C had had an opportunity of proving himself, yet the new environment was a world, in the words of one wartime official, 'as different from ours as anything could be'. [3] It is therefore possible to applaud Slessor's concern for the Mission's success, upon which so much depended, although his words appeared to sustain the Air Ministry's anti-Dowding sentiments. The note was passed on to Dowding with the explanation, 'I expect that Slessor himself has been plagued by the Press'. [4]

The intervention led to an exchange of letters between Beaverbrook and Portal. The new CAS wanted Slessor's suggestions to be implemented, pointing out that, although Dowding was working for the MAP, he would be seen by the Americans as a serving RAF officer. [5] Beaverbrook's hackles rose and, ever ready to joust with the Air Marshals, he replied that Dowding 'is seconded to this Ministry. He owes no responsibility to the Air Ministry.' [6] Portal in reply accepted that point, but claimed that in view of Dowding's RAF status he had a personal interest in the Mission's success and wanted Slessor's advice to be taken up. [7] Beaverbrook rounded off the correspondence by acknowledging that the MAP was influenced by the Air Ministry 'and we welcome it'. [8]

A. J. P. Taylor later suggested that Beaverbrook enjoyed moving 'men about from one office to another or in speculating how to do it', adding that he had been Lloyd George's errand-boy in such matters during the Great War and was delighted to be the same for Churchill. [9] Something of this propensity emerged in late December. When Portal became CAS he had pressed strongly for Freeman, with whom he had a good working relationship, to become his deputy, a move carried out on 4 November. The gap left at the MAP had to be filled, and on 19 December Beaverbrook wrote to Sinclair, asking him to name a successor. [10] The reply, two days later, contains the interesting statement, 'Assuming it is no longer your intention to appoint Sir Hugh Dowding', before going on to propose four names, one of whom was Salmond. [11] At that stage Dowding was on the high seas, on the SS *Leopoldville*, three days out from Glasgow and bound for Newfoundland. [12] There is no evidence to suggest why Sinclair thought that he was no longer a candidate, but it appears likely that he had at least been considered before being despatched to the United States.

The letter resurrected interest. In a Personal and Secret reply to Sinclair, Beaverbrook, still searching for a suitable haven for his friend, asked if the appointment would be well received by the RAF, since both Sinclair and Portal had stipulated that Freeman's successor should be an RAF officer. Had the appointment of Dowding been agreed, several of Beaverbrook's aims would have been achieved at one turn, particularly providing him with an ally in the inevitable controversies with the Air Ministry. [13] Sinclair's response shows that he had been put on the spot, and also adds weight to Beaverbrook's claim that he was governed by 'the bloody air marshals'. 'My own opinion,' he claimed, was that Dowding's appointment would meet the requirement of Freeman's successor being an RAF officer, a statement of the patently obvious. Then he added cautiously that he would consult Portal, who was away for a few days, before answering fully. [14]

The broader reply was dated 30 December, by which time Dowding had been ashore in Canada for two days. Sinclair hedged his bets over the appointment being well received in the RAF by suggesting that it would be preferred to the appointment of a civilian 'with the possible exception of Sir Henry Tizard'. Then honesty broke through. He felt 'bound to tell you frankly' that Sir John Salmond or Sir Edgar Ludlow-Hewitt 'would be more acceptable', a fact that Beaverbrook must have suspected all along. [15] What discussions ensued inside the Air Ministry in the days before Sinclair's reply was sent are unknown. Judging from previous episodes of the controversy, there must have been some fear within the Air Council that, like Banquo's ghost, Dowding might return to a different, yet powerful, position from which to haunt them. In the event those fears were unfounded, and Dowding remained in North America where, before long, further reservations were fuelled over his part in the Mission. [16]

Douglas had shown concern over his new role even before arriving to lead Fighter Command on 25 November. Five days earlier the *Daily Express* printed an article on night bombing which claimed that although 'some authority' said that the bomber was being beaten, the raiders were coming in great numbers and still getting back safely. People were being offered 'optimistic dope'. [17] Douglas at once wrote to Beaverbrook, fearing that a witch-hunt was being generated against him 'over the night bomber business'. He asked for help, together with time, in meeting the problem. In this he was appreciating the width and depth of Beaverbrook's influence. [18] Beaverbrook's reply was reassuring, confident that in time the 'night raiders' would be beaten. In his own hand he added that he would support Douglas as he had supported Dowding, 'to the limit of my capacity to do things'. Such a response was obviously reassuring for Douglas, who realized the extent of the burden he had shouldered. [19]

The width of that responsibility is shown by the continuing lack of success of the defences by the end of the year. Anti-Aircraft Command was still almost three times as successful as Fighter Command in shooting down bombers, claiming 102 enemy machines at night between June and December 1940, while fighters accounted for 35. General Pile referred to that period with justification as 'essentially a gun battle'. [20] At the same time German major raids decreased in December, with fewer on London but more on other cities. [21] Civilian casualties were still high; in that month 3,793 were killed and 5,044 injured, providing a worrying reminder both for politicians and the Air Ministry of what remained to be achieved. [22]

From the first days of his appointment Douglas prepared a more aggressive employment of Fighter Command than Dowding had used, and discussions were held at which Leigh-Mallory proposed the organization of Big Wings. In a long minute dated 17 December Douglas strongly approved of this, believing that the Command should try to outnumber the enemy in the air instead of itself being always outnumbered. He criticized No 11 Group, who 'have been rather hypnotised by the idea that they must meet the enemy before he reaches his objective'. [23] There was to be a new policy if the

Luftwaffe were to restart the day offensive in 1941. Also, on the afternoon of 20 December a small gesture of aggression was made when two Spitfires crossed the Channel and strafed Le Touquet airfield. [24] This was the first step in a series of operations which continued on an expanding yet, in terms of casualties, expensive scale. [25]

While Dowding was in the throes of his American Mission, the Fighter Command which he had done so much to create was 'leaning forward into France'. Park had moved to lead No 23 Group, Flying Training Command, in Gloucestershire, and Leigh-Mallory and Douglas were busily engaged in preparing to attack the Luftwaffe at every opportunity. All four men in different ways and to varying degrees had made contributions to their prime objective – namely to protect Britain from a German victory. This had been achieved in spite of the weaknesses of a CAS, Newall, whose work appeared to have a decreasing effect within the Service as the battle progressed. That factor was combined with a lack of authority from Sinclair, who failed to stamp his mark on the RAF at a time when firm decision was needed. Yet, although it was unknown at that stage, the aerial threat to the security of the Home Base was not to recur. During 1941 the course of the war would change radically, with the emergence of other dangers and opportunities.

Probably no instance of the treatment meted out to Second World War commanders has come under greater or more vigorous attack after the event than the case of Dowding and Park. Over half a century after the Battle of Britain the discussion continues with, generally, two distinct camps. This has occurred largely because hardened opinions, or prejudices, have been formed on hearsay, recollection and books, often unsupported by detailed evidence. Strongly divergent views have developed, and have been accepted uncritically. The orthodoxy has been unfair particularly to Leigh-Mallory who, alone of the main senior officers involved, did not survive the war to offer contributions to the debate. Few have drawn a distinction between the reasons for actions at the time and the later treatment, especially of Dowding, which was less than adequate.

Park's undoubted abilities were again recognized later in the war, when he was posted to Commands in the Middle East, especially the air defence of Malta in 1942. For him the greatest irony came in 1945, when he was sent to the Far East to take over the Command of his old rival, Leigh-Mallory, who had been killed in an air crash. Dowding's own disappointments were magnified in April 1941 when, at Churchill's insistence, he was called home early from the American Mission following complaints about his lack of tact and co-operation. In spite of Churchill's work on his behalf, during the following year he was once again at odds with the Air Ministry, and this led to his final resignation and retirement. Neither at that stage nor at the end of the war did he ever receive the just rewards for his service and loyalty. His subdued anger eventually emerged near the end of his life through Wright's biased book, which helped to form and fuel misguided opinions, still held by some.

PART 2: THE IMPORTANCE OF THE BATTLE OF BRITAIN

In many respects the Battle of Britain was, for Britain and a number of other countries, the most important battle of the war. It was an either/or battle. Either Britain did not lose, ensuring her a place in the remainder of the war, or she did lose and was forced out. Britain fought alone, having no powerful or active allies. Although British forces lost other battles later in the war, there were then unconquered companion nations in the conflict to share the burden. What would have been the results of defeat?

Firstly, with no opponent in western Europe, Germany would have had the opportunity, which undoubtedly would have been taken, of invading Russia earlier than June 1941. It is hardly stretching the realms of probability to believe that Moscow and Leningrad would both have been taken, Russia defeated and Bolshevism overthrown fifty years before it was.

In the Far East there is every chance that Japan would have launched attacks on the old European empires of France, Holland and Britain before December 1941. Japanese forces might well have advanced not only to the gates of India, but into the country. Invasion armies would have had a good chance of reaching Australia, a thought that still concentrates some minds there.

It is probable that the United States would have become more isolationist. There would have been no European springboard from which to hit back at Nazi Germany, in the way that Britain later became a type of floating aircraft carrier, naval base and military barracks. The Americans would, through force of circumstances, have turned their eyes and attention elsewhere, almost certainly to their interests in the Pacific.

In Britain, an enemy victory after the fighting of the Battle of Britain would have led to occupation and a severe regime. Undoubtedly there would have been some collaborators, but the establishment of German military law would have brought harsh conditions. That the German authorities intended this to be so can be deduced, for example, from a study of the Army Order of 9 September 1940, signed by General Halder. This ordered the death penalty for opposition and the removal of all men aged 17 to 45 to the Continent as soon as possible. In all likelihood they would have become slave labour. [26]

Probably the greatest effect of a British defeat would have been felt by European Jewry. There were, at the time, millions of Jews living on the Continent, and the chances of all would have been slender. There could have been a Holocaust far greater than the one that happened.

174

By fighting on without surrender, Britain gave hope to many nations in Europe which were conquered and occupied during the war years. Millions in the territories which fell under German domination regarded Britain as a beacon of light and hope amid the darkness of oppression. Although basically Britain fought alone, thousands of men and women from those countries came to the United Kingdom to continue the fight. That fact was particularly important during the Battle of Britain, when pilots from overseas served in Fighter Command, providing 15 per cent of the Command's strength. The largest European contingents came from two of Germany's earliest victims, Czechoslovakia and Poland.

The Command's effort from the summer of 1940 to May 1941 allowed Britain to remain in the war, and the German military machine suffered its first setback after a series of remarkable victories. The reverse for the Luftwaffe was particularly great because, although it played a prominent part in the early stages of the Russian campaign, its aircraft were never again an extensive threat to Britain. The holding operation by Fighter Command offered a breathing space for Bomber Command to build its power. Then, especially from 1942, in concert with the United States air forces, the bomber offensive was launched against the German homeland. A large part of the Luftwaffe's resources then had to be allocated to defending 'the fortress without a roof'.

For this alone, Dowding's men and women deserved praise and gratitude. The C-in-C's best work for the nation had been carried out before 1940 in the building of a system which, in a defensive campaign lasting several months, operated better than the Luftwaffe's haphazard offensive campaign. From the evidence at present available it appears that Dowding, Park, Douglas and Leigh-Mallory all had at heart the desire to defend their country in the best manner. In that respect it should be accepted that all acted honourably.

Nevertheless, in a Service suffering distinct weaknesses in leadership at the highest level, personal ambition played its part in filling the vacuum. Dowding tended to regard genuinely held differences as personal attacks and reacted abrasively. Park, always loyal, suffered from a lack of guidance and support from his C-in-C, whose strategy ensured that too heavy a burden fell on his Group. Leigh-Mallory met opposition when he rightly suggested that his squadrons could have been integrated more closely into the defensive system, and, without sound evidence, has drawn opprobrium as the result.

Through all of these events the impression grows that Douglas, an able and ambitious man, missed no opportunity of advancing his own cause as Dowding's reputation declined. He was well placed and took full advantage of his chances. If the Big Wing controversy is regarded as a battle for power, then Douglas was the winner. He, more than anyone, benefited from Salmond's plea that 'Dowding should go'.

APPENDIXES

APPENDIX A. WHO WAS WHO

The Four Principals

1   Air Chief Marshal Sir Hugh Dowding, 1882–1970

Born in 1882, Dowding was educated at Winchester and the Royal Military Academy, Woolwich, later serving abroad in the Royal Artillery. He gained his 'wings' in 1913 and fought with the RFC in France until 1916, when he was posted back to England. His post-war service in the RAF developed especially after 1926, with wide experience in departments of training, supply, development and research. His work on air defence, and especially his interest in single-seater fighters, Radio Direction Finding and control systems brought him the leadership of Fighter Command from its foundation in 1936.

Dowding then prepared and led the aerial defence of the United Kingdom, through the Battle of Britain, until November 1940, when he was sent on an air mission to the USA. After his return he headed a study into economies of RAF manpower, and retired in July 1942. Although not promoted to Marshal of the Royal Air Force, he was created 1st Baron Dowding in 1943. In retirement he became actively interested in Spiritualism, both as a writer and speaker, and later espoused the cause of animal welfare. He died in 1970.

2   Air Vice-Marshal Keith Park, 1892–1975

A New Zealander, Park served in the Army in Gallipoli and France until 1917. He then transferred to the RFC and flew in action over the Western Front. Between the wars he commanded RAF stations and was an instructor before becoming Dowding's Senior Air Staff Officer in 1938. He took over No 11 Group in April 1940 and organized fighter patrols over France during the Dunkirk evacuation. In the Battle of Britain, Park's Group bore the brunt of the fighting and he showed fine qualities of leadership. His disagreements with Leigh-Mallory at the time led to great bitterness. At the end of the daylight battle Park was removed and sent to Training Command.

He returned to action in January 1942, and for the next three years held commands in the Middle East, being posted in July 1942 to command the air defence of Malta. From there, his squadrons played a part in the North African and Sicilian campaigns. In early 1945 he was appointed Allied Air Commander, South-East Asia, and served there until the end of the war. Retiring in 1946, he returned to New Zealand, where he lived until his death.

3   Air Vice-Marshal William Sholto Douglas, 1893–1969

Sholto Douglas, educated at Tonbridge and Oxford, joined the Army in 1914. He transferred to the RFC as an observer, then became a pilot. Over the Western Front he gained wide experience in fighter combat, and by 1918 had been OC of two squadrons. Between the wars he was an RAF instructor, then served both at home and abroad, being especially interested in flying training.

In 1936 he moved to the Air Ministry, where he spent the next five years, covering most aspects of RAF work. By early 1940 he was Deputy Chief of the Air Staff, liaising with all operational Commands, so he was closely involved with Dowding throughout the Battle of Britain. He had always believed that fighters should operate in large numbers and that if sufficient enemy aircraft were destroyed their offensive would stop. Here he differed from

Dowding, whom he replaced in November 1940.

Douglas later served in many roles, including planning fighter sweeps over France and working in the Middle East and Coastal Command, and was a potential CAS. Instead he went to Germany, where he became Military Governor of the British Zone, but resigned in 1947. Granted a peerage, he turned to civil aviation, being chairman of British European Airways until 1964, five years before his death.

4 Air Vice-Marshal Trafford Leigh-Mallory, 1892–1944

Leigh-Mallory, born in 1892, was educated at Haileybury and Cambridge. He joined the Army in 1914, was wounded in action and later transferred to the RFC, where much of his work was connected with Army co-operation over the Western Front. After the war he was commissioned in the RAF, serving in Britain and then in Iraq. From late 1937 Leigh-Mallory commanded No 12 Group, Fighter Command. During the Battle of Britain he wanted his squadrons to be closely involved in action, and this led to disagreements with Park. He has been accused unjustly of forming a plot to overthrow Dowding.

Later, Leigh-Mallory took over the command of No 11 Group, and then, from December 1942, of Fighter Command itself. During preparations for Operation Overlord he became C-in-C of the Allied Expeditionary Force, which he led during the invasion. In August 1944 he was appointed to command air forces in South-East Asia, but while en route to take up the appointment his aeroplane crashed in the French Alps. All on board, including his wife, died. Leigh-Mallory, by then an Air Chief-Marshal, was the highest ranking British officer to be killed in the Second World War.

Others Involved

1 Bader, Douglas

Squadron Leader and OC No 242 Squadron in No 12 Group. He believed that his Duxford Wing should have been called earlier and more often into air battles south of the Thames.

2 Balfour, Harold

Member of Parliament and Under-Secretary of State for Air. As a former fighter pilot he favoured No 12 Group's case for greater involvement of their squadrons in the daylight battle.

3 Beaverbrook, Lord

A contentious and powerful newspaper owner who became Minister of Aircraft Production. In this role he was often at odds with the Air Ministry. He respected and befriended Dowding.

4 Brand, Sir Quintin

Air Vice-Marshal. He commanded No 10 Group, Fighter Command, which guarded south-west England in particular. Worked harmoniously with Park.

5 Churchill, Winston

As Prime Minister, Churchill showed great interest in the activities of Fighter Command. He wanted Dowding's squadrons to hold off the Germans until RAF bombers were ready to hit back. Was deeply worried by the effect of the night Blitz.

6 Crowe, H. G.

Group Captain and Deputy Director of Air Tactics at the Air Ministry. He was an advocate of Big Wings.

7 Evill, Douglas

Air Vice-Marshal. He was Dowding's Senior Air Staff Officer during the Battle of Britain and had a closer view than most of the disagreements between the C-in-C and the Air Ministry.

8 Goering, Hermann

Reichsmarschall. In the German State, second only to Hitler, with whom he had worked closely from the earliest days of the Nazi Party. A former First World War fighter pilot, he came to lead and control the Luftwaffe. Committed suicide in 1946.

9 Jeschonnek, Hans

General der Flieger and Chief of the Luftwaffe General Staff. He was a young man of brilliant promise and responsible for much of the planning of the air war against Britain. Committed suicide in 1943.

10 Joubert, Sir Philip
Air Marshal and Assistant Chief of the Air Staff. He was greatly interested in RDF and control systems, over which he often disagreed radically with Dowding.

11 Kesselring, Albert
Feldmarschall. He commanded *Luftflotte II*, which carried the main assault against south-eastern Britain between July and October 1940. His bases were in the Low Countries and north-eastern France.

12 Lindemann, Frederick
Oxford scientist and First World War aviator, greatly interested in air defence. He was a confidant of Churchill, who relied widely on his scientific judgement.

13 Macdonald, Peter
Member of Parliament. As a Flight Lieutenant he was Adjutant to Bader's No 242 Squadron. As an MP he was concerned with the air defence of the United Kingdom.

14 Milch, Erhard
Feldmarschall. After extensive service with civil airlines between the wars, he became State Secretary of Aviation in 1933. He was a hard-working organizer and deputy to Goering, though not always popular with other Staff officers.

15 Newall, Sir Cyril
Air Chief Marshal and Chief of the Air Staff. Newall held the RAF's senior Service position from 1937. There were many occasions when his views diverged from Dowding's.

16 Pile, Sir Frederick
General Officer Commanding-in-Chief, Anti-Aircraft Command. Pile worked closely and harmoniously with Dowding over air defence. His Command bore the main burden of countering the night Blitz during the winter of 1940–41.

17 Portal, Sir Charles
Air Chief Marshal. With one of the shrewdest brains in the RAF, he left Bomber Command to succeed Newall as CAS at the end of the daylight battle. He wanted to have Dowding replaced.

18 Salmond, Sir John
Marshal of the Royal Air Force. As Director of Armament Production at the Ministry of Aircraft Production, he was implacably opposed to Dowding and pressed hard to have him removed from Fighter Command.

19 Saul, R. E.
Air Vice-Marshal. He commanded No 13 Group, Fighter Command, guarding the most northerly parts of England and the whole of Scotland.

20 Saundby, R.
Air Vice-Marshal and Assistant Chief of the Air Staff, Technical Requirements, at the Air Ministry. An advocate of Big Wings and an opponent of Dowding's policies.

21 Sinclair, Sir Archibald
Member of Parliament and also leader of the Liberal Party. He was appointed Secretary of State for Air in Churchill's Coalition Government in May 1940. In the view of many, a perfect gentleman who lacked decisive leadership in his Ministry.

22 Slessor, J. C.
Air Commodore. He was Director of Plans at the Air Ministry and was particularly worried when Dowding was sent on the American Mission in late 1940.

23 Sperrle, Hugo
Feldmarschall. He commanded *Luftflotte III*, based largely in north-western France during the Battle of Britain.

24 Stevenson, D.
Group Captain. As Director of Home Operations at the Air Ministry, he had shown interest from pre-war days in the size of fighter formations to be employed in action.

25 Trenchard, Lord
Marshal of the Royal Air Force and 'Father of the RAF'. Trenchard did more than any other individual to create and mould the Service. In 1940 he worked with Salmond to have Dowding removed.

26 Udet, Ernst
Chief of Luftwaffe Supply and Procurement. A brilliant pilot, Udet found Staff duties demanding and unrewarding. Some of the Luftwaffe's weaknesses of production and supply must lie at his door. Committed suicide in 1941.

APPENDIX B. THE BADER NOTES

After the end of the Second World War, controversy developed over the activities of the Duxford Wing and the parts played in 1940 by Bader, Leigh-Mallory and Macdonald. According to Bader's brother-in-law, Wing Commander P. B. (Laddie) Lucas, 'Douglas would never be drawn *publicly* into criticism of those who were criticising him'. Nevertheless, after the publication of Wright's *Dowding and the Battle of Britain* in 1969, 'with its slanted content', notes were written privately for Lord Balfour of Inchrye (formerly Harold Balfour, MP) 'at the latter's request'. Balfour was starting to prepare his autobiography, *Wings Over Westminster*, and shared with Bader the feeling that Wright's criticisms were intemperate and inaccurate. These notes, dated 30 November 1969, are a clear exposition of Bader's views on the leadership, strategy and tactics employed during the Battle of Britain, and are also a rebuke to Wright. Their only error of fact is on page 5, where Bader believed, incorrectly, that Air Vice-Marshal R. Saul, AOC No 13 Group, was present at the Air Ministry meeting of 17 October 1940.

Section 1, p.1. 11 Group/12 Group – August/September 1940
In this section Bader showed disquiet at the publication of Wright's book. The author had mentioned him by name, quoting Dowding as his source, but Bader claimed that 'what is said is completely new to me. Frankly I do not believe what is said.' He was sure that Dowding's authorized biography, *The Leader of the Few*, by Basil Collier, published in 1957, was more accurate and characteristic than 'the sensationalism associated with Wright's version'.

Bader then widened his criticism. None of the post-war writers on the Battle of Britain, with the exception of 'Johnnie' Johnson, had 'taken the trouble to discuss matters with me'. For example, the authors of *The Narrow Margin*, which was widely acclaimed, 'failed completely in their views about the 12 Group Wing because they did not seek the facts'. This was relevant concerning the Duxford Wing, because 'I led it and my Group Commander of the time, Leigh-Mallory, died in a crash at Grenoble in 1944'.

Section 2, p.2. The Duxford Wing (No 12 Group)
Bader next explained the history and purpose of the Duxford Wing, which had originated in Leigh-Mallory's mind after No 242 Squadron was in action on 30 August 1940. Having been called off in good time, the squadron fought under favourable conditions near Epping. 'By favourable conditions is meant that we had position, height and sun in attacking an enemy bomber formation without Me 109 escort.' After the action, Bader had told Leigh-Mallory that if he had had more fighters, more enemy aircraft would have been destroyed. 'A few days later the Duxford Wing of 3 squadrons was born.'

Practices took place with Nos 19 and 310 Squadrons, then the Wing was ready. 'The method of operation was uncomplicated' and 'there was no joining up over the airfield'. The Hurricanes flew in line astern while the Spitfires (No 19 Squadron) were '3/4,000 feet above, behind and to one side'. The intention was that the Hurricanes would attack bombers, while the Spitfires 'with their better performance' would hold off Bf 109s. The Wing, claimed Bader, never took more than six minutes to leave the ground and 'frequently we were off in four minutes'. Thus, 20 minutes after take-off the Hurricanes were 'over the Estuary at 20,000 feet' with the Spitfires three to four thousand feet above.

The Wing's first action was on 7 September and, in the air, there was no more difficulty in controlling three squadrons than in controlling one. All squadrons were on the same radio telephone frequency and, after 'an occasional word' to the other commanders, 'my intentions' were given. Suggestions that the Wing 'was clumsy in operations are utter nonsense and completely without foundation', as was proved by fighter Wing operations over France in 1941.

Section 3, p.3. Problems

Bader spoke of 'one fundamental problem', which was 'the failure of the 11 Group operations room to get squadrons off the ground in time'. The inexperienced No 11 Group controllers failed to appreciate the fighters' need for 'height and position to dominate the battle'. The vulnerable, or fatal, position was to climb with the enemy above.

As German formations gathered near Calais at 15-17,000ft, then crossed the Channel, 'this virtually precluded a successful interception' by No 11 Group squadrons near the coast. However, Park's Controllers were reticent to call for the No 12 Group Wing, who were 'sent for as an afterthought or to do what we used to term "the lunch-time patrol" when there was no single aeroplane either German or British in the air at all'. The late call for aircraft was illustrated – '616 squadron on its first operational sortie out of Kenley lost 5 out of 12 on the climb without touching the enemy'.

Controllers in No 11 Group would not call squadrons off until the enemy aircraft were 'at operational height and leaving the French coast'. Bader stated that, 'the error of this thinking is self-evident'. Several times the Duxford Wing was at readiness as the Germans were building up over Calais, but when he asked for permission to take off, he was told to wait 'until 11 Group ask for you'. Had they taken off then, as 'Duxford to Tilbury is 43 miles', they could have arrived south of the Thames 'under favourable conditions to control a battle of our seeking'.

Section 4, pp.4-6. Politics

Bader examined the background to the controversy, which, he said, occurred over fourteen days, between 7 September, when the Wing was first in action, and 21 September, after which big air battles ceased. Troubles 'stemmed solely from mutterings in the Mess by the pilots of the Duxford

Wing against the No 11 Group habit of calling us off the ground late so that we inevitably arrived in the battle area at a disadvantage'. Nevertheless, Park's headquarters 'used to complain when we were late', leading to a 'vicious circle', with No 11 Group 'saying that we took so long to get off the ground'.

Some writers, specifically Wright, had suggested that the whole battle 'represented a continual and sustained intrigue by Leigh-Mallory to undermine the Commander-in-Chief, Dowding, using the big Wing formation led by Squadron Leader Bader as his spearhead'. Following this reasoning, Leigh-Mallory had won when he replaced Park and Douglas replaced Dowding. 'Nothing could be further from the truth', because an imputation of 'bad faith and dishonest dealing to the Air Council' was 'manifestly absurd'.

Bader then attacked another 'suggestion that has been accepted over the years', namely that Park should have used Wings, like No 12 Group, but this was 'nonsense'. He continued, 'You cannot operate large formations from close to an attacking enemy. At no time, and I say this with certainty, was it in Leigh-Mallory's mind.'

Turning to politicians, Bader mentioned that ministers visited airfields during the battle, and that he had commented to Balfour 'I wish they would get us off the ground sooner'. In addition, his own Adjutant, Flying Officer P. Macdonald, MP, 'would hear conversation in the Mess in the evening'. When in London, Macdonald 'used to pass on this sort of gossip' to other politicians, but 'I was not specifically aware of this until 1953 when Macdonald told my biographer, Paul Brickhill'. This was relevant only 'to would-be historians like Robert Wright', who fitted it into 'his pattern of intrigue' committed against Dowding.

The Air Staff meeting of 17 October, of which Wright 'makes much', was then explored. 'He only just avoids saying that Squadron Leader Bader called the meeting!', but in fact Bader was ordered to attend by Leigh-Mallory. When asked by Dowding to give his views on leading big formations, he 'did not speak for long', and 'in spite of my embarrassment' thought that it could be 'the only time that a fighter pilot might ever be asked for his views by the Air Staff'.

Wright, he believed, had twisted facts to suit his book and had 'damaged Stuffy Dowding in the eve of his life'. The 'derogatory references to Leigh-Mallory are distasteful since that very distinguished officer is dead'. Keith Park was 'a tired man since he alone conducted the Battle of Britain', which was fought by neither Dowding nor Leigh-Mallory. Park was not removed because he failed, but 'in the same way that tired fighter pilots were rested'. As for Dowding, of Wright's claim that Sinclair had retired him by telephone and that Churchill said that he knew nothing of it, Bader commented 'I do not believe it'. The true facts were given in Collier's authorized biography, which was 'more dignified, characteristic and as a result less sensational than Robert Wright's version'.

Section 5, pp.6-8. The Battle of Britain

Next, Bader assessed the battle itself. Dowding's two important contributions, he believed, were that he had prepared radar coverage and then had fought against sending more fighters to France in May 1940. Nevertheless, 'as Commander-in-Chief Fighter Command in August/September 1940 he failed', because he did not assume 'control of the air defence of Great Britain', which was his job. Instead, he left the business to Park, who fought 'an 11 Group battle which should have been a Fighter Command battle'.

Air defence in depth should have been arranged by Fighter Command Headquarters, which would have made 'life easier for controllers and less costly for pilots'. They would have seen 'the problem in its entirety'. Leigh-Mallory 'saw the problem with crystal clarity from the calm of his 12 Group headquarters; so did I from the quiet of Duxford'. The error was that 'the front line should have embraced the whole of Fighter Command not just 11 Group'.

Dowding should have 'seen the light' at the end of August, when German intentions 'became clear beyond doubt', as London was the obvious target. At that stage, Bader reckoned the Commander-in-Chief should have taken control, but 'it was not

to be'. In fact, Dowding failed and left a tired Group commander, who lacked authority and resources, to continue the struggle. 'It was as though General Montgomery had left a Corps Commander to fight the battle of Alamein and told him to call on other Corps commanders for assistance as necessary.' The battle, in his view, was won by the 'tired but resolute commanders and the immense courage of 11 Group pilots'. No 12 Group's Wing could have been used to attack enemy formations, 'creating havoc amongst them', giving No 11 Group pilots time to gain height and position. Sometimes Park's pilots climbed away northwards to gain tactical advantage. 'At the top level of Fighter Command,' Bader complained, 'there seemed an utter inability to grasp the basic and proven rules of air fighting'.

On 27 September, relations between the two Groups reached a very low ebb when the Duxford Wing, flying near Dover, destroyed some Bf 109s. Park, instead of offering congratulations, accused them of 'poaching on 11 Group's preserves'.

Bader then explained that Dowding's failure as a C-in-C possibly was caused by the pressure of his work, so that he was 'unaware of the changing circumstances of the Battle'. In that case, he failed by not appointing one overall deputy, an Air Marshal, 'to co-ordinate and direct the Battle'.

Section 6, pp.8-9. Dowding

Finally, Bader dealt with Wright's treatment of Dowding and Leigh-Mallory. He wrote of the high esteem in which their leader was held by his pilots, who were proud of 'this gruff, withdrawn, inarticulate Stuffy Dowding'. They were disappointed that he had not been promoted to Marshal of the Royal Air Force. 'We thought it, and some of us said it, long before Robert Wright wrote his book.'

Bader accused Wright of destroying the image, portraying Dowding as an embittered man, 'who for years had nursed a massive grudge against the Service which made him'. Wright's story was 'unattractive',`contributed nothing to history and damaged the reputations of Dowding and of Park.

Also it was 'viciously inaccurate' in referring to Leigh-Mallory. His 'rather pompous manner disguised a quick, questing mind and shielded a character of charm, kindness and understanding'. He was tough and honest with his juniors. 'My lasting impression of him was that he cared about people. They mattered to him.' Leigh-Mallory's death with his wife in an air crash in 1944 was a great loss. For his inaccurate portrayal, Wright 'will not be forgiven'.

APPENDIX C. WAS WRIGHT WRONG?

Questions relating to the treatment of Dowding and to the Big Wing controversy were raised several times during the years following the Second World War. From many examples, two are of interest here. When J. B. Collier was preparing his book *The Defence of the United Kingdom*, in 1955, he sent a draft to Sholto Douglas, who was by then Lord Douglas of Kirtleside. Douglas's commentary on the draft was returned to Collier on 14 February 1956. Among other matters it set out at length what he believed to be the virtues of employing Wings of fighters, his views on the disagreements between Park and Leigh-Mallory, various reflections on night-fighting in 1940, and a defence of the RAF's fighter sweeps over France in 1941.

In the following year, Robert Wright, one of Dowding's former Personal Assistants, wrote a review of Collier's authorized biography of Dowding, *Leader of the Few*. The review showed clearly that Wright had great sympathy for Dowding and, although offering some praise to the book, he commented that Collier had not always provided 'answers that do justice to Lord Dowding in a way that might be expected'. In particular, Wright felt that Dowding had been treated 'in a very shabby way', and said that the reason why he had not been 'promoted to the highest rank in the RAF is not explained'. Wright was then, as he had been earlier and would remain, a staunch supporter of the former Commander-in-Chief.

However, it was not until the publication of Wright's own book, *Dowding and the Battle of Britain*, and the first showings of the film, 'Battle of Britain', both in

1969, that the matter was brought sharply and critically to the attention of a wider public, many of whom had previously been unaware of events which had occurred 30 years earlier. Because of the effect of the book as a catalyst of controversy, some relevant and important deductions may be made about its author and his subject, as well as the circumstances under which it came to be written.

During the late 1950s Lord Douglas began to prepare his autobiography. To help in the gathering and presentation of his story, Douglas engaged the aid of Wright, an experienced author and journalist, who had served with him during the Second World War, part of the time as his Personal Assistant. Douglas's story appeared in two volumes, the first, *Years of Combat*, being published in 1963 and the second, *Years of Command*, emerging three years later. In the latter book Wright was referred to as 'an old friend', and discussion with him had 'helped me greatly in placing my story on record'.

Correspondence between the two men during 1961 shows that a tricky hurdle had to be surmounted when the events of 1940 were under investigation. The matter of particular interest was Churchill's claim that Dowding had told him that Britain could be defended by 25 squadrons, a statement which, although rejected by Dowding, he had never publicly denied. Douglas wanted a report, not only to learn the former C-in-C's opinion on the matter, but also in the hope that Dowding would contribute a short account for his forthcoming book. However, bearing in mind particularly the bitterness that had existed between the two leaders in 1940 over the Big Wing controversy, Wright offered to act as a 'go-between'.

On 10 March Wright informed Douglas that he had written to Dowding, but 'I have not yet told Stuffy that I am working with you on your book and will not do so until I have your permission'. A week later Wright disclosed to Dowding that he was helping Douglas. In a letter which may be described at best as emollient, at worst as oleaginous, he wrote of Douglas's belief that Dowding had been treated unfairly by Churchill's claim. A way of 'lodging a protest' would be for Dowding to offer an observation which could be inserted in the forthcoming book. Wright added that, to his delight, he knew that Douglas felt 'just as strongly as I do about the unfairness of the whole thing' and that Douglas also had paid 'a lengthy and fine tribute to you'. The letter went out of its way to stress Douglas's charitable feelings for the man he had replaced at Fighter Command.

Thus Dowding was persuaded to co-operate and received a letter of thanks from Douglas (27 March). In the letter, attempting to exorcise ghosts of the past, Douglas declared, 'I have always had the greatest respect and, indeed, affection for you', before continuing, 'I hope you will believe that, although at times I had to pass unpalatable instructions to you in 1940, I was always on your side and did my best inside the Air Ministry to fight your battles for you.' Dowding's reply (28 March) thanked Douglas for his 'friendly letter' and mentioned that he had agreed with Wright 'on the lines my contribution will take'. Then came a touch of Dowding's old spirit, when he added, 'It seems probable that Churchill, who never admits that he was wrong, dreamed up the absurd statement that *I* had told him that this Country cd. be successfully defended by 25 Squadrons'. Obviously, by using Wright to approach Dowding, Douglas was receiving dividends for the material of his book.

However, this policy had another effect, because Wright's letters start to show an increasing sympathy for Dowding. 'Nobody appears to have had the guts to stand up for Stuffy', he wrote to Douglas on 10 March, commenting, of Dowding's feeling of bitterness over his treatment, 'I think that he is justified'. Eleven days later he wrote of a 'rather distressing letter' which he had received from Dowding, saying 'I can well understand how he feels'. Wright was willing to 'accept his invitation to go and see him', because the research worker had to 'continue probing in spite of his inclination to beat a hasty retreat'. At the end of his note Wright announced that, although he felt uncomfortable over the business, he would continue investigations. 'I feel rather like a surgeon carving into something in order to cure it.'

On 27 March Wright reported that Dowding had been 'tremendously helpful' during a long talk held the previous afternoon. Next day, Wright mentioned the Big Wing controversy, saying that 'Stuffy would like to be involved in this as little as possible, because he knew nothing of the differences between Leigh-Mallory and Park until it had reached a fairly advanced stage, when, to his great surprise, the Secretary of State mentioned to him the views advanced to him by Leigh-Mallory based on the idea put forward by Bader'. Wright's letters give the impression of a growing concurrence with Dowding's opinions.

As work on the second volume of Douglas's autobiography progressed during late 1964 and the early months of 1965, Wright's correspondence showed a variety of worries. These included the lateness of the book, overwork, and the belief that he was being underpaid. Nonetheless, when the book emerged in 1966, Wright's name appeared on the front cover as co-author.

From this time Wright was drawn increasingly towards Dowding, who had, since the war, refused to offer to the public his version of the events of 1940. At some stage in the 1960s, when he was into his eighties, Dowding relented and Wright was taken on as friend, researcher and scribe to gather the story into print. By the time the venture was complete, together with the extensive preparations for the making of the film 'Battle of Britain', Wright stood as the former C-in-C's champion. Dowding, now aged 87 and often confined to a wheelchair, wrote, 'the author has been fair and faithful, endeavouring to render a full account, from both the personal and the historical point of view, of all that I should have liked to place on record'. That is a claim with which not all historians would agree. The book brought controversy at the time and has done so since.

One result of the publication of Wright's book, and the showing of the film, in the summer of 1969, was a passage of correspondence in *The Times* in January 1970, in which the events of late 1940 and the subsequent treatment of Dowding came under scrutiny. The steps by which Dowding was removed were discussed, with Wright and Dowding avowing that this had been done 'at the end of a telephone call', while Professor R. V. Jones and Marshal of the Royal Air Force Sir John Slessor suggested that such behaviour was foreign to the nature of the former Secretary of State for Air, Sir Archibald Sinclair (later Lord Thurso). The question was settled in the latter's favour when A. J. P. Taylor produced documentary evidence from the Beaverbrook Papers to prove that Sinclair *had* met with Dowding on 13 November 1940. Dowding's recollections and Wright's research were shown to be sadly at fault.

A further result was that another target of Wright's accusations, Group Captain Douglas Bader, wrote a private and unpublished set of notes in which he categorically refuted Wright's claims against No 12 Group in general, and against Churchill, the Air Staff, Harold Balfour, Leigh-Mallory and Bader himself in particular. Bader called it 'an unattractive story', portraying Dowding as 'an embittered man, with a gigantic chip on his shoulder', and said it was 'viciously inaccurate' to Leigh-Mallory. 'Robert Wright,' he wrote, 'will not be forgiven.' (See Appendix B.)

Subsequently an investigation was launched among the top echelons of the RAF, with officers of very high rank being asked to consider whether or not, 30 years on, Dowding should be promoted to MRAF and, perhaps, receive some other reward. Their findings, of course, are still classified, but obviously they recommended against it, because the promotion was never made. One question probably considered was whether such a promotion or award would have appeared to be the result of external pressure. In that case it would have been a belated and rather soured commendation. Possibly they felt that Dowding's main reward was the public recognition of what he had achieved in 1940, and that neither a promotion nor an award could have equalled that.

In the midst of the questions raised about the battle and its principals, both by book and film, Dowding died, on 15 February 1970, not far short of his 88th birthday. A month later a memorial service was held in Westminster Abbey, where his ashes were laid to rest below the Battle of Britain Memorial Window in the Royal Air Force Chapel. The address was given by the Rt. Hon. Denis Healey, MP, then Secretary of State for Defence, with a tribute both full and generous. In his belief, the 'true significance' of Dowding's service was to help preserve 'a form of democratic society which is Britain's greatest contribution to the history of man'. He added that the presence of a huge congregation was 'the surest proof of the British people's deep affection for Lord Dowding', who was about to take his place 'alongside the great Captains of the past'.

It is now clear that, as Wright drew closer to Dowding and learned more of his case, he came increasingly to suspect Douglas's motives and role in Dowding's dismissal at the end of 1940. That became obvious in 1977, when another participant in the RAF's wartime activities decided to put his recollections into print.

Sir Maurice Dean, an eminent civil servant, was, for many years, Permanent Under-Secretary of State at the Air Ministry. In retirement, in the 1970s, he began to write a book on the history of the RAF during both world wars. As part of the story he had to explore the development of Fighter Command, and especially the relationship between Dowding and the Air Council, which he had seen at first hand during his early work at the Air Ministry.

In general, Dean did not hold Dowding in the highest esteem, and believed that he was not an exceptional leader in the RAF. Dean particularly criticized the C-in-C's running of his Command at the time of the Big Wing controversy. Dowding had claimed that he did not know of the strong disagreement between Park and Leigh-Mallory until a late stage, but Dean asserted that it was the duty of a C-in-C to be aware of such happenings – 'Commanders-in-Chief have to know'.

As a result of reading Wright's book, particularly his version of the events of the Battle of Britain and Dowding's subsequent removal from his Command, Dean was anxious to present his story as correctly and fairly as possible. Knowing how closely Wright had worked with Dowding in the preparation of the book, Dean wrote to him on 25 August 1977, enclosing a photocopy of that part of his manuscript which dealt with Dowding and asking for Wright's comments on what he had written.

Wright replied on 5 September, and invested proceedings with an air of mystery by stating that he had some 'important information that I think you should know about', which he could not commit to paper. In fact, 'I doubt very much if I will ever put it on record'. It was, he claimed, too disturbing in its revelations of the workings of the minds of some men involved in the story. Group Captain Teddy Haslam, of the Air Historical Branch, Ministry of Defence, who broadly shared Dean's views of the events of 1940, had rung Wright, suggesting that all three might meet for a general discussion. Wright agreed to this, but requested that he might be allowed to bring along Group Captain Tom Gleave, 'one of my oldest and best friends', with whom he had served, and a man who shared his views over Dowding's treatment. Dean concurred, and the meeting took place over lunch at Dean's club on 13 November 1977. The gathering was of interest because the two pairs present represented opposite sides in their interpretation of Dowding's importance in 1940, his leadership, especially over the Big Wing controversy, and the reasons for his dismissal.

With the meticulous care to be expected of a senior civil servant, on the day after the meeting Dean made a list of notes of what was said by Wright.

First, Dean was told that in 1936 Dowding did not want the position of CAS, but was 'miffed because both Bowhill and Ellington had told him that he was going to get it'. On the third point, concerning Dowding's dismissal, Wright was convinced that the C-in-C had received a message telling him to be out in twenty-four hours; Dean wondered if the Air Ministry had been guilty of 'maladroit handling' of events.

He also learned that Portal, just before his death in 1971, had admitted that the question of making Dowding a Marshal of the Royal Air Force had been examined, possibly at the end of the war, but that he was not considered good enough. Dowding himself had only begun to be interested in becoming MRAF about the time of the making of the film.

Dean then looked again at the point concerning Dowding's removal 'at the end

of a telephone call', an accusation later shown to be incorrect. Obviously the fault of memory had worried Dowding, who 'was almost in a state of nervous collapse over the alleged telephone incident'. Dean incisively commented that there were two issues here. First, the posting had been 'clearly settled with great decorum'; second, however, he believed that the Air Ministry could have acted more carefully over the details of the move.

The last note referred to the relationship between Portal and Dowding, and in some ways summarized a widely held opinion of the latter's lack of co-operation with colleagues. 'When Portal was C-in-C, Bomber Command,' wrote Dean, 'he asked to visit Dowding at Fighter Command Headquarters. When he turned up Dowding said "What do you want?" and pushed him off on an aide.'

Eight days later Wright sent a list of comments in note form which he had made about the contents of Dean's photocopy. He pointed out that these were his personal views and, if proved wrong, he was open to correction. Also, he added significantly that in his book he had not been able to name Dowding's opponents in the Air Ministry 'because people concerned were still alive, and I was also working under the restraint of the old fifty-year rule'. Wright then criticized a number of points made by Dean, and from these criticisms several facts and opinions emerge.

First, he claimed that the 'wretched business of the intrigue' was worse than he believed when he wrote his book, and that he now had 'strong support from people involved' over the matter. However, he had not named them at his private meeting with Dean, nor did he here state who they were.

The failure to promote Dowding to Marshal was referred to as 'a very delicate matter', and it is clear that Dowding himself never suggested it. In later years, claimed Wright, he made only two comments on the matter; first, it would have been financially advantageous to him, but, secondly, he had a strong wish 'not to cause any embarrassment to the Queen'.

Next, Wright was bitter over the treatment shown to Dowding at the Royal Gala

Performance of the film 'Battle of Britain'. Before the film started, Dowding, who had been taken there in a wheelchair by Wright, was presented to the Queen. However, Wright claimed that in the interval, the 'top brass of the Service, and other so-called dignitaries of Dowding's time and later', were so anxious to get into a room at the back of the dress circle, to 'be in the presence of the royal family' that they ignored the former C-in-C. 'Not one of them saw fit to say a word to Dowding. No-one came near him.' Dowding was 'completely ignored', which was 'disgraceful', and only one senior officer showed any consideration.

These events, stated Wright, had made him and Tom Gleave bitter. He contrasted this treatment with that shown at an earlier première of the film, when the 'audience rose to their feet and applauded when I wheeled Dowding in in his chair and got him to his feet'. The reason, he suggested, was that they were aircrew who had actually taken part in the battle.

Wright disagreed with Dean's assessment of the importance of Dowding's leadership in the RAF as 'by no means exceptional'. He placed Dowding higher than Portal or Harris, 'although perhaps not Tedder' as a wartime leader. Of others, Wright felt that 'Courtney would have been a dam' sight better CAS than Newall'.

Dean had stated that the suggestion that Dowding faced an inept or malevolent Air Ministry was 'moonshine'. This enabled Wright to name names. It was true, he claimed, that mainly Sholto Douglas and Stevenson 'were up to their ears in the intrigue'. There was, he went on, proof of that in the record, 'and it has been confirmed for me by others who found themselves involved in it'. Wright's readiness at that time to name Douglas as an arch-offender is explained by the fact that the man who had referred to him as 'an old friend', and with whom he had worked closely in both war and peace, had died in 1969. Here, indeed, was proof of how Wright had become convinced that Douglas had played a prominent part in what he considered to be a plot to unseat Dowding. His former confidant was now relegated to the realms of the unworthy.

Wright affirmed that Dowding blamed Churchill, not the Air Ministry, for frittering away the resources of Fighter Command during the battle for France. Churchill, he believed, 'rode rough-shod over the Air Ministry'.

Concerning the Big Wing controversy, Wright claimed that the tension over tactics was not between Nos 11 and 12 Groups 'as whole Groups'. It was rather between 'Leigh-Mallory, using Douglas Bader, and Park, and Tom Gleave will tell you that most of those in all the Groups supported Park'. Wright was sure that this disagreement was 'the source of all the trouble'. He disagreed strongly with Dean's belief that 'either side could have been right', observing 'it is now firmly established that Leigh-Mallory and Bader were wrong, and events alone have proved that', a statement unsupported by any proof.

Dean's suggestion that Dowding was at fault, as C-in-C, for not knowing of the disagreement in his Command, was then explored and dismissed. Wright pointed the finger of accusation at 'one of the finest men ever to serve in the RAF, who was on Dowding's staff', whose 'misplaced loyalty and caution' had left the C-in-C ill-informed. Here he was referring to the then Air Vice-Marshal D. Evill, Dowding's Senior Air Staff Officer during the Battle of Britain. The impression has been accepted by a number of people that Evill failed to acquaint Dowding sufficiently with the extent of the quarrel between Park and Leigh-Mallory and that, consequently, the C-in-C was unable to intervene decisively in good time. This suggestion is less than just to Evill's work and reputation. Contemporary documents show clearly that the SASO consistently explained the position to his C-in-C, who *was* aware of the controversy. Evill appreciated that Dowding alone could act to resolve the crisis, but this the C-in-C failed to do.

Salmond's intervention was then mentioned. Wright, not having studied sufficiently the background to the controversy over night air defence, found Salmond's actions 'a complete mystery', standing to 'his final discrediting'. The criticism was extended to include another swipe at his old friend, 'Sholto Douglas as over "big wings". But Douglas, of course, acted as he did for a definite reason; his own interests.'

Next, Wright dealt with Portal and the sending of Dowding on a mission to the USA after he left Fighter Command. Portal's part in this, he suggested, was an 'intriguing question'. Wright had written to Portal about the events of 1940, but the reply he received 'amounted to a crude brush off'. He believed that, to find Portal's role in these events, 'you would have to dig deep into the files and private papers'.

Dowding's part in the American Mission was defended, even though documents of the time show clearly that he did not blend well with colleagues there, and also was outspoken over matters which lay outside his remit. In Wright's view, however, the trouble came from a 'clash between the Air Ministry representatives, and Beaverbrook's representatives in the United States, with Dowding unknowingly standing in the middle'. Wright had obviously not comprehended all of the correspondence on the case, written between December 1940 and the following April.

His complaints ranged wide, from criticism of Churchill over the sending of fighters to France, to Dowding's failure on the American Mission, where 'Churchill's minutes leave as bad a taste in one's mouth as those written by Beaverbrook'. Portal was criticized again, because of his 'attitude in the matter of honours and awards. And if that is true, how is it that he managed to do so well himself?' The answer to that, suggested Wright, was 'a most unpleasant one'. Then, on the controversy which led to Dowding's final resignation in 1942, he referred to the Air Ministry. 'I never ceased to wonder over the number of bitches – a word used advisedly – one could find at the top.'

At every turn, Wright charged at windmills, promoting the impression that Dowding himself seemed to hold, namely that his views were correct and different perceptions were held only by fools or knaves. In general, Dean was unimpressed by Wright's comments, as is proved by reading the text of his book, *The Royal Air Force in Two World Wars*. Nonetheless, with great care he explored the notes and listed his own reactions to the points Wright had made. The feeling is gained that, where Wright was moved by emotional responses to what he believed were injustices committed against Dowding, Dean had a wider and more balanced view.

Dean noted that Dowding 'clearly loathed the AM [Air Ministry], hated Sinclair, thought Newall lacking in guts and believed that the Big Wing controversy was a conspiracy. The fact is that a lot of people just didn't agree with Dowding on a number of important points.' Dean then offered a view quite ignored by Wright. 'Dowding never accepted the fact that the AM had a duty to control and where necy. criticise the policy of F.Cd.'

It is noticeable that when Dean's book appeared in 1979, shortly after his death, he had not altered his views. In the main, the opinions on which he had sought Wright's comments were maintained and were a clear refutation of some of the points made in the latter's book.

Also unpersuaded by Wright's comments and arguments was Group Captain Haslam, who in an article written in 1981 sustained the momentum of counterattack. Just after the celebration of the fortieth anniversary of the Battle of Britain, Haslam was disconcerted by an article and a book, both published in 1980, from the pen of Len Deighton. According to Haslam, Deighton had enhanced Dowding's reputation 'largely by denigration of senior members of the Air Staff and the "establishment" of 1940'.

Deighton's assertions over Dowding's removal from office were described as 'simplistic and inaccurate', and Haslam then advanced two arguments which had not been widely considered earlier. In these he showed the depth of his research and a clarity of thinking.

First, he emphasized that, although Deighton had praised Dowding's powers of leadership, it was 'precisely for his lack of control and leadership' that he was removed by the Air Staff. His vacillations during the Big Wing controversy proved the point.

Second, Haslam examined another area of difference between the C-in-C and the Air Ministry, saying he believed that 'it was not his handling of daytime raids but of night-time German attacks that eventually precipitated the call for Dowding's replacement by Sholto Douglas'. In this, Haslam was taking a wider view of the aerial war over Britain than those, including Dowding himself, who claimed that the day and the night campaigns should be viewed separately. Dowding believed that the two offensives had different aims, and that the night Blitz was no more than 'a sideline', which was how he described it in a letter to Liddell Hart in 1943.

Haslam explained in some detail the extent of the perceived threat from night bombing, which Fighter Command was unable to check. Many politicians, the Air Staff and, not unnaturally, civilians, regarded its effects with trepidation. Dowding, nonetheless, was at odds with his colleagues over the measures needed to defend the nation, and at times appeared to be obstructive when emergency plans were proposed. This attitude, combined with several other reasons, finally persuaded the Air Ministry that a new man was needed at the helm.

Haslam's article, written after a greater study of documents concerning night air defence than either Dean or Wright had made, was a model of balanced assessment. At the end, he summarized Dowding's contribution and avoided the trap which has ensnared those who fail to appreciate how events and characters of the past were viewed at the time. 'In the dark days of 1941 and 1942,' he wrote, 'the significance of his contribution to the history of the Royal Air Force was not so clearly visible as it is with hindsight.' He then concluded that Dowding was 'no easy compromiser or politician and he often aroused opposition, sometimes unwittingly. But no-one served his country more selflessly and courageously.'

APPENDIX D. DOWDING, SPIRITUALISM AND THE BATTLE OF BRITAIN

According to his biographer, Basil Collier, Dowding's interest in spiritualism dated from a series of newspaper articles on the subject that he had read during the First World War. His involvement, however, did not become widely evident until after his retirement in 1942. He then read extensively, attended and lectured at meetings, and formed friendships with like-minded people. In his own words, he became convinced 'of the fact of conscious survival of death and the possibility of communicating with dead people in certain circumstances'. Dowding traced much of his interest back to the Battle of Britain itself. 'For me,' he wrote in 1951, 'the experiences of the battle have paved the way towards an inquiry into the conditions which await us after physical death.'

This led to the writing of *Many Mansions* in 1943. A second book, *Lychgate*, appeared in 1945, followed later by two others, *The Dark Star* and *God's Magic*. He also wrote articles for newspapers and magazines. In these writings, Dowding set out his philosophy and beliefs, showing a rejection of the Church's conventional Christianity. He joined the Theosophical Society, which advocated belief in some form of reincarnation.

Reactions to his writings and lectures were mixed. For some people, especially those who had lost loved ones in the war, Dowding's words brought comfort and he became, in Collier's words, 'a peripatetic evangelist'. He carried hope to those who did not want death to be an irretrievable break with people they had known so well. They felt that he showed compassion and was a source of goodness.

Others disapproved of his interest in what they considered to be unconventional religion. A few found his claims bizarre. For example, in *Lychgate* he wrote of experiences during sleep, of being with his late wife, Clarice, of bringing help to prisoners in concentration camps and of visiting British prisoners in Japanese POW camps. He met dead 'RAF boys', who placed round his neck 'a deep mauve ribbon by which is suspended a lovely "medal", shining like crystal'. In this other world, he said, pilots flew fighters which took off from mountain-top runways, 'which are not of concrete but electrical vibrations (moving streams of light)'. One of his former pilots commented years later, 'At that stage we thought that Stuffy had gone ga-ga'.

Later, in 1964, Dowding wrote to his friend, Beaverbrook, reflecting on his role at Fighter Command before and during the Battle of Britain. He believed that a Divine Will had arranged for him, aided by Beaverbrook, to save the nation in 1940. This view of his destiny helps to explain his singular approach to command and the frustration he felt at the lack of recognition and reward he received after the battle.

'About a year after my retirement I was given a picture of the remote past. I was then chief of one of the Mongol tribes engaged in a great Westward sweep of conquest.

'I was very impetuous & always preferred to establish my tribe's footing in a new country by fighting rather than by negotiation.

'This led to my being mortally wounded in a battle against a tribe well armed with chariots and bows; and as I lay dying, the following message was given to me through my second in command.

'"Thou hast led thy people in haste: thou hast left them bereft. So in future ages thou must come again as a warrior to battle, and lead them alone. Then thou shalt serve me in spirit, and with the words of the spirit bring solace to my peoples."

'I don't know who was speaking, but it would be one high in the hierarchy of this planet.

'I am telling you this because I think it more than probable that your part in the Battle was laid down by the Lords of Karma as a result of some action of your own in times long past. Looking back on my own life I can see how events conspired to put me at the head of Fighter Command at the critical time, instead of succeeding Ellington as CAS, as I had been told in 1935 that I should. I don't know if you, with your widely differing views, will think that this is all nonsense; but to me it is an integral part of my life ...

'I think perhaps that the above will account for the way in which two such dissimilar characters as you and I were brought together and enabled to work harmoniously for the preservation of our dear country.'

From HLRO, Historical Collection 184, Beaverbrook Papers, C/120, 2 June 1964.

APPENDIX E. THE AIRCRAFT

	Wing span (ft in)	Length (ft in)	Maximum speed (m.p.h.)	Armament	Bomb load (lb.)	Range (miles)
Spitfire I	36 10	29 11	365	8 x .303in mg		
Hurricane I	40 0	31 4	316	8 x .303in mg		
Blenheim IV	56 4	39 9	260	6 x .303in mg		
Defiant	39 3	34 7	312	4 x .303in mg		
Bf 109E	32 4	28 4	354	3 x 7.9mm mg, 2 x 20mm cannon		
Bf 110	53 5	39 8	349	5 x 7.9mm mg, 2 x 20mm cannon		
He 111P	74 2	57 5	240	6 x 7.9mm mg	4,410	1,212
Do 17Z	59 0	51 9	260	3 x 7.9mm mg	2,205	720
Ju 87B	45 3	36 1	232	3 x 7 9mm mg	1,540	370
Ju 88	59 11	47 1	286	3 x 7.9mm mg	4,400	1,550

APPENDIX F. ABBREVIATIONS

AA	anti-aircraft
AAF	Auxiliary Air Force
AASF	Advanced Air Striking Force
ACAS	Assistant Chief of the Air Staff
ACM	Air Chief Marshal
ADGB	Air Defence of Great Britain
AHB	Air Historical Branch
AI	Airborne Intelligence
AM	Air Marshal
AMP	Air Member for Personnel
AMRD	Air Member for Research and Development
AMSO	Air Member for Supply and Organization
AOC	Air Officer Commanding
ASU	Aircraft Storage Unit
AVM	Air Vice-Marshal
BEF	British Expeditionary Force
CAS	Chief of the Air Staff
C-in-C	Commander-in-Chief
CHL	Chain Home Link
CID	Committee of Imperial Defence
CIGS	Chief of the Imperial General Staff
CO	Commanding Officer
COS	Chief of Staff
DCAS	Deputy Chief of the Air Staff
DCOS	Deputy Chief of Signals
DDAT	Deputy Director of Air Tactics
DDOI	Deputy Director of Intelligence
DDOps	Deputy Director of Operations
DDPlans	Deputy Director of Plans
D/F	direction finding
DHO	Director of Home Operations
DOI	Director of Intelligence
DOSS	Director of Staff Studies
DPlans	Director of Plans
FIU	Fighter Interception Unit
FTC	Flying Training Command
GCI	Ground Controlled Interception
GCOps	Group Captain (Operations)
G/L	gun laying
GOC-in-C	General Office, Commanding-in-Chief
HDC	Home Defence Committee
HF	high frequency
HQ	Headquarters
IAZ	inner artillery zone
IE	Initially Equipped
IFF	Identification Friend or Foe
JPC	Joint Planning Committee
MAF	Metropolitan Air Force
MAP	Ministry of Aircraft Production
MRAF	Marshal of the Royal Air Force
MTB	Motor Torpedo Boat
NADC	Night Air Defence Committee
NIC	Night Interception Committee
OC	Officer Commanding
OR	Operational Research
ORB	Operations Record Book
OTU	Operational Training Unit
PA	Personal Assistant
PPS	Parliamentary Private Secretary
PUS	Permanent Under-Secretary
QMG	Quartermaster-General
RA	Royal Artillery
RAFVR	Royal Air Force Volunteer Reserve
RDF	radio direction finding
RFC	Royal Flying Corps
R/T	radio telephone
SASO	Senior Air Staff Officer
VCAS	Vice-Chief of the Air Staff
VCNS	Vice-Chief of the Naval Staff
VHF	very high frequency
W/T	wireless telephone

NOTES

Introduction

1 See *The Times*, 31 October 1988, p.2.
2 Dowding Papers, Aviation Records Department, RAF Museum, Hendon, AC 71/17/2, HCTD/ S.305, 11 May 1943.
3 See H. Probert, *High Commanders of the Royal Air Force* (HMSO, 1991), p.22, who writes of 'a role for which he was quite unsuited and from which he soon had to be withdrawn'.
4 For example, see L. Deighton, *Fighter* (London, 1977), pp.271–73, and V. Orange, *Sir Keith Park* (London, 1984), p.121.
5 The 'Big Wing' referred to a formation of at least three squadrons flying as a unified force under one commander. It was also called a 'Balbo', after General Italo Balbo, who led a combined fleet of 24 Italian seaplanes on a two-way crossing of the Atlantic Ocean in 1933.
6 Orange, p.136.
7 B. Collier, *Leader of the Few* (London, 1957).
8 R. Wright, *Dowding and the Battle of Britain* (London, 1969).
9 Lord Douglas, *Years of Command* (London, 1966), pp.88–90.
10 See B. Newton Dunn, *Big Wing* (London, 1992), Chapters 18 and 19.
11 L. Lucas, *Flying Colours* (London, 1981).
12 Lord Balfour, *Wings Over Westminster* (London, 1973).
13 Sir Maurice Dean, *The Royal Air Force and Two World Wars* (London, 1979).
14 E. B. Haslam, 'How Lord Dowding Came to Leave Fighter Command', *Journal of Strategic Studies* (hereafter JSS), 4, 2 (1981), pp.175–86.

Chapter 1

1 AIR 8/863, Sir Hugh Dowding's Despatch, the Battle of Britain, 20 August 1941, Public Record Office (hereafter PRO), Kew; also published as a supplement to *The London Gazette*, 11 September 1946, pp.4543–71. See p.4544, paragraph 13.
2 AIR 19/572.
3 See Dowding Papers. In a letter from Newall on 30 March 1940, Dowding was requested to retire on 14 July.
4 Bruce Papers, Australian Archives, Belconnen, Canberra, Australia, M.100, 10 June, 2 and 10 July 1940.
5 Dowding Papers.
6 Wright, p.137.
7 Dowding Papers.
8 Ibid.
9 Ibid.
10 Ibid.
11 AIR 19/572.
12 Ibid.
13 Ibid.
14 Ibid.
15 Dowding Papers.
16 Ibid.
17 Ibid.
18 AIR 19/572.
19 Ibid.
20 Ibid.
21 J. Colville, *The Fringes of Power: Downing Street Diaries, 1939–1945* (London, 1985), p.194.
22 Interview, Wing Commander H. Ironside. His former Personal Assistant recollected that, when Dowding received Christmas presents from firms, he refused to accept them but had them returned, with a note of thanks.
23 See Collier, *Leader of the Few*, pp.72–75, and Wright, p.25.

24 Figures from *The Battle of Britain, Then and Now*, edited by W. Ramsey (London, 1980).

25 D. Richards and H. Saunders, *Royal Air Force, 1939–1945*, 3 volumes (HMSO, 1974), i, Appendices 1 and 2, show that between July 1936 and October 1940 Bomber Command had four Air Officers Commanding; between July 1933 and December 1940 there were five Air Members for Personnel (AMP).

26 See H. Montgomery-Hyde, *British Air Policy Between the Wars* (London, 1976), Appendix vi; Dean, Chapter 6; M. Smith, *British Air Strategy Between the Wars* (London, 1984), Chapters 8 and 9.

27 Dowding Papers.

28 Earl of Swinton, *Sixty Years of Power* (London, 1966), pp.230–31.

29 D. Saward, *'Bomber' Harris* (London, 1984), p.80.

30 H. Penrose, *British Aviation: Ominous Skies, 1935–1939* (HMSO, 1980), p.59.

31 Sir Philip Joubert, *The Third Service* (London, 1955), pp.129–30.

32 *The Times*, 16 February 1970, p.10.

33 Letter, Denis Richards.

34 Interview, Air Chief Marshal Sir Kenneth Cross.

35 Interview, Air Chief Marshal Sir Harry Broadhurst.

36 Orange, p.120. Wright, p.94, gives an account of Dowding's reaction to learning of this incident in 1968.

37 For Ludlow-Hewitt's relationship with the Air Ministry, see Sir Charles Webster and N. Frankland, *The Strategic Air Offensive Against Germany, 1939–1945*, 4 volumes (HMSO, 1961), i, Chapters 2 and 3; also see Dr M. Smith, 'Sir Edgar Ludlow-Hewitt and the Expansion of Bomber Command, 1939–40', *Journal of the Royal United Services Institute*, 126, 1(1981), pp.53–55.

38 J. Terraine, *The Right of the Line* (London, 1985), p.72.

39 A. Boyle, *Trenchard* (London, 1962), p.184; also see Wright, pp.35–36, and Collier, *Leader of the Few*, p.115.

40 270 H.C. Deb. 5s, c.632, 10 November 1932. Baldwin added, 'The only defence is offence, which means that you have to kill more women and children more quickly than the enemy, if you want to save yourselves'.

41 L. E. O. Charlton, *War From the Air*, (London, 1935), p.147.

42 See J.F.C. Fuller, *Towards Armageddon: The Defence Problem* (London, 1937), especially Chapter 10.

43 'Appreciation of the Situation in the event of War against Germany', Joint Planning Sub-Committee, 26 October 1936, (COS 513 [J.P.]).

44 CAB 4/29, 1499B, Committee of Imperial Defence, Sub-Committee on Emergency Reconstruction Report, 16 December 1938.

45 335 H.C. Deb. 5s, c.1752–53, 12 May 1938.

46 Webster and Frankland, i, pp.62–63.

47 Sir John Slessor, *The Central Blue* (London, 1956), p.151.

48 Papers of Lord Douglas of Kirtleside, Imperial War Museum, London, Box 2, File 2, 13 June 1963.

49 J. B. S. Haldane, *Air Raid Precautions* (London, 1938), p.7 and p.63.

50 112 H.L. Deb. 5s, p.235, c.1 and p.237, c.1, 15 March 1939.

51 AIR 16/255, 25 September 1939.

52 AIR 8/243, 26 November 1938.

53 See Slessor, Chapters VII and IX; also see AIR 20/313.

54 See AIR 19/524 and AIR 8/218.

55 AIR 16/255, 12 October 1938.

56 AIR 8/243, 26 November 1938; also see W.K. Wark, 'British Intelligence on the German Air Force and Aircraft Industry, 1933-1939', *Historical Journal* (hereafter HJ), 25, 3 (1982), pp.627–48.

57 AIR 8/277, 2 November 1938.

58 341 H.C. Deb. 5s, c.351, 10 November 1938.

59 344 H.C. Deb. 5s, c.2388, 9 March 1939.

60 AIR 8/240.

61 AIR 8/863, p.4544, paragraph 16. The background to the figure of 52 squadrons is shown in Marquess of Londonderry, *Wings of Destiny* (London, 1943), Chapter II.

62 Wright, p.72.

63 See AIR 20/252, 7 July 1939.

64 See AIR 20/393, pp.57–63.

65 AIR 16/116, figures for 31 August 1939.

66 For example, see Terraine, pp.150–52; Deighton, pp.61–64; Wright, pp.103–7.

67 Reasons for the decision to create separate Commands are shown in AIR 41/14, Air Defence of Great Britain (hereafter ADGB), i, pp.15–23 and 30–34; also in AIR 41/40, Bombing Offensive Against Germany (hereafter BOAG), i, pp.110A-110E.

68 AIR 20/220, 6 April 1939.

69 CAB 53/49, COS 912, 13 May 1939.

70 See AIR 16/255, 12 and 21 September 1939.

71 R. Hough and D. Richards, *The Battle of Britain* (London, 1989), pp.76–77.

72 Douglas, *Years of Command*, p.51.

73 Wright, p.87.

74 See AIR 16/255, 5 October 1939; also see AIR 20/293, pp.87–88.

75 See A. Horne, *To Lose a Battle* (London, 1969), pp.70–73.

76 Interview, Wing Commander H. Ironside.

77 Terraine, pp.119–20; see also C. Dunning, *L'Armée de l'Air, 1939–40* (London, 1989), p.22.

78 D. Wood and D. Dempster, *The Narrow Margin* (London, 1961), Appendix 16.

79 Ibid, p.186, and Horne, pp.195–96.

80 For problems of Anglo-French cooperation, see J.C. Cairns, 'Great Britain and the Fall of France: A Study in Allied Disunity', *Journal of Modern History* (hereafter JMH), 27, 4 (1955), pp.365–410.

81 V. Goddard, *Skies to Dunkirk* (London, 1982), pp.135–36.

82 For example, see *The Ironside Diaries, 1937–1940*, edited by R. Macleod and D. Kelly (London, 1962), pp. 346 and 351.

83 AIR 41/14, ADGB, i, Appendix 10, 14 May 1940, also Appendix 16, 24 May 1940.

84 Dowding attended two meetings on 15 May. First was the Chiefs of Staff Committee No 133 at 10am, and second was War Cabinet No 123 at 11am. Some of the words he spoke at the first meeting have been attributed to the second, where Newall, as CAS, put the RAF's case. Nevertheless, the gist of Dowding's sentiments is plain. See M. Gilbert, *Winston S. Churchill*, vol. vi, *Finest Hour, 1939–1941* (London, 1981), pp.340–43, who refers to CAB 79/4, COS(40), 133rd meeting, 15 May 1940, 10am and CAB 65/7, W.M. 123(40), 123rd meeting, 15 May 1940, 11am. Compare CAB 65/13, W.M. 153(40), Confidential Annexe, 3 June 1940. The overall confusion has ensnared several.

85 Dowding Papers, 16 May 1940.

86 See above, note 84, and Gilbert, vi, pp.455–58.

87 Halifax diary, 8 February 1941, quoted in *The Diaries of Sir Alexander Cadogan*, edited by D. Dilks (London, 1971), p.299. Dowding was not alone in these sentiments, but his view must be tempered by the realization that the French collapse brought German forces to within 22 miles of southern England.

88 For views on the virtues and weaknesses of different types of fighter in action, see for example A. Galland, *The First and the Last* (London, 1955), pp.64–65; A. Deere, *Nine Lives* (London, 1959), p.52; P. Richey, *Fighter Pilot* (London, 1941), pp. 105–8; AIR 41/15, ADGB, ii, p.100.

89 Air Historical Branch (AHB) Translation, VII/83, 'German Aircraft Losses, September 1939-December 1940'.

90 R. Suchenwirth, *Command and Leadership in the German Air Force* (New York, 1970), p.160.

91 For RAF pilot losses and their effect, see AIR 16/352; AIR 19/162; and AIR 41/15, ADGB, ii, p.9.

92 See Douglas, *Years of Command*, pp. 40–42, for a description of the crash, in which he was involved.

93 On achieving power in a Ministry and the Cabinet, Beaverbrook was described as acting like 'the town tart who has finally married the Mayor', see *The Diaries of Sir Henry Channon*, edited by R. R. James (London, 1967), p.257; also see A. J. P. Taylor, *Beaverbrook* (London, 1972),

pp.415-17. H. Dalton, *The Fateful Years, Memoirs, 1931–45* (London, 1957), p.300, mentions his 'utter disregard of all rules or orders except his own'. Beaverbrook often referred to 'the bloody Air Marshals', which Slessor, p.308, translated as 'a generic term applied by Lord Beaverbrook to the senior officers of His Majesty's Air Force'. See also House of Lords Record Office (HLRO), Historical Collection 184, Beaverbrook Papers, BBK C/120.

94 Beaverbrook Papers, BBK D/414, vol.i, 8 July 1940.

95 Sinclair, leader of the Liberal Party, was appointed to Churchill's all-Party Coalition on 10 May 1940. See Gilbert, vi, p.317.

Chapter 2

1 F. Hinsley, *British Intelligence in the Second World War*, 4 volumes, (HMSO, 1979), i, pp.61, 78–79 and 299–300 shows variations in Intelligence estimates of the size of the Luftwaffe; see also AIR 40/2321.

2 See W. Churchill, *History of the Second World War*, 6 volumes (London, 1948–58), i, p.212.

3 M. Bloch, *Strange Defeat*, translated by G. Hopkins (Oxford, 1949), pp.54–55.

4 See Air Ministry, *The Battle of Britain* (HMSO, 1941), p.9, and *Ironside Diaries*, p.385.

5 See H. Schliephake, *The Birth of the Luftwaffe* (London, 1971), p.31; Lord Tedder, *Air Power in War* (London, 1947), p.94; W. Murray, *Luftwaffe* (London, 1985), p.47; R.J. Overy, *The Air War, 1939–1945* (London, 1980), pp.23–25.

6 See D. Irving, *Goering* (London, 1989), p.190.

7 See Suchenwirth, *Command and Leadership*, pp.82–83. German air leaders 'accepted Hitler's erroneous belief that there would be no war with Britain for the simple reason that Germany did not want it'.

8 See *Luftwaffe*, edited by H. Faber (London, 1979), Chapter XII; also see

R.J. Overy, *Goering, 'The Iron Man'* (London, 1984), pp.102–4.

9 D. Irving, *The Rise and Fall of the Luftwaffe* (London, 1974), p.64; also see T. Taylor, *The Breaking Wave* (London, 1967), p.105.

10 Suchenwirth, *Command and Leadership*, p.230; Second Air Group Study, 'Planning Case, Green', 22 September 1938, in Irving, *Rise and Fall*, p.64.

11 Schliephake, pp.48–50.

12 R. Suchenwirth, *Historical Turning Points in the German Air Force War Effort* (New York, 1968), p.31.

13 Ibid, pp.36–38 shows the effect of the pressure to have dive-bombers; see also Suchenwirth, *Command and Leadership*, pp.75–77. This policy restricted the Luftwaffe's ability to launch a strategic bombing offensive against Britain.

14 Suchenwirth, *Turning Points*, p.43; see also R.J. Overy, 'German Air Strength, 1933 to 1939: A Note', *HJ*, 27, 2 (1984), pp.465–71.

15 W. Baumbach, *Broken Swastika* (London, 1960), pp.30–33; Wood and Dempster, pp.101–2.

16 Suchenwirth, *Command and Leadership*, p.240; also ibid, pp.23 and 325, quoting Karlsruhe Document 'High Command of the Air Force, Chief of the General Staff, 1st (Operations) Branch, No 5095 of 1939, Top Secret Command Matter', 22 May 1939, G/V.2a; also, *Kesselring Memoirs*, pp.41–42.

17 Eng. General G. Hubner, 'The engineer problem in the Luftwaffe, 1933-1945', p.21, in Irving, *Rise and Fall*, p.74; Suchenwirth, *Command and Leadership*, pp.232–33.

18 Lloyd George's doubts of Britain's abilities to help Poland are shown in 345 H.C. Deb. 5s, c.2505-11, 3 April 1939; see also J. Douglas-Hamilton, 'Ribbentrop and War', *JCH*, 5, 4 (1970), pp.45–63.

19 *Hitler's War Directives*, edited by H. Trevor-Roper, (London, 1964), pp.3–5.

20 A summary of the German Air Force's role during the Polish campaign is given in Murray, pp.31–33; see also Air Ministry, *The Rise and Fall of the*

German Air Force, Pamphlet No 248 (London, 1948), pp.53–57.

21 Trevor-Roper, pp.12-14.

22 AHB Translation, volume 2, No VII/30, General Schmid, 'Proposal for the Conduct of Air Warfare against Britain', German Air Force Operations Staff (Intelligence), 22 November 1939.

23 AHB Translation, volume 2, No VII/26, Luftwaffe 8th Abteilung report, 'The Course of the Air War against England', 22 November 1939. Variants of the He 111 used during the Battle of Britain could carry 4,407lb. of bombs. Later, the Lancaster Mk.I carried 14,000lb, the Halifax Mk.II 13,000lb and the B-17D Flying Fortress 10,500lb. In addition, German bombers had a weak defensive armament.

24 According to T. Taylor, *Breaking Wave*, p.107, 'The Luftwaffe did not attack during these months because its leaders saw no prospect of decisive results'.

25 See H. Allen, *Who Won the Battle of Britain?* (London, 1974), pp.71–73; E. Sims, *Fighter Tactics and Strategy* (London, 1972), pp.87–92; Galland, *First and Last*, pp.68–69.

26 M. Spick, *Fighter Pilot Tactics* (Cambridge, 1983), p.43; *Pamphlet No 248*, p.14.

27 See AHB Translation, volume 9, No.VII/121, A. Galland, 'The Battle of Britain', February 1953, p.6; also Galland, *First and Last*, pp.37–38; also see Overy, *Air War*, p.14.

28 AHB Translation, volume 4, No.VII/83, 'German Air Losses (in the West only), September 1939-December 1940'; see also Murray, pp.42–45.

29 Suchenwirth, *Turning Points*, pp.66–67; Terraine, pp.188–94; Beaverbrook Papers, BBK D/362, Reports to the War Cabinet, 19 June, 27 October and 24 December 1940.

30 Suchenwirth, *Turning Points*, p.86.

31 A. Bullock, *Hitler, a Study in Tyranny* (London, 1962), pp.588–89.

32 For a list of Churchill's speeches, see Gilbert, vi, p.1283; also see Taylor, *English History*, p.473.

33 *Secret Session Speeches*, compiled by C. Eade (London, 1946), pp.9-10; for British optimism see N.Frankland, *The Bombing Offensive Against Germany* (London, 1965), p.48, and W. N. Medlicott, *The Economic Blockade, vol.i, 1939–1941* (HMSO, 1952), p.411; see also *Memoirs: Ten Years and Twenty Days, by Admiral Doenitz*, translated by R. H. Stevens (London, 1959), pp.113-14 – 'The British never give up the struggle half way through; they fight on to the end'.

34 Irving, *Rise and Fall*, pp.91–92; see also Deere, p.71. For an opposite view, see AIR 41/15, ADGB, II, p.24.

35 See Townsend, *Duel of Eagles*, pp.277–78 and Deere, Chapter VI. Also see AIR 20/3457.

36 See *Kesselring Memoirs*, p.65.

37 E. P. von der Porten, *The German Navy in World War Two* (London, 1972), p.95.

38 Trevor-Roper, p.29.

39 Ibid, p.33.

40 Taylor, *Breaking Wave*, pp.44–46.

41 On Oran, see Hinsley, i, pp.149–54; also see Gilbert, vi, Chapter 31.

42 For German naval losses in the Norwegian campaign, see Porten, p.92; see also D. Grinnell-Milne, *The Silent Victory* (London, 1976), chapters 4 and 5, and R. Wheatley, *Operation Sea Lion* (Oxford, 1958), p.112.

43 Goering's Directive, from Ob.d.L.Fust 1a. No 5835/40g.K.(Op.1) chefs, 30 June 1940. See K. Klee, 'The Battle of Britain', in *Decisive Battles of World War II*, edited by H. Jacobsen and J. Rohwer (London, 1965), pp.79–80.

44 W. Kreipe, 'The Battle of Britain', in *The Fatal Decisions*, edited by W. Richardson and S. Freidin (London, 1956), p.10.

45 *Kesselring Memoirs*, p.63.

46 Bekker, p.173.

47 For relative strengths of the two sides, see Suchenwirth, *Turning Points*, p.64; AIR 16/116; Wood and Dempster, Appendix 6; Terraine, p.725; A. Robinson, *Fighter Squadrons in the Battle of Britain* (London, 1987), p.15.

48 T. Taylor, *Breaking Wave*, pp.129–34, 'Deployment and Order of Battle'

49 See AHB Translation, volume 7, No.VII/107, 'Luftwaffe Quartermaster General's Returns'.

50 For Hitler's lack of understanding of air power, see R.J. Overy, 'Hitler and Air Strategy', *JCH*, 15, 3 (1980), pp.405–22.

51 For Hitler's mood at the time, see B. Liddell Hart, *The German Generals Talk* (London, 1948), pp.145–47; see also A. Hillgruber, 'England's place in Hitler's plans for world dominion', *JCH*, 9, 1 (1974), pp.5–22.

52 For Hitler's power within the German State, see League of Nations, *Armaments Year Book* (Geneva, 1938), p.387; also see F.L. Carsten, 'The German Generals and Hitler', *History Today* (hereafter HT), 8, 8 (1958), pp.556–64.

53 Goering's movements from June to September 1940 are shown in Asher Lee, *Goering: Air Leader* (London, 1972); L. Moseley, *The Reich Marshal* (London, 1974); Irving, *Goering*; Overy, *Goering*. All passim.

54 Murray, p.6.

55 Galland, *First and Last*, p.127 and Bekker, p.292.

56 Suchenwirth, *Command and Leadership*, pp.215-19.

57 Ibid, pp.31–32.

58 *Kesselring Memoirs*, p.67.

59 AHB Translation, volume 2, No.VIII/40, 'The Effects of Air Power', 12 July 1940.

60 Trevor-Roper, pp.33–37.

61 An eyewitness account is given by W. Shirer, *Berlin Diary* (New York, 1941), pp.452–57.

62 Halifax broadcast, BBC Home Service, 22 July 1940. See also Churchill, ii, pp.229–30; also Gilbert, vi, p.672.

63 Goering conference, 'Besprechung Reichsmarschall am 21 July 1940'.

64 See S. Cox, 'A Comparative Analysis of RAF and Luftwaffe Intelligence in the Battle of Britain'; H. Boog, 'German Air Intelligence in World War II', *Aerospace Historian*, June 1986, p.122; Wood and Dempster, p.120.

65 Cox, 'Intelligence', pp.3–4.

66 Ibid, pp.11–12 and Wood and Dempster, pp.106-10.

67 Overy, *Air War*, Table 3; see also M.M. Postan, *British War Production* (HMSO, 1952), p.485.

68 OKL Intelligence Report, 16 July 1940: See F.K. Mason, *Battle Over Britain* (London, 1969), Appendix K.

69 Overy, *Goering*, p.170.

Chapter 3

1 K. G. Wynn, *Men of the Battle of Britain* (Norwich, 1989), p.2, shows that 2,927 airmen, from 67 squadrons and two flights, were awarded the Battle of Britain Clasp for service in action between 10 July and 31 October 1940.

2 The British were 'better at battle management' than the Germans. Lecture, Group Captain I. Madelin, 'The Battle of Britain', Royal Aeronautical Society, 20 November 1990.

3 See Dean, Chapter 14.

4 Slessor, p.298.

5 COS Paper No 168 of 1940.

6 See Gilbert, vi, pp.602–3. Churchill wanted people to treat raids 'as if they were no more than thunderstorms'.

7 Churchill, ii, p.214 and Gilbert, vi, p.655.

8 See Terraine, pp.141–44.

9 AIR 16/347 and Gilbert, vi, p.656.

10 For manifestations of the relationship, see Beaverbrook Papers, BBK D/21, BBK C/311 and BBK D/390; also see Gilbert, vi, pp.759–60 and p.811; also Slessor, p.305; also Dean, pp.137–38.

11 CAB 66/8, W.P. (40) 213.

12 See AIR 41/14, ADGB, i, Section 8; also see Dowding's confidence at meeting attacks in AIR 16/261, 24 February 1939.

13 AIR 8/863, p.4543, paragraph 7; also see AIR 41/15, ADGB, ii, pp.33–34.

14 Gilbert, vi, p.577.

15 Lord Ismay, *The Memoirs of General the Lord Ismay* (London, 1960), p.159.

16 AIR 16/347; AIR 20/2061; for Dowding's mistrust of the Air Ministry, see AIR 16/659, 3 July 1940.

17 AIR 41/14, ADGB, i, pp.1–22.

18 See ELMT 2/1, German Air Force Order of Battle. A.I.3b, 1 August 1940, in Elmhirst Papers, Churchill

College, Cambridge; also see Hinsley, i, Chapter 5.

19 Allen, *Who Won?* p.110.

20 Table based on AIR 8/863, pp.4560–61, Appendix A. However, Sir Peter Masefield, 'After the 120-Day Battle', in *Aerospace Historian* (October, 1990), pp.16–21, has a more guarded view of numbers.

21 AIR 41/15, ADGB, ii, p.40.

22 Dowding's Despatch, AIR 8/863, contained thinly veiled criticisms of Air Ministry policy, and although written in 1941 was not published until 1946. See Beaverbrook Papers, BBK D/440, 9 February 1944, which called it 'the record of a disappointed man'.

23 See PREM 3/38, folios 52–53, June 30, 1940.

24 Figures given in C. Bowyer, *Fighter Command* (London, 1980), p.56.

25 Gilbert, vi, pp.605–6. For a background to the problem, see Wood and Dempster, Chapter 3.

26 See Hough and Richards, p.290 and Wynn, p.2.

27 See AIR 41/15, ADGB, ii, p.40 and p.565.

28 Allen, *Who Won?* pp.111–13.

29 Interviews, Air Chief Marshal Sir Harry Broadhurst and Air Marshal Sir Denis Crowley-Milling.

30 See *The Battle Re–thought*, edited by H. Probert and S. Cox (London, 1991), p.18 (Dr H. Boog) and p.97 (Air Chief Marshal Sir Christopher Foxley-Norris).

31 See A. Price, *Luftwaffe Handbook, 1939–1945*, (London, 1977), Chapter 7.

32 AIR 8/863, p.4546, paragraphs 47 and 48; also Sir Frederick Pile, *Ack–Ack* (London, 1949), p.116.

33 Pile, pp.132–33.

34 AIR 8/863, p.4563, Appendix C, col. 1.

35 Ibid, pp.4564–65, Section 7, cols. 1 and 2.

36 See D.J. Smith, 'Balloon Barrages', in *The Blitz: Then and Now*, vol.1, edited by W. G. Ramsey (London, 1987), pp.86–95.

37 For workings of the 'Dowding System', see AIR 8/863, pp.4547–48, paragraphs 68–86; Wood and Demp-

ster, Chapter 10; A. Andrews, *The Air Marshals* (London, 1970). pp.107–8. Kreipe, the Chief Operations Officer of *Luftflotte III* later wrote, 'Radar at least doubled the efficacy of their own fighting force' – Richardson and Freidin, pp.16-17.

38 See Robinson, p.24. 'Well-established Kent radar stations' could give about twenty minutes' warning.

39 Terraine, p.180.

40 Overy, *Air War*, p.32.

41 See Cox, 'Intelligence', p.6.

42 See A. Clayton, *The Enemy is Listening* (London, 1980); also, Hinsley, i, pp.179–80.

43 See Hinsley, i, pp.11–12.

44 See AIR 40/2321; also see W. Wark, 'British Intelligence on the German Air Force and the Aircraft Industry, 1933-1939', *HJ*, 25, 3 (1982), p.648, who believes that British Intelligence officers 'failed to climb into the skulls of their German opponents'.

45 Hinsley, i, p.177.

46 AIR 40/2321, Minute 77; see also AHB Translation, volume 2, No.VII/39, Appendix A.

47 AIR 40/2321; see also Hinsley, i, p.177.

48 Ibid.

49 F. Winterbotham, *The Ultra Secret* (London, 1974), pp.65–80; R. Lewin, *Ultra Goes to War* (London, 1978), pp.84–87; Terraine, pp.178–79.

50 Gilbert, vi, p.849.

51 Hinsley, i, p.178.

52 Interview, Wing Commander H. Ironside.

53 Interview, Air Chief Marshal Sir Kenneth Cross.

54 Probert and Cox, p.64.

55 Air Ministry, *Royal Air Force Training Manual, Pt.II, Applied Flying. Air Publication 928* (February 1933); R.T. Bickers, *The Battle of Britain* (London, 1990), pp.97-102, gives a visual presentation of the attacks.

56 B. Gunston, *Fighters, 1914–1945* (London, 1951), pp.51–63, shows the development of fighters in all major air forces during the 1930s.

57 See Allen, *Who Won?* p.72.

58 J. Quill, *Spitfire* (London, 1985), p.122.

59   See *Air Publication 928*, Chapter 8; AIR 16/74; Deere, p.34; Spick, pp.46–51.

60   AIR 16/281.

61   Ibid.

62   Beaverbrook Papers, BBK D/330, 29 May 1940.

63   AIR 16/281.

64   Interview, Air Marshal Sir Kenneth Porter.

65   AIR 16/281; also see N. Franks, *The Air Battle of Dunkirk* (London, 1983) p.121.

66   AIR 8/863, p.4558, paragraph 220.

67   Interview, Group Captain H. Darley.

68   Franks, p.120.

69   AIR 16/281.

70   Ibid.

71   AIR 2/7281.

72   'Higher Authority' probably refers to Dowding; see Orange, p.87.

73   See Robinson, p.68; Franks, p.17; AIR 27/252 and AIR 27/424, for the period of the Dunkirk evacuation.

74   Wood and Dempster give five phases; Hough and Richards four; Robinson offers four; Galland, AHB Translation, vol.9, VII/121, proposes six; Dowding's Despatch chooses four.

75   One example was the later Air Vice-Marshal G. Lott, OC 43 Squadron. After action from September 1939 to Dunkirk, then over the Channel, he was shot down on 9 July. 'I tangled with a Messerschmitt 110 as a result of which I subsequently lost my right eye'. He was not entitled to the Battle of Britain Clasp. Letter, AVM G. Lott.

76   See, for example, *Kesselring Memoirs*, Chapter 11.

77   Irving, *Rise and Fall*, pp.100–1.

78   T. Taylor, *Breaking Wave*, pp.127–28.

79   Richardson and Freidin, pp.11–12.

80   See AIR 41/15, ADGB, ii, pp.71–78; also see W. P. Crozier, *Off the Record, Political Interviews, 1933–1943* (London, 1973), p.182, interview with A. V. Alexander; also see C.I. Savage, *Inland Transport* (HMSO, 1957), pp.214–21.

81   See AIR 41/15, ADGB, ii, pp.71–72.

82   See Gilbert, vi, p.718.

83   See Hough and Richards, pp.357–58; also see Wood and Dempster, pp.239–56; also AIR 41/15, ADGB, ii, p.36.

84   Trevor-Roper, pp.37–38.

85   AHB Translation, vol.2, No.VII/26.

86   For a critical review of RAF tactics, see N. Gelb, *Scramble* (London, 1986), pp.88–90.

87   See A. Price, *The Hardest Day* (London, 1979), p.23. For Defiant losses, see Ramsey, *Battle of Britain*, pp.326–27; also see AIR 41/15, ADGB, ii, p.62; for the Defiant's weaknesses, see AIR 8/863, p.4553, paragraph 154; also see AIR 2/2964, 25 June 1938.

88   For Ju 87s in action, see AIR 50/22, 13 July 1940; also see Galland, *First and Last*, pp.71–73. For weaknesses of the Me 110, see Townsend, *Duel of Eagles*, p.297 and Robinson, pp.146–47.

89   Murray, p.50.

90   AHB Translation, volume 2, VII/121, pp.13-14.

91   *Pamphlet No.248*, p.80.

92   See Gilbert, vi, p.650 and p.710; also see Hinsley, i, Chapter 5.

93   See AIR 41/15, ADGB, ii, p.81.

94   See Suchenwirth, *Turning Points*, pp.63–65; also see AHB Translation, vol. 2, No.VII/83; compare, however, figures in Ramsey, *Battle of Britain*, p.707.

95   Postan, pp.116 and 484.

96   Suchenwirth, *Turning Points*, p.66.

97   Suchenwirth, *Command and Leadership*, p.87.

98   Their optimism is shown in T. Taylor, *Breaking Wave*, p.133.

99   For Goering's methods in staff conferences, see ibid., pp.130–32; also see *Kesselring Memoirs*, pp.67–68.

100 See H. Boog in Probert and Cox, pp.22–23 and p.26.

101 See AIR 2/7281, 12 September 1940; also see P. Wykeham, *Fighter Command* (London, 1960), pp.117–22.

102 See Irving, *Rise and Fall*, p.100; also see Wood and Dempster, p.285.

103 Hough and Richards, pp.157 and 160–62.

104 See R. Collier, *Eagle Day* (London, 1980), pp.50–51; also see Bekker, pp.194–95; also see U. Steinhilper and P. Osborne, *Spitfire on my Tail* (Bromley, 1989), p.264.

105 See Hough and Richards, Appendix

VII and Price, *Hardest Day*, Appendix C.

106 T. Taylor, *Breaking Wave*, pp.137 and 140.

107 See Price, *Hardest Day*, Appendices E and F. Compare these figures with Ramsey, *Battle of Britain*, pp.581–90.

108 AHB Translation, vol. 9, No.VII/123; also see Price, *Hardest Day*, Appendix C.

109 Allen, *Who Won?*, p.149 shows the extent of the burden.

110 Orange, p.101.

111 See AIR 2/7355, 12 September 1940; also see Orange, p.102.

112 See C. Shores, *Duel for the Sky* (London, 1985), p.54.

113 AIR 8/863, p.4554, paragraphs 169–72.

114 AIR 41/15, ADGB, ii, p.219; also see Allen, *Who Won?*, p.149.

115 Gilbert, vi, p.711.

116 AIR 19/572.

117 Ibid.

118 Ibid.

119 Dowding Papers, S.305, 13 August 1940.

120 Ibid, 21 August 1940.

121 Earl of Avon, *The Eden Memoirs: The Reckoning* (London, 1965), p.137.

122 Gilbert, vi, p.726.

123 *Ismay Memoirs*, pp.179–80.

124 Gilbert, vi, pp.736–37.

125 364 H.C. Deb. 5s, c.1167, 20 August 1940.

126 *Crozier Interviews*, 23 August 1940.

127 There are 197 boxes of the Thurso Papers at Churchill College, Cambridge. However, many wartime papers were destroyed by fire. The first was at the Liberal Club during the Blitz and the second, accidental, blaze occurred at his Scottish home. For Sinclair, Dowding was an inherited problem.

128 J. Colville, in *Action This Day: Working with Churchill*, edited by Sir John Wheeler-Bennett (London, 1968), p.195.

129 *Channon Diaries*, p.264.

130 *Crozier Interviews*, p.198.

131 *A Party Politician, The Memoirs of Chubby Power*, edited by N. Ward (Toronto, 1966), pp.196–97.

132 Douglas, *Years of Command*, p.278.

133 Air Marshal Sir Robert Saundby, in *The Ampleforth Journal* (1970), p.84.

134 Colville, *Action This Day*, pp.105–6.

135 Beaverbrook Papers, BBK D/430.

136 *Crozier Interviews*, p.199.

137 PREM 4/3/6 and Beaverbrook Papers, BBK D/328.

138 See D. Richards, *Portal of Hungerford* (London, 1977), pp.168–69.

139 H. Dalton, *The Fateful Years, Memoirs, 1931–1945* (London, 1957), pp.344–45.

Chapter 4

1 AIR 16/25.

2 CAB 3/8, CID, 308A; also see AIR 16/129; for No 12 Group, see AIR 16/294; Wykeham, pp.76–77 explains that 'though a procedure was standardized for handover, it remained a troublesome problem for many years'.

3 'The Forgotten Pilots: The Women Who Flew in the Second World War', television programme, BBC South, 25 May 1984.

4 See Spick, Chapter 4, for tactics used and lessons learned.

5 CAB 55/8, CID.

6 AIR 16/91.

7 AIR 2/3034, 11 August 1938; also see AIR 16/367, 17 December 1940; also see Douglas Papers, File 2, 14 February 1956.

8 AIR 2/3034.

9 AIR 16/261. Dowding's optimism is supported by comparing the top speeds of the Heinkel He 111P (247mph) and the Dornier Do 17Z (265mph), with those of the Hurricane I (328mph) and the Spitfire IA (362mph). See Mason, *Battle Over Britain*, Appendix C.

10 AIR 16/254, 10 March 1939; also see AIR 16/45, 28 June 1939; also see Douglas, *Years of Command*, p.43.

11 AIR 16/254, 14 March 1939.

12 AIR 16/131, 15 August 1939.

13 For a background of Park's RAF service, see Orange, passim.

14 AIR 16/131, 15, 17 and 19 August 1939.

15 For example, see on the one hand

Wright, especially Chapter 10, Orange, Deighton and Terraine, all passim. On the other hand, see Allen, *Who Won?* and Lucas, *Flying Colours*, both passim; also see Bader Notes, Appendix B.

16 Allen, *Who Won?*, p.178, believes that the Germans had gained local air superiority by 1 September.

17 See 'Parrying the Blitz', *The Aeroplane*, 6 September 1940. 'The frequency of attacks increased and more fighters were sent with fewer bombers.'

18 See Price, *Luftwaffe Handbook*, p.14.

19 SKL KTB, 18 August 1940.

20 See Irving, *Rise and Fall*, pp.100–1. For a German pilot's reaction see R. Jackson, *Douglas Bader: a biography* (London, 1953), p.74.

21 See Hough and Richards, p.219; Allen, *Who Won?* p.150; Wood and Dempster, p.300.

22 See Hough and Richards, Chapter 15; Wood and Dempster, Chapter 16.

23 See AIR 16/635, 3 November 1940.

24 Robinson, pp.189–90.

25 See Gelb, p.177.

26 Hough and Richards, p.251.

27 AHB Translation, Volume 9, No.VII/121, p.18; also see K. Bartz, *Swastika in the Air* (London, 1956), pp.70–71.

28 See T. Taylor, *Breaking Wave*, pp.149–51.

29 P. Stahl, *The Diving Eagle: A Ju 88 Pilot's Diary* (London, 1984), pp.58–59; also see Murray, p.43.

30 Gilbert, vi, p.759.

31 Ibid, p.760.

32 Ibid, p.761.

33 CAB 65/14, War Cabinet No 238.

34 *Colville Diaries*, p.235.

35 Ibid, p.238.

36 See AHB Monograph, R. E. Skelley, Signals (3), vol.4, *Radar in Raid Reporting*, CD 1063, AHB/II/116/21(C) (London, 1950), pp.112-13, also issued as AIR 41/12; also see J. Nissen, *Winning the Radar War* (London, 1989), p.84

37 See T. Taylor, *Breaking Wave*, pp.80–81.

38 Robinson, p.24.

39 See R. Hillary, *The Last Enemy* (London, 1942), p.103.

40 D. Crook, *Spitfire Pilot* (London, 1942)

41 See AIR 16/659, 20 and 28 June 1940.

42 See Crook, p.64; also Gelb, pp.187–91; also see R. Beamont in RAF Benevolent Fund's publication, *So Few*, edited by M. Pierce et al. (London, 1990), pp.32–34.

43 AIR 2/7281, 12 September 1940.

44 See AIR 41/15, ADGB, ii, Appendix 6, Instructions to Controllers, No 4.

45 See, for example, Mason, *Battle Over Britain*, pp.257–84; Price, *Hardest Day*, Chapter 5; *The Blitz, Then and Now*, vol. i, edited by W.G. Ramsey (London, 1987), p.211; Richards and Saunders, i, pp. 173–74.

46 Price, *Hardest Day*, p.60.

47 See AIR 8/863, p.4554, paragraphs 169–75.

48 AIR 41/15, ADGB, ii, Appendix 9, Instructions to Controllers, No 6.

49 AIR 16/330.

50 Ibid.

51 See Ramsey, *Blitz*, i, pp.232–38 and pp.247–51 for the raids on North Weald and Debden respectively.

52 For events on the 24th, see D. Sarkar, *Spitfire Squadron* (New Malden, 1990), pp.56–58; also see AIR 27/252, 24 and 26 August 1940.

53 AIR 16/330, Instructions to Controllers, No 7, 27 August 1940.

54 Ibid, 28 August 1940.

55 Ibid, 9 October 1940; also see Lucas, *Flying Colours*, Chapters 9-12 inclusive; and Bader Notes, Appendix B.

56 AIR 16/330.

57 See Crozier, pp.197 and 199–201; also see Slessor, p.305.

58 See Hinsley, i, p.184; also see AIR 40/2321, 2 September 1940.

59 AIR 16/330.

60 AIR 41/15, ADGB, ii, Instructions to Controllers No 10.

61 For Dowding's own view, see AIR 8/863, pp.4554–55, paragraphs 169–78. For one pilot's recollections, see H.R. Allen, *Spitfire Squadron* (London, 1979), pp.66–72; also see AIR 16/330.

62 See AIR 16/330, 8 September and 8 October 1940; for the shortage of pilots, see Deere, pp.150–52; also see

Orange, pp.105–6.

63 AIR 16/330, The three named squadrons were Nos 3, 232 and 245.

64 Ibid; also see Burns, p.87.

65 Ibid, 14 September 1940.

66 For a detailed background of the London raid, see *The Blitz, Then and Now*, vol.ii, edited by W. G. Ramsey (London, 1988), pp.41–61; see also Ministry of Information, *Front Line* (HMSO, 1942), pp.10-12; for an individual view, see Mrs R. Henrey, *London Under Fire, 1940–45* (London, 1969), pp.33–34; for a vivid diary account, see C. Perry, *The Boy in the Blitz* (London, 1972), pp.106-17. See also A. Calder, *The People's War* (London, 1969), pp.154–59; Sir Aylmer Firebrace, *Fire Service Memories* (London, 1949), pp.168–69; Sir Harold Scott, *Your Obedient Servant* (London, 1959), pp.126–27. A German pilot's account is given in Steinhilper and Osborne, pp.291–92.

67 See, for example, Taylor, *English History*, p.499 and Gelb, p.288. For a German view of RAF bombing, see *The Berlin Diaries, 1940–1945, of Marie 'Missie' Vassiltchikov*, edited by G. H. Vassiltchikov (London, 1987), pp.28–33, entries for the period 28 August–26 October 1940. See also K. W. Koch, 'The Strategic Air Offensive Against Germany: The Early Phase, May-September 1940', in *HJ*, 34, 1 (1991), pp.117–39. Although containing several inaccuracies of quotation, the article shows that, while the Battle of Britain was in progress, the RAF bombing of Germany had some effect.

68 AHB Translation, German Air Force General Staff/8th Abteilung, 'German Air Force Operations Against Great Britain, Tactics and Lessons Learnt, 1940-1941', 2 February 1944.

69 'Reasons of Luftwaffe for changing over to mass attacks on London', General P. Deichmann, Chief Control Officer of the Karlsruhe Study, 1953–58. See also Murray, p.54; see also AHB Translation, vol.4, VII/83, which shows that by 30 September Luftwaffe bombers had suffered a 69 per cent casualty rate; see also *Kessel-*

ring Memoirs, pp.75–78.

70 See T. Taylor, *Breaking Wave*, pp.157–58. Hitler announced a policy of retribution.

71 See Orange, pp.107–8; also see Gilbert, vi, p.774.

72 See Galland, *First and Last*, p.83.

73 See *Colville Diaries*, p.235 and Collier, *Defence of the United Kingdom*, p.237; also see Terraine, p.208.

74 See Orange, p.107 and Gelb, p.234.

Chapter 5

1 AIR 2/7281, 14 October 1940.

2 See, for example, Terraine, pp.214-17; Wright, Chapter 13; Deighton, pp.271–73; Taylor, *English History*, p.500.

3 See Orange, pp.120–39; Terraine, pp.196 and 199–201; Wright, Chapters 11 and 12; Wood and Dempster, pp.309-10 and 411–14; Collier, *Leader of the Few*, pp.212 and 220–27; Deighton, pp.228–31, 262–63 and 271–73; *The Times*, 7 February 1975, p.16.

4 Interview, Air Marshal Sir Kenneth Porter.

5 Interviews, Air Chief Marshal Sir Kenneth Cross and Professor D. Wiseman.

6 Dr V. Orange, in Probert and Cox, p.36.

7 Air Vice-Marshal S. Johnstone in *Thanks for the Memory*, edited by L. Lucas (London, 1989), pp.205–6.

8 Joubert, p.137.

9 Interview, Air Marshal Sir Kenneth Porter.

10 Interview, Air Chief Marshal Sir Kenneth Cross.

11 Interview, Air Marshal Sir Denis Crowley-Milling.

12 Interview, Air Marshal Sir Kenneth Porter.

13 Interview, Air Chief Marshal Sir Harry Broadhurst, and letter, Professor R.V. Jones.

14 AIR 28/232, 31 August 1940.

15 See AIR 41/15, ADGB, ii, pp.567–74; also see N. Monks, *Squadrons Up!* (London, 1940), p.246; also see AIR 25/219, July and August 1940.

16 See Air Ministry, *The Air Force List*, February 1940, Index, Nos.221 and 222–23; also see Orange, p.83; also, *The Times*, 7 February 1975, p.16; also Douglas Papers, File 2, 14 February 1956.

17 For Bader's impatience at being called late into action, see Air Marshal Sir Denis Crowley-Milling in *So Few*, p.69.

18 See Lucas, *Flying Colours*, p.106; also see H. Dundas, 'Sir Douglas Bader', in Lucas, *Thanks for the Memory*, p.337.

19 See Bader Notes, Appendix B.

20 Interview, Air Chief Marshal Sir Kenneth Cross.

21 J. Johnson, *Wing Leader* (London, 1956), Foreword.

22 Lucas, *Flying Colours*, pp.83–84 and 95; see also Burns, pp.28–29.

23 Interviews, Air Chief Marshal Sir Harry Broadhurst, Air Chief Marshal Sir Kenneth Cross and Air Marshal Sir Denis Crowley-Milling; also see Terraine, p.198.

24 See Deighton, p.276, 'Table 3. Comparison of British and German figures for aircraft lost'.

25 P. Brickhill, *Reach for the Sky* (London, 1956), p.186; also see Lucas, *Flying Colours*, p.120.

26 See Mason, *Battle Over Britain*, pp.320–27.

27 See Ramsey, *Battle of Britain*, pp.606–9.

28 See Ramsey, *Blitz*, i, pp.269–76.

29 See Bader Notes.

30 AIR 16/281.

31 Ibid.

32 AIR 16/330.

33 Ibid, 10 September 1940.

34 Ibid.

35 AIR 16/842, Instructions to Controllers, No 16, 11 September 1940.

36 See AIR 41/15, ADGB, ii, p.392.

37 Ibid.

38 AIR 16/281, 17 September 1940.

39 AIR 28/232.

40 See W. Ansel, *Hitler Confronts England* (New York, 1964), pp.252 ff, quoting SKL KTB, Part A, 17 September 1940 and STL KTB, 12 October 1940; also see Hinsley, i, p.168 for British caution.

41 See AHB Translation, vol.4, No.VII/83; also see Ramsey, *Battle of Britain*, p.707.

42 See Bekker, p.224; AIR 41/15, ADGB, ii, Appendix 36 shows discrepancies of claims.

43 See Richards and Saunders, i, p.186; see also Gelb, p.234.

44 See AIR 41/15, ADGB, ii, pp.454–55; also see Leigh-Mallory's beliefs in co-ordinated attacks in AIR 25/219, 15 September 1940; also see Hough and Richards, pp.277–83; also see Ramsey, *Blitz*, ii, pp.95-104.

45 AIR 41/15, ADGB, ii, Instructions to Controllers, No 18, 16 September 1940.

46 AIR 16/281.

47 See Robinson, pp.151–52, using particularly AIR 50/32 to show that the reality of battle for No 74 Squadron differed from the plan laid down.

48 See Mason, *Battle Over Britain*, Chapter 8.

49 See Ramsey, *Battle of Britain*, pp.706–7.

50 AIR 16/281.

51 Ibid.

52 See AIR 2/7281, Enclosure 1A, 20 September 1940 and AIR 16/281, Enclosure 101A, 24 September 1940.

53 AIR 2/7281.

54 Ibid, Minute 2. This minute reinforces the contention that there were two Big Wing theories.

55 Ibid, Minute 3.

56 See especially AIR 16/387, 25 September 1940 and AIR 2/7341, 25 September 1940.

57 AIR 16/281. For an account of the pilots of No 310 Squadron and their general approval of Big Wing tactics, see Johnson, pp.34–36.

58 Ibid.

59 AIR 2/7281.

60 Ibid.

61 Ibid, 27 September 1940.

62 Ibid.

63 AIR 41/15, ADGB, ii, Appendix 25, Instructions to Controllers, No 19.

64 AIR 16/330.

65 AIR 2/7281.

66 Park's Senior Controller was Air Commodore Baron Willioughby de Broke. For references to him, see

Orange, pp.107, 122, 146 and 148.
67 Interview, Group Captain H. Darley.
68 AIR 2/7281.
69 Ibid, 1 October 1940.
70 AIR 28/232.
71 AIR 16/330, 3 October 1940.
72 Ibid.
73 See Bader Notes, Appendix B.
74 AIR 16/330.
75 Wright, p.199.
76 AIR 16/330.
77 Ibid.
78 For German disappointment, see for example, *The Goebbels Diaries, 1939–1941*, edited by F. Taylor (London, 1982), diary entry for 12 October, p.140. Certainly the German euphoria of June had been dampened by Fighter Command's tenacity.
79 See T. Taylor, *Breaking Wave*, pp.166–67.
80 Galland, *First and Last*, p.88.
81 For examples of raids on aircraft factories, see C.R. Russell, *Spitfire Odyssey* (Southampton, 1985), pp.72–83.
82 Beaverbrook Papers, BBK D/28.
83 Ibid, BBK D/32.
84 AIR 16/635.
85 See AIR 2/7281, Minute 7, Douglas to Saundby, 29 September 1940.
86 AIR 16/635, 24 October and 1 November 1940.
87 AIR 2/7281, 14 October 1940.
88 See Beaverbrook Papers, BBK D/35, 29 September 1940.
89 AIR 2/7281.
90 AIR 16/375, 15 October 1940.
91 AIR 28/232.
92 AIR 16/330, 16 October 1940.
93 Ibid.
94 See Douglas Papers, File 2, 28 March 1961.

Chapter 6

1 E. B. Haslam, 'How Lord Dowding Came to Leave Fighter Command', *JSS*, 4, 2 (1981), pp.175–86.
2 See L. Deighton, *Fighter: The True Story of the Battle of Britain* (London, 1977), and L. Deighton, 'Forty Years On', *Sunday Times* colour supplement, 14 September 1980.

3 See Air Chief Marshal Lord Dowding, 'Night Fighters Hunt the Bombers', *Star*, 24 September 1951, p.3.
4 See AIR 41/17, ADGB, iii, pp.1–4, for a background to night air defence.
5 Captain J. Morris, *The German Air Raids on Great Britain, 1914–1918* (London, 1927), Preface.
6 Ibid.
7 For details of the early development of bombers, including the Gotha, see Cooper, pp.35–45.
8 P. R. C. Groves, *Behind the Smoke Screen* (London, 1934), pp.154–55.
9 See Taylor, *English History*, pp.427–28. At the time of Munich, 'thirty-eight million gas masks' were distributed in Britain.
10 See Morris, Part II, chapters 3 and 4.
11 Pile, p.166.
12 *Roof Over Britain*, p.48.
13 The need was great. AIR 6/55, 25 October 1938 showed that 24 of the 29 squadrons in Fighter Command then were obsolete. R. Higham, *Armed Forces in Peacetime* (London, 1962), gives spending on the RAF between 1937 and 1940.
14 See Webster and Frankland, i, p.125.
15. Wykeham, p.150.
16 AHB Translation, vol.9, No.VII/121, p.28.
17 See H. A. Jones, *The War in the Air* (Oxford, 1934), vol.5, p.159.
18 AIR 41/17, ADGB, iii, Home Defence Committee Paper No 270, 9 February 1937.
19 AIR 16/260, 24 May 1937.
20 See Pile, p.151.
21 Wood and Dempster, Appendix VIII show the slowness of gun production.
22 See Pile, p.152.
23 For an excellent background summary, see E. Munday, 'Chain Home: Radar and the Blitz', in Ramsey, *Blitz*, i, pp.124–37.
24 See AIR 41/17, ADGB, iii, Chapter 1, p.4.
25 For difficulties involved, see C. F. Rawnsley and R. Wright, *Night Fighter* (London, 1957), Chapter 2; also see Wykeham, pp.158–60.
26 The Bawdsey station, northeast of Felixstowe, began experiments in 1936. See Wykeham. pp.151–52.

27 See ibid., p.153. Dowding believed that a night-fighter should carry a crew of two – see AIR 2/2964, 16 November 1938.

28 See Wykeham, pp.160–61; also see Gunston, pp.98–99; for shortages, see AIR 41/17, ADGB, iii, p.6.

29 See AHB Monograph, C. Stephenson, Signals (3), vol.5, *Fighter Control and Interception*, CD 1116, AHB/II/116/21(D), (London, 1950), p.9.

30 See R. Clark, *Tizard* (London, 1965), pp.159–60.

31 AHB monograph, Signals (3), vol.5, p.113. See Dowding's worries in AIR 8/863, p.4558, paragraph 232.

32 Wykeham, p.153.

33 For details of night raids, see Ramsey, *Blitz*, i, pp.24–76.

34 Air Vice-Marshal Peck was an Assistant Chief of the Air Staff (ACAS, O and I) with a special interest in night defence.

35 See Wykeham, pp.155–56.

36 See AIR 41/17, ADGB, iii, pp.11–12. The squadrons were Nos 23, 25, 29, 219, 600 and 604.

37 Ibid., p.9, quoting COS(40), 4 May 1940. For the work of the Night Interception Committee, see AIR 16/247.

38 See Ramsey, *Blitz*, i, pp.108-10.

39 See R. V. Jones, *Most Secret War* (London, 1979), Chapters 10 and 11; also see Churchill, ii, pp.339–41; also Gilbert, vi, pp.580–84. German beams could have been 'bent' deliberately, but were not, although the effect was sometimes achieved accidentally. See A. Price, *Instruments of Darkness* (London, 1967), pp.36–38.

40 See R. V. Jones, 'The Electronic War', in Ramsey, *Blitz*, i, pp.282–93; also see AIR 20/1623, 20 June 1940; also see AIR 41/17, ADGB, iii, p.27, where *Knickebein* was 'found to be 400 Yards in width, with a range of approximately 300 miles'; also see Stahl, pp.82–83.

41 See AIR 41/17, ADGB, iii, p.26, 16 June 1940; letter, Professor R. V. Jones.

42 For a background to the work, and rivalry, of Tizard and Lindemann, see Jones, *Secret War*, especially pp.38–47.

43 See Trevor-Roper, pp.18–21; also see Frankland, *Bombing Offensive*, pp.55–56; also see Saward, p.104. For Kesselring's view, which carefully avoids mention of failures, see *Kesselring Memoirs*, p.75.

44 AIR 41/17, ADGB, ii, p.34 shows that in June, RAF and AA Command claimed sixteen German aircraft at night, of which eleven were confirmed. In reply, the RAF lost ten.

45 See Webster and Frankland, i, pp.144–45 and 213–33.

46 See 'The Unceasing Offensive', in *The Aeroplane*, 14 June 1940, which gave 5 June for the start of the offensive.

47 See Wood and Dempster, pp.239 and 283; also see Ramsey, *Battle of Britain*, p.549. For Dowding's warnings to Churchill, see Gilbert, vi, pp.668–69.

48 See T. Taylor, *Breaking Wave*, pp.145–46, and Price, *Instruments of Darkness*, p.35.

49 See Ramsey, *Battle of Britain*, pp.385–86.

50 See Elmhirst Papers, ELMT 2/1, 3 September 1940; also see 'Parrying the Blitzkrieg', in *The Aeroplane*, 6 September 1940; also see AIR 41/17, ADGB, iii, p.44.

51 *Front Line*, p.12; see also AIR 41/17, ADGB, iii, p.55; also see Earl of Birkenhead, *Halifax* (London, 1965), p.460; also see I. Maisky, *Memoirs of a Soviet Ambassador* (London, 1967), p.107.

52 See *Ismay Memoirs*, pp.183–84; also see Gilbert, vi, pp.760 and 764.

53 See Gilbert, vi, p.774, and Hough and Richards, p.263.

54 See Pile, p.149. On 12 September, one headline ran, 'Terrific London Barrage Meets Greatest Raid', *Daily Express*, 12 September 1940, p.1.

55 Wood and Dempster, pp.341–42.

56 *Roof Over Britain*, p.48, and *Channon Diaries*, p.266.

57 E.H. Gombrich, *Myth and Reality in German War–Time Broadcasts* (London, 1970), p.9.

58 Gilbert, vi, p.777, and AIR 41/17, ADGB, iii, p.55.

59 See Pile, p.173.

60 See 'Charioteer', 'The Need for

Research', *The Aeroplane*, 20 September 1940.

61 For example, see AIR 2/7281, 28 September 1940.

62 AIR 41/17, ADGB, iii, pp.49–50 and 55.

63 Douglas, *Years of Command*, pp.103–4.

64 See AIR 16/379.

65 AIR 20/4298, 11 September 1940.

66 See AIR 19/230, 11 September 1940.

67 See Douglas, *Years of Command*, pp.106–7; also see Douglas Papers, File 2, 21 November 1961. Details of 'Mutton' are in A. Price, *Blitz on Britain, 1939–1945* (London, 1977), pp.107-10.

68 Beaverbrook Papers, BBK D/442, 14 September 1940.

69 AIR 2/7341, 14 September 1940.

70 AIR 16/387, 14 September 1940.

71 Beaverbrook Papers, BBK D/414, 11 and 12 September 1940.

72 See Boyle, p.675; also see the papers of Marshal of the Royal Air Force Sir John Salmond, Aviation Records Department, RAF Museum, Hendon, B2638, 27 October, 6 and 30 November 1939. For words in praise of Salmond, see Dean, p.87. For a general biography, see J. Laffin, *Swifter Than Eagles* (Edinburgh, 1964).

73 Ibid., 12 September 1940.

74 AIR 20/4298, 16 September 1940.

75 Ibid., 17 September 1940.

76 Ibid., 18 September 1940.

77 *Colville Diaries*, pp.245 and 248. For a summary of Lindemann's interventions, see Ramsey, *Blitz*, ii, p.310.

78 AIR 19/230, 22 September 1940.

79 AIR 20/4298, 25 September 1940.

80 AIR 16/387 and AIR 2/7341, both 25 September 1940.

81 Salmond Papers, B2638, 25 September 1940.

82 Ibid.

83 See Douglas, *Years of Command*, p.91.

84 AIR 16/387, 17 September 1940.

85 AIR 2/7341, 27 September 1940.

86 Ibid.

87 Beaverbrook Papers, BBK D/442, 27 September 1940.

88 AIR 2/7341, 30 September 1940.

89 AIR 20/4298, 1 October 1940.

90 AIR 16/387, 3 October 1940.

91 AIR 41/17, ADGB, iii, Appendix 1/B.

92 See Gilbert, vi, pp.812, 814 and 824.

93 Ibid., p.823.

94 Salmond papers, B2638.

95 Ibid., 5 October 1940.

96 Beaverbrook Papers, BBK D/327 and BBK C/311.

97 Ibid., BBK D/28 and BBK D/414. See also BBK C/311, 14 and 16 October 1940, which show the problems facing the C-in-C. In Dowding's letter it is noticeable how, in paragraph 19, he shows antipathy towards Salmond.

98 See Pile, pp.165–66.

99 CAB 81/22.

100 See AIR 20/4298, 7 October 1940.

101 AIR 16/387, 8 October 1940.

102 AIR 20/4298, 12 October 1940.

103 See *Colville Diaries*, p.265, and Gilbert, vi, p.841.

104 For details of this large raid, see Gilbert, vi, pp.842–44; also see Pile, p.175; also see Stahl, pp.73–80; also see Wykeham, pp.170–72, who remarks on Fighter Command's 'guilt complex'; a close examination of the raid is given in AIR 41/17, ADGB, iii.

105 See Gilbert, vi, p.849.

106 Ibid, p.855.

107 AIR 16/387.

108 See Wood and Dempster, pp.365–66.

109 AIR 20/4298.

110 AIR 16/330.

111 AIR 16/387.

Chapter 7

1 For example, see Wright, Chapters 12 and 13; Deighton, pp.238–39; Orange, pp.127–33; Terraine, pp.194–205 and 220–22; Wood and Dempster, pp.411–13; Bowyer, pp.86–87; Wykeham, pp.145–47; Townsend, *Duel of Eagles*, pp.469–71; Gelb, p.266.

2 Orange, p.136.

3 Wright, passim.

4 Balfour, p.135.

5 For contrasting views, see Lucas, *Flying Colours*, pp.151–53 and Terraine, pp.215-17.

6 See AIR 2/7281, 1 November 1940.

7 For Park's later recollections of what he said, see Townsend, *Duel of*

Eagles, pp.470–71.

8 In Wright, Chapter 13, the impression is given that Dowding supported Park, but this is not apparent in the minutes.

9 See Townsend, *Duel of Eagles*, pp.470–71.

10 AIR 2/7281.

11 Ibid., 21 October 1940.

12 Ibid., 22 October 1940.

13 Ibid., 24 October 1940.

14 Ibid., 28 October 1940.

15 Ibid., 31 October 1940.

16 Ibid., 31 October 1940.

17 Ibid., 1 November 1940.

18 Ibid., 1 November 1940.

19 See Ramsey, *Blitz*, ii, pp.147–51.

20 See *Kesselring Memoirs*, p.75; also see AHB Translation, vol.4, No.VII/83.

21 See Hough and Richards, p.292 for the dangers of this new work.

22 AIR 16/330.

23 Ibid, 20 October 1940.

24 Ibid., 22 October 1940.

25 Ibid., 26 October 1940.

26 Ibid., 27 October 1940.

27 Ibid., 24 October 1940.

28 Ibid., 25 and 26 October 1940.

29 AIR 16/901, Instructions to Controllers, No 35.

30 AIR 16/330, 26 October 1940.

31 Ibid., 29 October 1940.

32 Ibid.

33 Ibid., 2 November 1940.

34 Ibid., 4 November 1940.

35 Ibid., 5 November 1940.

36 Ibid., 13 November 1940.

37 AIR 16/635, 7 November 1940.

38 Ibid., 17 November 1940.

39 Ibid., 15 November 1940.

40 AIR 16/676, 16 and 17 October 1940.

41 Ibid., 17 October 1940.

42 AIR 20/4298, 12 and 20 October 1940.

43 Ibid., 20 October 1940.

44 CAB 81/22.

45 AIR 20/4298, 21 October 1940; also see AIR 41/17, ADGB, iii, p.53.

46 P. Townsend, *Duel in the Dark* (London, 1986), p.95.

47 AIR 16/677, 24 October 1940.

48 See Price, *Instruments of Darkness*, p.41.

49 See *The Aeroplane*, 25 October 1940.

50 See AIR 16/379.

51 Beaverbrook Papers, BBK D/28.

52 See AHB Monograph, signals (3), vol.4, p.131.

53 AIR 2/7341.

54 AIR 16/635, 7 November 1940.

55 AHB Monograph, Signals (3), vol.4, p.127.

56 See AIR 41/17, ADGB, iii, p.194 for October figures.

57 Interview, Air Marshal Sir Kenneth Porter.

58 See above, Chapter 3.

59 Balfour, pp.132–33.

60 Letter, Dr Martin Gilbert.

61 See AIR 28/232.

62 H. Dundas, *Flying Start* (London, 1988), p.53.

63 Interview, Air Marshal Sir Denis Crowley-Milling.

64 See Bader Notes; Lucas, *Flying Colours*, Chapter 13; J. Foreman, *Battle of Britain: The Forgotten Months, November and December, 1940* (London, 1988), p.32; H. Halliday, *242 Squadron* (London, 1982), p.87.

65 AIR 16/375, 2 November 1940.

66 Ibid., 3 November 1940.

67 Ibid., 4 November 1940.

68 Ibid., 6 November 1940.

69 Ibid., 17 November 1940.

70 Ibid., 17 November 1940.

71 *Channon Diaries*, p.244. Although the Balfour Papers in the House of Lords Record Office (HLRO, Balfour Papers, No 199, Historical Collection) contain a typescript, 'Dunkirk Days – Battle of Britain: As seen from desk of US of S For Air', pp.128–40, the following section on the Battle of Britian is not included.

72 Bruce Papers, M/100/1, 5 November 1940.

73 See Gilbert, vi, p.909, and PREM 4/3/6.

74 Minute Book of the Conservative Party 1922 Committee, 1938-1943, Bodleian Library, Oxford.

75 *The Second World War Diary of Hugh Dalton, 1940–1945*, edited by B. Pimlott (London, 1986), p.102.

76 See Wright, pp.241–44.

77 Collier, *Leader of the Few*, p.227, also remarks 'Mr Churchill expressed

surprise that this change should be made "in the hour of victory"'.

78 See Wright, pp.255–57.
79 *The Times*, 14 January 1970.
80 Ibid., 20 January 1970.
81 Ibid., 19 January 1970.
82 Ibid., 22 January 1970.
83 Ibid., 22 January 1970.
84 On Churchill's worries over missions to the USA, see Gilbert, vi, pp.796–99, 869–75 and 926–2,
85 Beaverbrook Papers, BBK D/21, 16 October 1940.
86 See Slessor, pp.318–24.
87 AIR 19/572.
88 PREM 3/466.
89 See Terraine, pp.220–21.
90 AIR 19/572.
91 Ibid.
92 Orange, p.136.
93 Bader Notes suggest that Park was tired 'since he alone conducted the Battle of Britain'. Others, too, noted his tiredness. Interviews, Air Marshal Sir Kenneth Porter and Professor D. Wiseman.
94 See Terraine, pp.254–55; also see N. Longmate, *The Bombers* (London, 1983), pp.91–92.
95 Douglas's story is told in two volumes of autobiography, *Years of Combat* (London, 1963), and *Years of Command*. While writing, he was helped by Robert Wright. See Douglas-Wright correspondence in Douglas Papers, Box 2. See also Denis Richards in Probert and Cox, p.77.
96 Douglas, *Years of Command*, p.278.
97 Slessor, p.241.
98 Douglas Papers, Box 2, 3 November 1961.
99 Douglas, *Years of Command*, p.91.
100 See Gilbert, vi, p.820 on changes in the Chiefs of Staff.

Epilogue

1 See Dowding Papers, AC 71/17/8, 21 and 28 November 1940.
2 Ibid., Secret Cypher Message, Briny 1763, 4/12.
3 H. D. Hall, C.C. Wrigley and J.D. Scott, *Studies of Overseas Supply* (HMSO, 1956), p.312.

4 Dowding Papers, AC 71/17/8, 5 December 1940.
5 Beaverbrook Papers, BBK D/29, 5 December 1940.
6 Ibid., 6 December 1940.
7 Ibid., 7 December 1940.
8 Ibid., 8 December 1940.
9 Taylor, *Beaverbrook*, pp.458–59.
10 AIR 19/572.
11 Ibid.
12 See Dowding Papers, AC 71/17/8, Diary list, 'Visit to Canada and USA', sent to Dowding on 21 June 1941 by F. H. X. Gwynne.
13 Ibid., 23 December 1940.
14 Ibid., 24 December 1940.
15 Ibid., 30 December 1940.
16 For the background to these difficulties, see PREM 3/466, and Beaverbrook Papers, BBK D/29. Also see Portal Papers, Christ Church, Oxford, especially Slessor's letter to Portal, 25 January 1941.
17 See Beaverbrook Papers, BBK D/29, quoting *Daily Express*, Opinion column, 20 November 1940. The comment was written less than a week after the Coventry raid.
18 Ibid., 20 November 1940.
19 Ibid., 22 November 1940.
20 See AIR 41/17, ADGB, iii, p.94.
21 Ibid., Appendix 5.
22 See Gilbert, vi, p.963 and Ramsey, *Blitz*, ii, p.313.
23 AIR 16/367.
24 See Wykeham, p.183.
25 See ibid., Chapter 13, for details of early 'Rhubarb' and 'Circus' operations; also see AIR 41/18, ADGB, iv, especially Part 4 and Appendices 2, Part 4; also see Terraine, pp.282–88.
26 Milch Papers, RAF Museum, Hendon, Microfiche 565, IV/58/3, 'The Secret Dossier on the Military Administration of England', 9 September 1940.

Appendix C

References here are from:

1 The Papers of Lord Douglas of Kirtleside, Imperial War Museum, London. Box 2, File 2.

2   *The Times*, 14, 19, 20 and 22 January 1970.

3   Bader Notes, Appendix B, above.

4   Address given by the Rt. Hon. Denis W. Healey, MP, Secretary of State for Defence, at the Memorial Service for Air Chief Marshal Lord Dowding at Westminster Abbey on 12 March 1970.

5   The Papers of Sir Maurice Dean, Liddell Hart Centre for Military Archives, King's College, London.

6   E. B. Haslam, 'How Lord Dowding Came to Leave Fighter Command', *JSS*, 4, 2(1981), pp.175–86.

BIBLIOGRAPHY

Key:

A Unpublished Sources
1 Government records: Public Record Office
2 Private and unpublished collections
3 Air Historical Branch: monographs, narratives and translations

B Published Sources
1 Parliamentary records
2 Memoirs, autobiographies, diaries
3 Contemporary publications: books
4 Official publications: HMSO
5 Biographies
6 Books
7 Articles

UNPUBLISHED SOURCES

1 Government Records: Public Record Office

AIR 2	Correspondence
AIR 6	Meetings of the Air Council
AIR 8	Chief of the Air Staff Papers
AIR 16	Fighter Command
AIR 19	Private Office Papers
AIR 20	Unregistered Papers
AIR 27	Operations Record Books, Squadrons
AIR 28	Operations Record Books, Stations
AIR 40	Directorate of Intelligence
AIR 41	Air Historical Branch: Narratives and Monographs
AIR 50	Squadron Combat Reports
CAB 3	Committee of Imperial Defence, Memoranda, Series A
CAB 4	Committee of Imperial Defence, Memoranda, Series B
CAB 13	Home Defence Committee, Memoranda
CAB 53	Committee of Imperial Defence,

	Chiefs of Staff Sub-Committee, Minutes and Memoranda
CAB 55	Committee of Imperial Defence, Joint Planning Committee, Minutes and Memoranda
CAB 65	War Cabinet, Minutes
CAB 66	War Cabinet, Memoranda (WP) Series
CAB 79	War Cabinet, Chiefs of Staff Committee, Minutes
CAB 81	Chiefs of Staff Committee and its sub-committees
PREM 3	Prime Minister's Office: Operational Papers
PREM 4	Confidential Papers

2 Private and Unpublished Collections

Bader Notes: From the papers of Air Marshal Sir Denis Crowley-Milling
Balfour Papers: Papers of Lord Balfour, House of Lords Record Office, London
Beaverbrook Papers: Papers of Lord Beaverbrook, House of Lords Record Office, London
Bruce Papers: Papers of Stanley Bruce, Australian Archives, Belconnen, Canberra, Australia
Conservative Party: The Minute Book of the Conservative Party 1922 Committee, 1938-1943, Bodleian Library, Oxford
Cox Intelligence: From the papers of Mr Sebastian Cox, Air Historical Branch, Ministry of Defence, Whitehall, London
Douglas Papers: Papers of Marshal of the Royal Air Force Lord Douglas, Department of Documents, Imperial War Museum, London
Dowding Papers: Papers of Air Chief Marshal Lord Dowding, Department of Aviation Records, Royal Air Force Museum, Hendon
Ellender Notes: The workings of Anti-Aircraft defence, from the papers of Cap-

tain A. R. Ellender, Maidstone, Kent, formerly of AA Command

Elmhirst Papers: Papers of Air Vice-Marshal Sir Thomas Elmhirst, Churchill College, Cambridge

Evill Papers: Papers of Air Chief Marshal Sir Douglas Evill, Department of Aviation Records, Royal Air Force Museum, Hendon

Leigh-Mallory Papers: Papers of Air Chief Marshal Sir Trafford Leigh-Mallory, Department of Aviation Records, Royal Air Force Museum, Hendon

Newall Papers: Papers of Marshal of the Royal Air Force Lord Newall, Department of Aviation Records, Royal Air Force Museum, Hendon

Ogilvie Notes: Notes on Lord Dowding, from the papers of Squadron Leader D. B. Ogilvie, Tunbridge Wells, Kent

Portal Papers: Papers of Marshal of the Royal Air Force, Lord Portal, Christ Church College, Oxford

Salmond Papers: Papers of Marshal of the Royal Air Force Sir John Salmond, Department of Aviation Records, Royal Air Force Museum, Hendon

Saundby Papers: Papers of Air Marshal Sir Robert Saundby, Department of Aviation Records, Royal Air Force Museum, Hendon

Slessor Papers: Papers of Marshal of the Royal Air Force Sir John Slessor, formerly at the Department of Aviation Records, RAF Museum, Hendon

Thurso Papers: Papers of Lord Thurso, formerly Sir Archibald Sinclair, Churchill College, Cambridge

Dean Papers: Papers of Sir Maurice Dean, Liddell Hart Centre for Military Archives, King's College, London

Liddell Hart Papers: Papers of Sir Basil Liddell Hart, Liddell Hart Centre for Military Archives, King's College, London

3 Air Historical Branch: Monographs, Narratives and Translations

Monographs

J. M. Spaight, *The Expansion of the RAF, 1914–1939*, AHB/II/116/17 (1945), also as PRO AIR 41/8

R. E. Skelley, Signals (3), vol. 4, *Radar in*

Raid Reporting, CD 1063, AHB/II/116/21 (C) (1950), also as PRO AIR 41/12

C. Stephenson, Signals (3), vol. 5, *Fighter Control and Interception*, CD 1116, AHB/II/116/21(D)

Narrative

A. C. Bell, *The Campaign in France and the Low Countries, September 1939–June 1940*, also as PRO AIR 41/21 and AIR 41/22 (Appendices and Maps)

Translations

AHB Translation, vol. 2, No. VII/26, Luftwaffe 8th Abteilung report, 'The Course of the Air War against England', 22 November 1939, first study

AHB Translation, vol. 2, No. VII/26, 'The Course of the Air War against England', prepared by the 8th Abteilung, 7 July 1944, second study

AHB Translation, vol. 2, No. VII/30, General Schmid, 'Proposal for the Conduct of Air Warfare against Britain', German Air Force Operations Staff (Intelligence), 22 November 1939

AHB Translation, vol. 2, No. VII/39, 'Battle of Britain', August 1940

AHB Translation, vol. 2, No. VII/40, 'The Effects of Air Power', document No. WC/87, 12 July 1940

AHB Translation, vol. 4, No. VII/83, 'German Air Losses (in the West only), September 1939-December 1940', records of VI Abteilung Quarter-Master General's Department of the German Air Ministry

AHB Translation, vol. 7, No. VII/107, 'Luftwaffe Quartermaster-General's Returns', Luftwaffe Strength/Serviceability Aircraft Tables, August 1938-April 1945

AHB Translation, vol. 9, No. VII/121, A. Galland, 'The Battle of Britain' (1953)

AHB Translation, vol. 9, No. VII/132, 'German bombing of Warsaw and Rotterdam'

AHB Translation, K15410, Hauptmann Otto Bechtle, Operations Officer of KG2, 'German Air Force Operations against Great Britain: tactics and lessons learnt, 1940–41', lecture given for German Air Force General Staff/8th Abteilung, Berlin-Gatow, 2 February 1944

PUBLISHED SOURCES

1 Parliamentary Records

Parliamentary Debates (House of Commons), Official Report, 5th Series
Parliamentary Debates (House of Lords), Official Report, 5th Series

2 Memoirs, Autobiographies, Diaries

All books are published in London unless otherwise stated

H. R. Allen *Spitfire Squadron* (1979)
Anon (P. Gribble) *The Diary of a Staff Officer* (1941)
Avon, The Earl of *The Eden Memoirs: The Reckoning* (1965)
Balfour, Lord *Wings Over Westminster* (1973)
M. Bloch, trans. by G. Hopkin *Strange Defeat* (Oxford, 1949)
A. Calder *The People's War* (1969)
W. Churchill *Second World War*, vol. i, *The Gathering Storm* (1948); vol. ii, *Their Finest Hour* (1949)
A. Clayton *The Enemy is Listening* (1980)
J. Colville *The Fringes of Power: Downing Street Diaries, 1939–1945* (1985)
D. Crook *Spitfire Pilot* (1942)
W. P. Crozier *Off the Record: Political Interviews, 1933–1943* (1973)
H. Dalton *The Fateful Years: Memoirs, 1931–45* (1957)
Sir Maurice Dean *The Royal Air Force and Two World Wars* (1979)
A. Deere *Nine Lives* (1974)
D. Dilks (ed.) *The Diaries of Sir Alexander Cadogan, 1938–1945* (1971)
Douglas, Lord *Years of Combat* (1963)
– *Years of Command* (1966)
Dowding, Lord *Lychgate* (1945)
H. Dundas *Flying Start* (1988)
Sir Aylmer Firebrace *Fire Service Memoirs* (1949)
A. Galland *The First and the Last* (1955)
R. Gehlen *The Gehlen Memoirs* (1972)
N. Gelb (ed.) *Scramble* (1986)
Sir Gerald Gibbs *Survivor's Story* (1956)
Sir Victor Goddard *Skies to Dunkirk* (1982)
H. Guderian *Panzer Leader* (1979)
Sir Arthur Harris *Bomber Offensive* (1947)
J. Harvey (ed.) *The Diplomatic Diaries of Oliver Harvey, 1937–1940* (1970)
E. Heinkel *He 1000* (1956)
Sir Nevile Henderson *Failure of a Mission* (1940)
Mrs R. Henrey *London Under Fire, 1940–45* (1969)
R. Hillary *The Last Enemy* (1942)
Sir Brian Horrocks *A Full Life* (1960)
L. Hudson (trans.) *The Memoirs of Field–Marshal Kesselring* (1953)
Ismay, Lord *The Memoirs of General the Lord Ismay* (1960)
R. R. James (ed.) *Chips: The Diaries of Sir Henry Channon* (1967)
J. Johnson *Wing Leader* (1956)
S. Johnstone *Enemy in the Sky* (1976)
R. V. Jones *Most Secret War* (1979)
Sir Philip Joubert *The Third Service* (1955)
J. Kemp *Off to War with '054* (Braunton, 1989)
H. Knoke *I Flew for the Fuhrer* (1954)
B. Liddell Hart *The German Generals Talk* (1948)
A. M. Lindbergh *War Within and Without: Diaries and Letters of Anne Morrow Lindbergh, 1939–1940* (New York, 1980)
P. B. Lucas (ed.) *Wings of War* (1985)
– *Thanks for the Memory* (1989)
R. MacLeod & D. Kelly (eds.) *The Ironside Diaries, 1937–1940* (1962)
I. Maisky *Memoirs of a Soviet Ambassador* (1967)
Moran, Lord *Winston Churchill* (1966)
M. Muggeridge (ed.) *Ciano's Diary, 1939–1943* (1947)
J. Nissen *Winning the Radar War* (1989)
C. Perry *The Boy in the Blitz* (1972)
Sir Charles Petrie (ed.) *The Private Diaries of Paul Baudouin* (1948)
Sir Frederick Pile *Ack–Ack* (1949)
B. Pimlott (ed.) *The Second World War Diary of Hugh Dalton, 1940–1945* (1986)
J. Quill *Spitfire* (1985)
C. F. Rawnsley & R. Wright *Night Fighter* (1957)
P. Richey *Fighter Pilot* (1941)
C. R. Russell *Spitfire Odyssey* (Southampton, 1985)
Sir Harold Scott *Your Obedient Servant* (1959)
W. Shirer *Berlin Diary* (New York, 1941)

Sir John Slessor *The Central Blue* (1956)
C. B. Smith *Evidence in Camera* (1958)
A. Speer *Inside the Third Reich* (1970)
P. Stahl *The Diving Eagle: a Ju 88 Pilot's Diary* (1984)
U. Steinhilper & P. Osborne *Spitfire on my Tail* (Bromley, 1989)
R. H. Stevens (trans.) *Memoirs: Ten Years and Twenty Days, by Admiral Doenitz* (1959)
Swinton, The Earl of *Sixty Years of Power* (1966)
F. Taylor (ed.) *The Goebbels Diaries, 1939–1941* (1982)
Tedder, Lord *With Prejudice* (1966)
Templewood, Viscount *Nine Troubled Years* (1955)
P. Townsend *Duel of Eagles* (1974)
– *Duel in the Dark* (1986)
J. Tremayne *War on Sark* (Exeter, 1981)
G. H. Vassiltchikov (ed.) *The Berlin Diaries, 1940–1945, of Marie 'Missie' Vassiltchikov* (1987)
N. Ward (ed.) *A Party Politician: The Memoirs of Chubby Power* (Toronto, 1966)
W. Warlimont *Inside Hitler's Headquarters* (1964)
R. Watson-Watt *Three Steps to Victory* (1957)
J. Wheeler-Bennett (ed.) *Action This Day: Working with Churchill* (1968)
F. W. Winterbotham *Secret and Personal* (1969)
– *The Ultra Secret* (1974)

3 Contemporary Publications: Books

Air Ministry *Royal Air Force Training Manual. Part II, Applied Flying, Air Publication 928* (1933)
– *The Air Force List* (1940)
– *The Battle of Britain* (1941)
– *The Battle of Britain*, Pamphlet 156 (1943)
E. B. Ashmore *Air Defence* (1929)
A. B. Austin *Fighter Command* (1941)
L. E. O. Charlton *War From the Air* (1935)
G. Douhet *The Command of the Air* (1943)
J. F. C. Fuller *Towards Armageddon: The Defence Problem* (1937)
C. G. Grey *A History of the Air Ministry* (1940)

P. R. C. Groves *Behind the Smoke Screen* (1934)
J. B. S. Haldane *Air Raid Precautions* (1938)
T. Harrison (ed.) *War Begins at Home: Mass Observation* (1940)
Hauptmann Hermann *The Rise and Fall of the Luftwaffe* (1943)
H. A. Jones *The War in the Air* (1934)
League of Nations *Armaments Year Book* (Geneva, 1938)
B. Liddell Hart *The Defence of Britain* (1939)
Londonderry, Marquess of *Wings of Destiny* (1943)
N. Monks *Squadrons Up!* (1940)
J. Morris *The German Air Raids on Great Britain, 1914–1918* (1927)
A. P. de Seversky *Victory Through Air Power* (New York, 1942)
J. M. Spaight *The Sky's the Limit* (1940)
F. Sternberg *Germany and a Lightning War* (1938)
F. Tuohy *Twelve Lances for Liberty* (1940)

4 Official Publications: HMSO

J. R. M. Butler *Grand Strategy, vol. ii, September 1939–June 1941* (1957)
B. Collier *The Defence of the United Kingdom* (1957)
T. K. Derry *The Campaign in Norway* (1952)
L. F. Ellis *The War in France and Flanders, 1939–1940* (1953)
M. R. D. Foot *S.O.E. in France: An Account of the Work of the British Special Operations Executive in France, 1940–1944* (1966)
N. H. Gibbs *Grand Strategy, vol. i, Rearmament Policy* (1976)
F. Hinsley *British Intelligence in the Second World War, vol. i* (1979)
H. Duncan Hall, North American Supply (1953)
– C. C. Wrigley & J. D. Scott *Studies of Overseas Supply* (1956)
W. N. Medlicott *The Economic Blockade, vol. i, 1939–41* (1952)
T. H. O'Brien *Civil Defence* (1955)
H. Penrose *British Aviation: Ominous Skies, 1935–1939* (1980)
Ministry of Information *Front Line* (1942)
– *Roof Over Britain* (1943)

– *Atlantic Bridge* (1945)

M. M. Postan *British War Production* (1952)

M. M. Postan, D. Hay & J. Scott *Design and Development of Weapons* (1964)

H. Probert *High Commanders of the Royal Air Force* (1991)

D. Richards & H. Saunders *Royal Air Force, 1939–1945, vol. i* (1961)

C. I. Savage *Inland Transport* (1957)

Sir Charles Webster & N. Frankland *The Strategic Air Offensive Against Germany, 1939–1945, vol. i* (1961)

5 Biographies

A. Andrews *The Air Marshals* (1970)

Birkenhead, The Earl of *Halifax* (1965)

A. Boyle *Trenchard* (1962)

S. Bradford *George VI* (1989)

P. Brickhill *Reach for the Sky* (1956)

A. Bullock *Hitler: a Study in Tyranny* (1962)

M. G. Burns *Bader: The Man and His Men* (1990)

R. Clark *Tizard* (1965)

B. Collier *Leader of the Few* (1957)

J. Colville *Churchillians* (1981)

J. Cross *Lord Swinton* (Oxford, 1983)

W. Newton Dunn *Big Wing: the biography of Air Chief-Marshal Sir Trafford Leigh-Mallory* (1992)

C. Edwards *Bruce of Melbourne: Man of Two Worlds* (1965)

M. Gilbert *Winston S. Churchill, Prophet of Truth*, vol. v,(1976)

– *Winston S. Churchill, Finest Hour, vol. vi* (1983)

D. Irving *The Rise and Fall of the Luftwaffe: The Life of Luftwaffe Marshal Erhard Milch* (1974)

–, *Goering* (1989)

R. Jackson *Douglas Bader: a biography* (1953)

J. Laffin *Swifter Than Eagles: The Biography of Marshal of the Royal Air Force Sir John Maitland Salmond* (Edinburgh, 1964)

A. Lee *Goering: Air Leader* (1972)

P. B. Lucas *Flying Colours* (1981)

L. Moseley *The Reich Marshal* (1974)

V. Orange *Sir Keith Park* (1984)

R. J. Overy *Goering: The Iron Man* (1984)

M. Pierce et al. *So Few* (1991)

D. Richards *Portal of Hungerford* (1977)

A. Roberts *'The Holy Fox': A Biography of Lord Halifax* (1991)

D. Saward *'Bomber' Harris* (1984)

A. J. P. Taylor *Beaverbrook* (1972)

– *The War Lords* (1972)

R. Wright *Dowding and the Battle of Britain* (1969)

K. Young *Churchill and Beaverbrook* (1966)

6 Books

Air Ministry *The Rise and Fall of the German Air Force*, Pamphlet No. 248 (1948)

H. R. Allen *Who Won the Battle of Britain?* (1974)

W. Ansel *Hitler Confronts England* (New York, 1964)

C. Barnett *The Collapse of British Power* (1972)

K. Bartz *Swastika in the Air* (1956)

R. Batt *The Radar War* (1991)

W. Baumbach *Broken Swastika* (1960)

C. Bekker *The Luftwaffe War Diaries* (1969)

R. T. Bickers *The Battle of Britain* (1990)

C. Bowyer *Fighter Command* (1980)

P. Calvocoressi *Top Secret Ultra* (1980)

R. Collier *Eagle Day* (1980)

B. Cooper *The Story of the Bomber, 1914–1945* (1978)

G. Craig *Germany, 1866–1945* (1978)

R. Cross *Spitfire* (Cambridge, 1971)

L. Deighton *Fighter: The true story of the Battle of Britain* (1977)

W. Dierich *Kampfgeschwader 'Edelweiss'. The History of a German Bomber Unit, 1939–1945* (1975)

C. Dunning *L'Armée de l'Air, 1939–40* (1989)

C. Eade (ed.) *Secret Session Speeches of Winston Churchill* (1946)

H. Faber (ed.) *Luftwaffe* (1979)

J. Foreman *Battle of Britain: The Forgotten Months, November and December, 1940* (1988)

N. Frankland *The Bombing Offensive Against Germany* (1965)

N. Franks *The Air Battle of Dunkirk* (1983)

E. H. Gombrich *Myth and Reality in German War–Time Broadcasts* (1970)

D. Grinnell-Milne *The Silent Victory* (1976)

B. Gunston *Fighters, 1914–1945* (1951)

L. Hagen *Follow My Leader* (1951)

P. Haining *The Spitfire Log* (1985)

H. Halliday *242 Squadron* (1982)

B. Liddell Hart *History of the Second World War* (1970)

R. Higham *Armed Forces in Peacetime* (1962)

F. Hinsley *Hitler's Strategy* (1951)

A. Horne *To Lose a Battle* (1969)

R. Hough & D. Richards *The Battle of Britain* (1989)

D. Irving *Hitler's War* (New York, 1977)

A. von Ishoven *The Luftwaffe in the Battle of Britain* (1980)

H. Jacobsen & J. Rohwer (eds.) *Decisive Battles of World War II* (1965)

W. F. Kimball *The Most Unsordid Act* (Baltimore, 1969)

W. E. Langer & S. E. Gleason *The Undeclared War* (New York, 1953)

J. M. Lee *The Churchill Coalition, 1940–1945* (1980)

R. Lewin *Ultra Goes to War* (1978)

N. Longmate *Air Raid* (1976)

– *The Bombers* (1983)

F. Mason *The Hawker Hurricane* (1962)

D. Middleton *The Sky Suspended* (1960)

C. L. Mowat *Britain Between the Wars, 1918–1940* (1955)

W. Murray *The Luftwaffe* (1985)

R. J. Overy *The Air War, 1939–1945* (1980)

E. P. von der Porten *The German Navy in World War Two* (1972)

A. Price *Instruments of Darkness* (1967)

– *Luftwaffe Handbook, 1939–1945* (1977)

– *Blitz on Britain, 1939–1945* (1977)

– *The Hardest Day* (1979)

H. Probert & S. Cox (eds.) *The Battle Re-Thought* (1991)

W. G. Ramsey (ed.) *The Battle of Britain, Then and Now* (1980)

– *The Blitz, Then and Now*, vol. i (1987)

– *The Blitz, Then and Now*, vol. ii (1988)

W. Richardson & S. Freidin (eds.) *The Fatal Decisions* (1956)

A. Robinson *RAF Fighter Squadrons in the Battle of Britain* (1987)

D. Sarkar *Spitfire Squadron* (1990)

R. Schleiter & S. D. Heron *Development of Aircraft Engines and Fuels* (Boston, 1950)

J. Scutts *Luftwaffe Fighter Units, Europe, 1939–41* (1977)

– *Luftwaffe Bomber Units, 1939–41* (1978)

C. Shores *Duel for the Sky* (1985)

E. Sims *Fighter Tactics and Strategy* (1972)

M. Smith *British Air Strategy Between the Wars* (1984)

M. Spick *Fighter Pilot Tactics* (Cambridge, 1983)

R. Suchenwirth *Historical Turning Points in the German Air Force War Effort* (New York, 1968)

– *Command and Leadership in the German Air Force* (New York, 1970)

A. J. P. Taylor *English History, 1914–1945* (Oxford, 1965)

Telford Taylor *The March of Conquest* (New York, 1958)

– *The Breaking Wave* (1957)

J. Terraine *The Right of the Line* (1985)

H. Trevor-Roper (ed.) *Hitler's War Directives* (1964)

R. Wheatley *Operation Sea Lion* (Oxford, 1958)

M. Williamson *The Luftwaffe, 1939–1945* (New York, 1986)

J. Willis *Churchill's Few* (1985)

D. Wood & D. Dempster *The Narrow Margin* (1961)

P. Wykeham *Fighter Command* (1960)

K. G. Wynn *Men of the Battle of Britain* (Norwich, 1989)

7 Articles

U. Bialer 'Humanization of Air Warfare in British Foreign Policy on the Eve of the Second World War', *Journal of Contemporary History* (hereafter JCH), 13, 1 (1978)

G. Bonnet 'Pourquoi j'ai approuvé les accords de Munich', *Historama*, No 238, (Paris, 1971)

H. Boog 'German Air Intelligence in World War II', *Aerospace Historian*, June 1986

– 'German Air Intelligence in the Second World War', *Intelligence and National Security* (hereafter INS), 5, 2 (1990)

J. C. Cairns 'Great Britain and the Fall of France: A Study in Allied Disunity', *Journal of Modern History* (hereafter JMH), 27, 4 (1955)

– 'Some Recent Historians and the "Strange Defeat" of 1940', *JMH*, 46,1 (1974)

215

F. L. Carsten 'The German Generals and Hitler', *History Today*, 8, 8 (1958)

S. Cox 'A Comparative Analysis of RAF and Luftwaffe Intelligence in the Battle of Britain, 1940', *INS*. 5, 2 (1990)

J. Crossland 'Britain's Air Defences and the Munich Crisis', *History Today*, 38, 9 (1988)

J. Davis 'ATFERO, The Atlantic Ferry Organisation', *JCH*, 20, 1 (1985)

J. Douglas-Hamilton 'Ribbentrop and War', *JCH*, 5, 4 (1970)

Dowding, Lord 'I Believe', *Sunday Chronicle*, 18 March 1945

– 'The Real Story of the Spitfire', *Star*, 13 September 1951

– 'At Last I Knew It Was Victory', *Star*, 25 September 1951

D. Farrer 'A Very Great Man', *Sunday Express*, 15 September 1946

E. B. Haslam 'How Lord Dowding Came to Leave Fighter Command', *Journal of Strategic Studies* (hereafter JSS), 4, 2 (1981)

A. Hillgruber 'England's place in Hitler's plans for world dominion', *JCH*, 9, 1 (1974)

H. Montgomery-Hyde 'Lord Trenchard: Architect of victory in 1940', *The Times*, 15 September 1973

E. J. Kingston-McCloughry 'The Strategic Air Offensive', *Journal of the Royal United Services Institute* (hereafter JRUSI), 107, 1 (1962)

K. W. Koch 'The Strategic Air Offensive Against Germany: The Early Phase, May-September 1940', *Historical Journal* (hereafter HJ), 34, 1 (1991)

H. Michel 'La Seconde Guerre Mondiale',Tome 1, *Peuples et Civilisations, XXI* (Paris, 1968)

R. J. Overy 'Hitler and Air Strategy', *JCH*, 15, 3 (1980)

– 'German Air Strength, 1933 to 1939: A Note', *HJ*, 27,2 (1984)

D. Porch 'French Intelligence and the Fall of France,1939–40', *INS*, 4, 1 (1989)

Sir Robert Saundby 'Dowding and the Battle of Britain', *The Ampleforth Journal*, 1970

M. Smith 'Sir Edgar Ludlow-Hewitt and the Expansion of Bomber Command', *JRUSI*, 126, 1 (1981)

O. Thetford 'On Silver Wings', *Aeroplane Monthly*, 12, 9 (1991)

W. K. Wark 'British Intelligence on the German Air Force and Aircraft Industry, 1933-1939', *HJ*, 25, 3 (1982)

INDEX